TAKE CHARGE!

IMPROVE YOUR READING AND STUDY SKILLS

Patricia Glenn-Cowan, Ph.D.
Director, Academic Development Program
Baltimore City Community College

Formerly, Associate Director, Center for Learning Assistance
New Mexico State University, Las Cruces

GLENCOE
Macmillan/McGraw-Hill

New York, New York   Columbus, Ohio   Mission Hills, California   Peoria, Illinois

Jacob Lawrence (1917-) is the creator of the cover art, *The Library*. This work in tempera on fiberboard is housed in the National Museum of American Art, Washington, D.C. Lawrence was born in Atlantic City, New Jersey. He moved to Harlem with his family around 1930, shortly after the years of the Harlem Renaissance and near the beginning of the Great Depression. Lawrence began taking art classes at a local settlement house and continued his studies at the Harlem Art Workshop and at the American Artists School in New York. The first exhibition of his work took place in 1937. Lawrence has devoted his artistic career to representing the history and culture of the African-American community.

PHOTO CREDITS: Cover, Lawrence, Jacob. *The Library*. 1960. Tempera on fiberboard. National Museum of American Art, Washington, DC/Art Resource, NY; 2-3, Chuck Savage/The Stock Market; 11, Paul Conklin/Monkmeyer Press Photo Service; 34-35, Michael Kagan/Monkmeyer Press Photo Service; 54-55, David Young-Wolff/PhotoEdit; 58, Michael Kagan/Monkmeyer Press Photo Service; 78-79, Stephen Ogilvy; 100, Andy Levin/Photo Researchers; 104-105, Pete Saloutos/Tony Stone Images; 118-119, Ian O'Leary/Tony Stone Images; 123, Paul Conklin/PhotoEdit; 137, Deborah Davis/PhotoEdit; 146-147, Arlene Collins/Monkmeyer Press Photo Service; 151, David Young-Wolff/PhotoEdit; 162-163, Merritt Vincent/PhotoEdit; 172, Rhoda Sidney/PhotoEdit; 186, David Weintraub/Photo Researchers; 189, David Weintraub/Photo Researchers; 194-195, David R. Frazier/Photo Researchers; 204, Mimi Forsythe/Monkmeyer Press Photo Service; 208-209, Junebug Clark/Photo Researchers; 215, Joseph Nettis/Photo Researchers; 240-241, Michael Kagan/Monkmeyer Press Photo Service; 256-257, George E. Jones/Photo Researchers; 261, Jeff Greenberg/Photo Researchers; 278-279, Renee Lynn/Photo Researchers; 290, Joyce Wilson/Photo Researchers; 302-303, David Young-Wolff/PhotoEdit; 318-319, Bill Aron/PhotoEdit; 327, Charles Gupton/The Stock Market; 328, Victor Englebert; 335, Bruce Smith & The Chicago Bulls; 342, Robert Brenner/PhotoEdit; 346-347, Stephen Ogilvy; 378-379, Freda Leinwand/Monkmeyer Press Photo Service; 392, Springer/Bettmann Film Archive; 416-417, Susan Leavines/Photo Researchers; 438-439, George Zimbel/Monkmeyer Press Photo Service.

All text illustrations by Philip A. Scheuer.

Send all inquiries to:
GLENCOE DIVISION
Macmillan/McGraw-Hill
936 Eastwind Drive
Westerville, OH 43081

ISBN 0-02-802027-8

Printed in the United States of America.

00 99 98 97 96 95 94 HESS-HESS 9 8 7 6 5 4 3 2 1

TABLE OF CONTENTS

To the Instructor

Improve Your Reading and Study Skills provides a holistic plan for developing reading and study skills at the college level. The holistic approach is inclusive, engaging students' valuable prior experience (their knowledge, feelings, observations, and skills) and using this experience as the basis for introducing and developing essential academic skills. Drawing from materials used successfully with many classes and from the real-life issues that incoming college students present, *Improve Your Reading and Study Skills* helps students develop skills and habits that contribute to success in college. The presentation in the book is simple, direct, respectful, and thorough. The text is highly interactive, requiring students to respond continually to the concepts and examples through group activities and independent writing. Skills are presented as strategies or sequential steps rather than as rote memorization, enabling students to obtain a deep understanding that fosters mastery. In a wide variety of activities and assignments, students practice new skills, applying what they've learned to classroom and other real-life situations.

ORGANIZATION OF *IMPROVE YOUR READING AND STUDY SKILLS*

In working through the six sections and twenty chapters of this book, students will find straightforward content and user-friendly features that support their desire to succeed in college. *Improve Your Reading and Study Skills* covers a range of skills, from setting personal goals to taking tests.

- **Section 1. Taking Charge.** This section helps students set goals, stay motivated, develop assertiveness, and deal effectively with various "systems."

- **Section 2. Analyzing Your Strengths.** This section helps students identify the circumstances under which they learn best. After assessing their learning style and study skills, students will have a clear idea of their strengths and weaknesses.

- **Section 3. Managing Time and Resources.** This section helps students gain control of their time—an important skill in all aspects of life. This section will also help identify personal and institutional systems of support. How to get help is a critical skill not only in one's college career but also in one's personal life.

- **Section 4. Taking Notes.** This section focuses on the critical skill of note taking, a three-step process involving preparing before class, taking notes during class, and using notes after class.

- **Section 5. Improving Your Reading Skills.** This section addresses reading skills and provides strategies for increasing vocabulary, previewing textbooks, identifying main ideas, improving your reading rate, reading textbooks effectively, and developing critical thinking and critical reading skills.

- **Section 6. Improving Your Memory and Test-Taking Skills.** This section covers techniques for increasing the ability to organize and remember information and strategies for taking tests.

The Appendix to *Improve Your Reading and Study Skills* includes helpful materials to be used with specific chapters.

FEATURES OF THE STUDENT EDITION

Each chapter of *Improve Your Reading and Study Skills* includes these special features:

- **Chapter Opener.** The chapter opener includes the chapter title, objectives, focusing question, brief introductory paragraphs, and a picture. The chapter opener engages students' interest and builds on their current knowledge.

- **Getting Started.** This feature helps students identify what they already know about the content of the chapter and helps them get the greatest benefit from the chapter. *Getting Started* includes checklists, inventories, and questionnaires that help students assess their prior knowledge.

- **In Your Journal.** Each chapter has journal-writing activities that encourage students to identify personal goals for developing and improving skills. Journal-writing activities also guide students in describing their progress toward those goals.

- **Group Activities.** The peer group activities guide students' work with other students. Group work has several important benefits: students share tasks and contribute both ideas and skills to the group; they learn to appreciate other people's ideas and skills; they take pride in both their ability to work with others and the outcome of group efforts.

- **Discovery Activities.** These activities guide students in using their prior knowledge to improve skills they already have and to learn new concepts and skills.

- **Questions.** Every chapter poses questions that invite students to respond to the material presented. Some questions are informal, drawing on students' prior knowledge and experience; some questions check students' understanding of the chapter content.

- **Assignments.** Every chapter offers opportunities to apply skills to real-life situations. Because the assignments are valuable evidence of skills, students are directed to save these assignments in a portfolio or folder.

- **Wrapping It Up.** Each chapter concludes with a summary, questions, and a journal-writing activity. The summary restates key points from the chapter. The questions invite students to describe what they found most useful in the chapter and how they will use what they've learned. The journal-writing activity encourages students to assess their progress toward goals they set in the first journal activity of the chapter.

- **Conversational Writing Style.** The style of writing is relaxed and conversational. The tone is warm and supportive, which helps make learning easy and enjoyable.

- **Real-Life Vignettes.** Realistic examples provide insight and encouragement. These examples provide alternative ways of approaching problems.

- **College-Level Examples.** Reprinted from published sources, numerous examples reflect a variety of college-level subjects. The examples recognize the diversity of your students and the unique contributions each of them brings to the classroom.

FEATURES OF THE INSTRUCTOR MATERIALS

The Instructor's Wraparound Edition of *Improve Your Reading and Study Skills* is a unique teaching guide that combines the student edition with the instructor's edition to provide a wealth of teaching support. Positioned adjacent to the appropriate student material, teaching suggestions, solutions, and strategies specifically focus on each major concept.

The transparency package for *Improve Your Reading and Study Skills* includes instructional examples to enhance the presentation of new material.

TAKE CHARGE! SERIES

Glencoe's *Take Charge!* series provides comprehensive support for success in college-level studies. The set of four books—each with a student text, an Instructor's Wraparound Edition, and transparencies—includes *Improve Your Reading and Study Skills* and:

- *Improve Your Sentences* presents a logical and thorough treatment of sentence structure.

- *Improve Your Paragraphs* helps students integrate and develop skills and knowledge in using the writing process to create sound, well-organized paragraphs.

- *Improve Your Essays* incorporates the latest techniques of writing theory, providing students with a thorough immersion in the writing process as it applies to essay writing.

Your decision to use *Improve Your Reading and Study Skills* reflects a commitment to facilitating your students' success in college. The text, used with the Instructor's Wraparound Edition and the transparency package, provides a complete and empowering tool for setting students on the path toward success.

Patricia Glenn-Cowan

To the Student

Congratulations! You've decided to pursue college-level studies, perhaps eventually to earn a college degree. Your decision shows that you are committed to higher education and to taking charge of your life. Your commitment is vital; it supplies the motivation you need to achieve your goals. Commitment and motivation are not enough, however, to guarantee your success in college. You also need skills and frequent opportunities to practice those skills to meet the many challenges ahead. *Improve Your Reading and Study Skills* is designed to help you identify, develop, and improve the skills you need to succeed in college.

The majority of the challenges you'll meet in your college career will be academic challenges, requiring specific skills. Your success in meeting academic challenges, however, depends very much on taking charge of your personal life—knowing who you are, recognizing your unique style, and asserting yourself. In addition to helping you with academic skills, *Improve Your Reading and Study Skills* supports your effort to take charge of your personal life. You'll find valuable information and activities that will help you develop self-awareness, assertiveness, and other sources of support. By combining academic skills with activities that engage your emotions and experiences, *Improve Your Reading and Study Skills* provides a powerful and well-rounded program of skills essential to college success.

As you work through the six sections and twenty chapters of this book, you'll find straightforward content and user-friendly features that support your desire to succeed in college. *Improve Your Reading and Study Skills* covers a range of skills, from setting personal goals to taking tests.

- **Section 1. Taking Charge.** This section helps you set goals, stay motivated, develop assertiveness, and deal effectively with various "systems."

- **Section 2. Analyzing Your Strengths.** This section helps you identify the circumstances under which you learn best. After assessing your learning style and your study skills, you will have a clear idea of your strengths and weaknesses, which will benefit you as you work through the remaining sections of the book and through your college career.

- **Section 3. Managing Time and Resources.** This section helps you gain control of your time—an important skill in all aspects of your life. This section will also help you identify personal and institutional systems of support. How to get the help you need is a critical skill not only in your college career but also in your personal life.

- **Section 4. Taking Notes.** This section focuses on the critical skill of note taking, a three-step process involving preparing before class, taking notes during class, and using notes after class.

- **Section 5. Improving Your Reading Skills.** This section addresses reading skills and provides strategies for increasing your vocabulary, previewing textbooks, identifying main ideas, improving your reading rate, reading textbooks effectively, and developing critical thinking and critical reading skills.

- **Section 6. Improving Your Memory and Test-Taking Skills.** The final section covers techniques for increasing your ability to organize and remember information and strategies for taking tests.

The Appendix to *Improve Your Reading and Study Skills* includes helpful materials that you will use with specific chapters.

The key to making the best use of this book is to take charge—to read actively. Active reading involves comparing new information to what you already know, discussing the information, and applying what you learn in an active way such as writing. The activities and assignments enable you to apply what you learn. Use the activities. Then apply what you learn in this book to your other courses.

Patricia Glenn-Cowan

ACKNOWLEDGMENTS

The author thanks the following educators for reviewing the manuscript and offering suggestions for enhancing *Improve Your Reading and Study Skills*.

CONSULTANTS

Hunter R. Boylan
Appalachian State University
Boone, North Carolina

Pura G. Gonzalez
Microcomputer Technology Institute
Houston, Texas

Bertha Murray
Tallahassee Community College
Tallahassee, Florida

Lettie Wong
De Anza College
Cupertino, California

REVIEWERS

Francine L. DeFrance
Cerritos College
Norwalk, California

Paul Calocino
Bergen Community College
Wood-Ridge, New Jersey

Sigrun Coffman
Truckee Meadows Community College
Reno, Nevada

Daniel Gallagher
Laredo Junior College
Laredo, Texas

Faith Heinrichs
Central Missouri State University
Warrensburg, Missouri

Barbara Henry
West Virginia State College
Dunbar, West Virginia

David Hopkins
Rio Hondo College
Whittier, California

Joy Lester
Forsyth Technical Community College
Winston-Salem, North Carolina

Dolores Mirabella
South Seattle Community College
Seattle, Washington

Michael W. Radis
The Pennsylvania State University
University Park, Pennsylvania

Charoline Simmons
Motlow State Community College
Tullahoma, Tennessee

David A. Strong, Jr.
Dyersburg State Community College
Dyersburg, Tennessee

Joseph Thweatt
State Technical Institute at Memphis
Memphis, Tennessee

Kimberly A. Tyson
Marian College
Indianapolis, Indiana

Taking Charge

Your decision to attend college shows that you are taking charge of your life. As you work toward achieving your academic goals, two of your greatest assets are the aptitudes and skills that you bring with you. Section 1 of *Improve Your Reading and Study Skills* will help you focus, apply, and expand these resources so that you are prepared for the hard work that lies ahead. Chapter 1 focuses on setting and achieving goals. This chapter will help you appreciate your ability to set goals and will help you develop strategies for achieving your goals. Chapter 2 explores motivation. This chapter will help you become aware of how motivated you are and will offer tips for increasing and maintaining your motivation. Chapter 3 centers on assertiveness. In this chapter you will examine the strategies you already have for identifying and expressing your needs, and you'll learn some new techniques for getting what you want in a positive and nonaggressive way. Chapter 4 helps you understand and work with "the system." This chapter will draw on your experience with large organizations and will help you develop skills to negotiate with such organizations.

1

SETTING GOALS

OBJECTIVES:

- To identify steps in the goal-setting process.

- To set appropriate personal and academic goals.

- To describe personal goals and achievements toward those goals.

How Can I
Succeed?

For most of us, setting goals and working toward achieving those goals is the way to make our dreams come true. What dreams have come true for the people in the picture? What kinds of work made those dreams come true?

Achievements usually start as ideas, daydreams, or fantasies. Then the hard work begins. This chapter will help you identify steps you can take toward achieving your goals.

GETTING STARTED

Before you can work toward achieving goals, you must decide what your goals are.

- Goals begin in your imagination. What kinds of things have you imagined or daydreamed about doing recently?

  _____

  _____

  _____

- Which of these daydreams could become real goals for you?

  _____

  _____

  _____

- Describe a goal you achieved or are on the way to achieving. When did you first imagine this goal?

  _____

  _____

  _____

- Has the goal you described above changed since you first imagined it? Describe any changes that have taken place.

  _____

  _____

WRITING IN YOUR JOURNAL

As you read this book, you'll have opportunities to record your thoughts and ideas in a journal. Expressing yourself on paper will help you clarify and focus your thinking.

Your journal is a place to express yourself freely: to try out ideas; to jot down impressions of people, places, and things; or to experiment with different kinds of writing. In your journal you can explore possible writing topics, note your reactions to political or social issues, or simply comment on everyday events. Often you'll be able to use the thoughts from your journal as a springboard for writing.

Journal entries may take various forms. Sometimes you may want to express yourself by writing sentences or whole paragraphs. Other times a few scribbled words and phrases—or even a drawing—will be sufficient. At times you may want to clip or staple newspaper or magazine articles or photocopied book excerpts in your journal, perhaps with your comments attached. You may also want to record in your journal amazing facts that you encounter, notable quotations, and thought-provoking statistics. Any of these items may later inspire your thinking when you're searching for a writing topic.

The writing you do in your journal is for yourself. What you write is not graded and need not be perfect. Your journal also provides a place to write specific goals. As you develop and polish your writing skills, you can monitor your progress toward the goals you have set.

IN YOUR JOURNAL

What ideas do you have about how to achieve your most important goal? Keep a journal to record some of the things you can do to try to make your dreams come true. In your journal, record the steps you're taking and the events that happen as you move toward your goal. Also record your personal responses. If you get disappointed, for example, describe your feelings in your journal. Expressing your feelings in writing is an excellent way to work through setbacks.

YOUR COLLABORATIVE GROUP

Throughout this book you will have many opportunities to work within a collaborative group to discuss ideas and carry out activities. A collaborative group works together—collaborates—to achieve a common goal. As a member of a group, you have certain responsibilities that will enable the group to function effectively.

- Be an active participant, contributing ideas and examples from your experience and observations.
- Carry out your part of the activity or assignment to the best of your ability.
- Be considerate of other members of the group. Avoid interrupting other group members when they are speaking. Try not to dominate the group.

GROUP ACTIVITY

Goal setting is something people do throughout their lives. A goal may be as simple as unwrapping a piece of candy or as complex as discovering the cure for a deadly disease. Many factors affect progress toward achieving goals. **Ambition**—the strong desire to have or do something—and luck play important roles in achieving goals.

In your group, discuss at least two goals from the Data Bank. How important are ambition and luck in achieving these goals? Describe the work and the "lucky breaks" that may be necessary to reach each goal.

- Become a millionaire by the age of 40.
- Open my own business.
- Buy a house.
- Start a family.
- Win the lottery.
- Graduate from college.

DATA BANK

- Work only six months a year.
- Make the dean's list in college.
- Get a job in my chosen career right after college.
- Buy a car.
- Put myself and my child through college.

SETTING AND ACHIEVING GOALS

DREAM A LITTLE

Daydreaming is an act of imagination. Some people dismiss day-dreaming as a waste of time, particularly when they think they—or you—should be doing something else, like paying attention to a lec-ture. Daydreaming is still not appropriate in every situation.

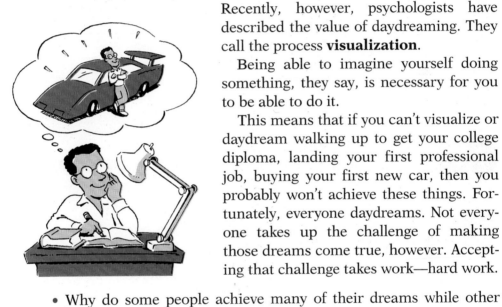

Recently, however, psychologists have described the value of daydreaming. They call the process **visualization**.

Being able to imagine yourself doing something, they say, is necessary for you to be able to do it.

This means that if you can't visualize or daydream walking up to get your college diploma, landing your first professional job, buying your first new car, then you probably won't achieve these things. For-tunately, everyone daydreams. Not every-one takes up the challenge of making those dreams come true, however. Accept-ing that challenge takes work—hard work.

- Why do some people achieve many of their dreams while other people achieve few of their dreams? Give an example that sup-ports your opinion.

DISCOVERY
ACTIVITY

_____

_____

_____

_____

_____

_____

Two factors are important in moving from daydreams to goals. They are motivation and belief in yourself. The two work together. **Motivation** is the positive attitude or drive toward achieving your goal. You're motivated if your dream is a powerful one—one you really want to achieve. You might be so tired of your present life situation, for example, that you know you *have* to make a change. To make your dreams become reality, you also need to believe you can make them come true. Then you are motivated enough to set goals and begin taking steps to achieve them.

- Even with the strongest motivation and belief in yourself, you will still face obstacles to achieving your goals. What are some obstacles you might need to overcome in reaching a goal?

_____

_____

_____

_____

GOAL ACHIEVEMENT: A FIVE-STEP PROCESS

Achieving your goal involves these five steps:
1. Dream, imagine, visualize.
2. Change your dream into a goal statement.
3. Analyze and use goal-related resources.
4. Make a goal-achievement plan.
5. Keep track of progress toward your goal.

STEP 1: DREAM, IMAGINE, VISUALIZE

In the space provided on the next page, describe at least four daydreams that you'd like to turn into goals. Don't put any limits on your dreaming right now. See yourself as you want to be. For each daydream, describe the knowledge, skills, jobs, or possessions you would like to have. Tell what you would like to have time to do. Identify the person or people you would want to be with.

- Daydream 1

  _____

  _____

  _____

- Daydream 2

  _____

  _____

  _____

- Daydream 3

  _____

  _____

  _____

- Daydream 4

  _____

  _____

  _____

Kinds of Goals

Goals are generally either short-term or long-term. **Short-term goals** are those that you can achieve in a short period of time. Such goals include studying for an upcoming test, getting an assignment done on time, meeting with your advisor, and writing a letter. **Long-term goals** naturally take longer to achieve. Such goals might include graduating from college, becoming a public official, building your own house, and starting your own business.

- Which of your dreams could be short-term goals?

  _____

  _____

  _____

  _____

  _____

- Which of your dreams could be long-term goals?

_____

_____

_____

_____

The Goal You're Really Going After 〜〜〜

You've considered how much time achieving some of your dreams may require. What impact has the time factor had on your motivation and on your belief in your ability to make your dreams come true? Look at your dreams again, and cross out the ones that seem not important enough for you to work really hard for. You might have thought that owning a sailboat or earning a master's degree would be nice, for example, but not worth the time and work required to get them. Write the remaining "serious" dreams here.

_____

_____

_____

_____

STEP 2: CHANGE YOUR DREAM INTO A GOAL STATEMENT

A dream is vague. The main point of a dream is to describe what you want. A **goal statement** names a specific achievement and time element or deadline. The main point of a goal statement is to set you on the path toward achieving that goal. The time factor is sometimes hard to estimate, but it is important to keep you on track. Mandy is a college student using her dreams to plan her long-term goals. One of Mandy's dreams was the following:

> I dream of having my own business where I can learn about all the countries in the world.

Expressed as a goal, Mandy's dream became

I will own my own travel agency in ten years.

Questions

1. What is specific and concrete about Mandy's goal statement?

_____

_____

_____

2. How are the ideas "goal" and "dream" different?

_____

_____

_____

Activity A: Stating Your Goal

Turn one of your "serious" dreams into a goal statement.

_____

_____

_____

_____

STEP 3: ANALYZE AND USE GOAL-RELATED RESOURCES

In this step, think carefully about what skills, money, and other resources you need to meet your goal. You may need to do some research. Use Mandy's goal of owning a travel agency as an example.

• How can Mandy find out what resources she might need to buy and run a travel agency?

_____

_____

_____

_____

Did any of the following ideas occur to you?

- Talk to experts in the travel industry.
- Survey the college catalog for courses that are related to the travel industry.
- Read books and magazines on travel.
- Attend seminars on some aspect of the business.
- Write to special schools that provide instruction in travel.

Activity B: Listing Your Resources

For your goal, make a list of sources of information. Be specific.

_____

_____

_____

_____

_____

_____

_____

_____

Among your resources, include people whose knowledge can help you achieve your goals. Interviews with experienced people can provide you with valuable information.

STEP 4: MAKE A GOAL-ACHIEVEMENT PLAN

Even with all the research in the world, you will never reach your goal without a plan. Your plan should be in writing and should include specific stages. Here is Mandy's plan for owning a travel agency, a long-term goal.

> *Stage 1: Graduate from travel agency school in Phoenix by May 199-.*
>
> *Stage 2: Work in a travel agency in a major eastern city for two years to get maximum experience with international travel.*
>
> *Stage 2-A: While working, save $150 per month to accumulate capital. Invest in mutual growth fund.*
>
> *Stage 3: Begin to shop around for travel agencies that might be affordable. Alternative: become a partner in the business I'm working in, if that is an option. Find financial backers, including parents. Deadline: 199-.*
>
> *Stage 4: By 20--, have my own business, purchased from partner or bought outright.*

To achieve a short-term goal, use the same kind of plan. Lay out the stages of work required and indicate appropriate time limits. Suppose you had a short-term goal of writing a term paper due at the end of a 14-week course. Your plan might look like this:

> *Stage 1: Decide on a topic by Week 2.*
>
> *Stage 2: Complete research and outline by Week 6.*
>
> *Stage 3: Complete first draft by Week 10.*
>
> *Stage 4: Complete edit by Week 12.*
>
> *Stage 5: Proofread, complete bibliography, and final edit by Week 13.*

Activity C: Make a Plan for Achieving Your Goal

Write a plan for the stages of your goal. Whether your goal is short-term or long-term, describe the stages and indicate about how much time each stage would take. Be specific. If you're not sure about a certain stage, use your resources. Add more stages if you need to.

Stage 1: _____

_____

_____

_____

Stage 2: _____

_____

_____

_____

Stage 3: _____

_____

_____

_____

Stage 4: _____

_____

_____

_____

STEP 5: KEEP TRACK OF PROGRESS TOWARD YOUR GOAL

Once you have your written plan and are working through the stages, keep track of how you're doing. This is especially important when your goal is long-term. When you're trying to achieve a long-term goal, you're likely to encounter setbacks. Keeping track of where you've been can help you evaluate your accomplishments. Keeping track of where you're going can help you achieve your goal.

Recording Your Progress in a Journal

In addition to recording your important, long-term goals in your journal, you should keep track of the steps along the way. To make keeping your journal easier, you can divide the journal into sections, with each section relating to a step in your overall process. You will also want to record everything important that happens as you pursue your goal.

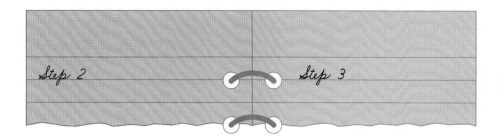

When Mandy has a short talk with a local travel agent about the business, she will record the date and the talk under the resources step of her plan, Step 3. If that talk was not very productive, Mandy wouldn't dwell on the time wasted but would immediately arrange to talk to someone more helpful. In your journal, praise yourself for every small step you make in the right direction. Being your own cheerleader may not come naturally to you. You may be more accustomed to being your own critic. Remember, however, that there are lots of critics in the world and few cheerleaders. Notice how Mandy handles a setback in the following journal entry.

I got a reply from the Henderson Foundation today. They turned down my application for a grant. I was really disappointed, but I'm glad that I applied for six other grants. I'm sure one of them will come through. I'm not going to let one disappointment set me back.

• How do you feel about your ability to praise yourself?

_____

_____

_____

_____

Allow Others to Support You 〜〜〜〜〜

Telling other people about your goal is a good way to keep your motivation high and to receive support when you need it. Share your goal only with people who are likely to be positive and helpful. Tell them what you're doing and ask for encouragement, especially when you face a roadblock. If you are not sure about someone, take time to get to know the person better before you share your goal with that person.

PORTFOLIO

Assignment: 〜〜〜〜〜〜〜
Beginning Your Portfolio

Write a paragraph or two describing a time when you told someone about one of your goals. What was the goal? Whom did you tell? Why did you choose that person as someone to describe your goal to? How did telling that person help you achieve your goal?

This is the first of the assignments in which you will write on a separate sheet of paper and not in the book. These assignments will help you and your instructor evaluate your progress in the course. You can also refer to the items in your portfolio at any time to reexamine and compare the work you've completed. Keep your assignments in a folder or portfolio that you use only for this course.

Recording Your Progress on a Chart 〜〜〜〜〜

Another way to track your progress and to keep up your motivation is to make a chart of your progress. Design a chart that shows all the stages of your plan. You can use a single sheet of paper for the whole chart, or you can have a page for each stage of your goal. Record each time you do some research, make a deposit of money, or whatever you have planned to do. If it doesn't seem too silly to you, get a box of stick-on stars or other ornaments to show when you've made progress. Your chart might look something like this:

Step 2. Goal Statement: I will keep up my motivation to stay in college and graduate.

Step 3. Resources: Instructors, advisors, people who have recently graduated from this college, friends and family members.

★ Stage 1: Went to student orientation. Learned a lot about the college and what's expected of me.

★ Stage 2: Met my advisor and talked about my goals.

★ Stage 3: Talked to Ronnie who graduated last year. She said the hardest thing for her was deciding on a major and keeping up with her course work. Talking to someone who's been there really helped my motivation.

Stage 4: Discussed college with my uncle Roy.

WRAPPING IT UP

SUMMARY

- Goals begin in your imagination as daydreams and visualizations.

- Visualizing your goal is essential to achieving it.

- Motivation and belief in yourself are important factors in achieving your goals.

- Goal achievement is a five-step process:

    1. Dream, imagine, visualize.
    2. Change your dream into a goal statement.
    3. Analyze and use goal-related resources.
    4. Make a goal-achievement plan.
    5. Keep track of progress toward your goal.

- Goals are either short-term or long-term, depending on the amount of time required to achieve them.

- Your goal-achievement plan should include stages that identify how you will achieve your goal.

- A journal and chart are good ways to record your goals and your progress toward achieving them.

- Sharing your goal with supportive people is a good way to keep your motivation high.

THINKING IT OVER

- What ideas and information in this chapter did you find most useful?

  _____

  _____

  _____

  _____

  _____

- How will you apply the ideas and information from this chapter in achieving your short- and long-term goals?

  _____

  _____

  _____

  _____

  _____

IN YOUR
JOURNAL

Describe the progress you've made so far toward one of your goals. Set a new goal based on something you learned from this chapter.

2

STAYING MOTIVATED

OBJECTIVES:

- To evaluate your motivation.
- To assess your behavior to see whether it gives an impression of motivation.
- To evaluate your self-esteem.

How Do I Stay Motivated?

Motivation is the positive attitude that keeps you going when the going gets tough. You can't accomplish anything difficult without motivation. How are the people in the picture showing their motivation?

    This chapter will help you identify your own sources of motivation and will help you discover ways to keep your motivation strong in order to accomplish your goals.

All of us want to achieve certain goals. Just wanting, however, is not enough. If you're serious about what you want, you must also take specific actions. As an example, think about your desire for an education and what action you're taking to achieve that goal. Respond to each statement to get more insight into your motivation. Circle *A* for "always," *F* for "frequently," or *N* for "seldom or never."

1. I know why I'm in college.   A   F   N

2. I am able to keep myself going despite
     setbacks.   A   F   N

3. I want to do my best in college.   A   F   N

4. I am determined to graduate from
     college.   A   F   N

5. I have specific plans for the future.   A   F   N

If you answered *A* for all five statements, you are highly motivated. More than two *N* answers indicate that you need to improve your motivation.

IN YOUR JOURNAL

Based on the statements you responded to so far, choose at least one area of motivation that you would like to improve. Set a personal goal for yourself in that area. Write the goal in your journal. You might, for example, want to improve your attitude about doing your best in college.

DISCUSSING MOTIVATION

GROUP ACTIVITY

Motivation is a very important factor in goal achievement.

A. Share with group members some of the goals you've been motivated to achieve. Describe where you think the motivation came from. Did the motivation come from enjoyment of the task itself? Did it come from the pride you feel after accomplishing something? Did it come from the hope of pleasing someone important to you or from doing something good for someone else? Write the three most common sources of motivation among people in your group.

_____

_____

_____

B. Discuss at least three of the goals listed in the Data Bank. For each goal, write two or more reasons that someone may be highly motivated to achieve the goal.

_____

_____

_____

_____

_____

- Graduate from college.
- Work for civil rights.
- Help reduce poverty.
- Practice a musical instrument.
- Learn to cook.
- Meet new people.
- Settle an argument with a friend.

DATA BANK

- Run for political office.
- Improve eating habits.
- Stop smoking.
- Travel in foreign countries.
- Learn a new computer program.
- Take careful lecture notes.

Motivation—One of Your Resources

By making the decision to go to college, you have taken charge of the course of your own life. You have chosen to take positive action toward your goal. You may have begun college directly after high school; or you may have spent time working, doing military service, or achieving other goals. You have one thing in common with other college students: you see college as a step to becoming successful.

As you move toward your goals, you'll draw upon skills that you've learned in school, at work, and from life in general. Applying what you already know to new information will give you a fast start in creating a successful college experience for yourself. You already have a wealth of information and experience that will be of tremendous help in your college career.

In the movie *Stand and Deliver*, the calculus instructor, Jaime Escalante, uses the Spanish term *ganas*, "desire or wanting," to explain to his students what it takes to be successful.

Instructor Jaime Escalante, played by actor Edward James Olmos, challenged students to use *ganas*—"desire" or "wanting"—to take charge of their lives and achieve success.

- Describe a recent experience you've had with *ganas*. You might think of *ganas* as "desire" or "motivation" or "ambition."

_____

_____

_____

_____

_____

SKILLS—ANOTHER RESOURCE

Now read about Doris, someone who learned she had skills that would help her succeed in college.

After I left high school, I got married almost right away and began to work as a secretary in an accounting office. I was a pretty good secretary after a few years, and I was proud of my work. When I was 27, tragedy struck: my husband Larry was killed in an accident on the job, and I was left to support two children. It didn't take me long to realize that I couldn't support us on my salary.

One day, on our local television channel, I saw a public service announcement about Pell Grants for college. I called the number and found out that I would qualify. I had always thought that I'd like to be an accountant. I thought I could do the work, having worked all these years with accountants. I applied for the grant, and three months later, I was sitting in my first college class! I was scared. I had been out of school for nine years, and a voice in my head kept saying, *Are you crazy? You're not a student. You're a secretary.*

But for my kids' sake, I kept going to class.

One day, a young girl who sat beside me said, "Could I borrow your notes? They look so great, so much better than mine." Do you know what? She was right. Taking good, neat notes was an important part of being a secretary. This incident started me thinking about other skills from my job that could help me do well in college.

First, I already knew that being there and being on time was bottom line. I never missed or was late to class. I noticed that people who came in late to accounting class missed out on the problem solutions. Second, I already knew how to budget my time, and I always carried a time planner, which I also took to class. This way I never missed assignments or tests. Third, I knew how to take complete notes. In fact my notes brought me to one of the proudest moments of my life.

For the midterm test, I carefully studied my notes. When I took the test, I had no problem with any of the questions. I was able to answer them in detail because my notes were so complete.

When the instructor handed back the papers he congratulated me on mine, pointing out that it was ten points higher than any other score in the class. As I looked over my paper—I'll never forget—I thought to myself, "You *are* a student, and a good one."

GROUP
ACTIVITY

Activity A: Your Hidden College Skills

Like Doris, you probably have skills that can help you in college. Discuss them with your group, then list some of them.

_____

_____

_____

_____

_____

_____

_____

PORTFOLIO

Assignment 1:
Sharing Your Experience

Write a brief letter to Doris telling her your response to her story. When have you had similar fears, experiences, triumphs? Save this assignment in your portfolio.

GETTING MOTIVATED, STAYING MOTIVATED

Setting the curve on a midterm as Doris did is one excellent motivator. Even if you don't ace a test, however, your aim must be to develop or fuel your motivation from inside, from *ganas*, and keep your motivation strong even in the face of setbacks.

IN YOUR JOURNAL

Keep track of your small daily successes to keep your motivation high.

Even famous people have had to face roadblocks and overcome them. Albert Einstein proved to be a genius in mathematics and physics. When he was in the sixth grade, however, his parents were told that he was mentally retarded. Winston Churchill became the prime minister of England. His stirring speeches gave heart to the British people during World War II. As a youth, however, Churchill had to overcome a severe learning disability and was never a great student.

In more recent times, Cesar Chavez overcame extreme shyness and a poor education to become a spokesperson for Mexican-American farm workers. Basketball star Michael Jordan was cut from his high school varsity basketball team.

PORTFOLIO

Assignment 2:
Overcoming Obstacles

Think of someone you know or someone famous who overcame obstacles to become a success. In writing, share the story of this person. Point out what kept the person going when faced with difficulties. Save this assignment in your portfolio.

SELF-ESTEEM AND MOTIVATION

As the stories of successes of ordinary and famous people illustrate, what others think of you and your abilities is not as important as what you think and believe about yourself. The way you feel about yourself is called **self-concept** or **self-esteem**.

Having high but realistic self-esteem is important to how you see your potential for success. An informal self-esteem inventory like the one that follows lets you evaluate your self-esteem. Remember that self-esteem comes from within and can be changed from within. If the results of the informal inventory show that your self-esteem is not very high, remember that you can change it—especially by rethinking and concentrating on your strengths.

SELF-ESTEEM INVENTORY

To complete this inventory, circle the A for "always," F for "frequently," or N for "seldom or never."

1. I like the way my body looks.   A   F   N

2. I feel comfortable around my friends.   A   F   N

3. I'm comfortable with myself, regardless
   of what others think of me.   A   F   N

4. I am cheerful and friendly.   A   F   N

5. I take care to look my best.   A   F   N

6. I can master any reasonable task I set
   my mind to.   A   F   N

7. Other people seem to like me.   A   F   N

8. I don't want to change anything about
   the way I look.   A   F   N

9. I am polite and caring toward others.   A   F   N

10. I like my personality.   A   F   N

11. Making mistakes from time to time does
    not bother me.   A   F   N

12. I am as capable as anyone else my age.   A   F   N

Count the letters you circled. If you circled *A* ten or more times, you have high self-esteem. If you circled *F* ten or more times, you have a moderate amount of self-esteem. If you circled *N* six or more times, you probably have low self-esteem.

- Did the results surprise you? Explain why.

  _____

  _____

  _____

  _____

  _____

- Regardless of the results, what three things about yourself are you proudest of?

  _____

  _____

  _____

  _____

  _____

To raise your self-esteem, go back to the statements on the inventory for which you answered *F* or *N*. Use each statement as an **affirmation**—a positive statement about yourself. Repeat the affirmations to yourself often throughout the day.

CONTROL AND MOTIVATION

Success is within your control. You succeed or fail based on your attitudes and actions. You have control when you take responsibility for what happens to you.

Read what Mark, a first-year college student, wrote about his experience.

> My parents were set on my getting a college degree since neither one of them had. They were the ones who made the decision. As soon as I got to college, things started to go against me. I was given classes that were not interesting to me and that met too early in the morning. Each professor seemed to think his or hers was the only class we were taking. The homework was too much to keep up with.
>
> I missed the first test in anthropology because my room-mate told me the wrong date for the test. Since I had missed class the day the test was announced, I believed him. Missing that test made me have to drop the class, and I was short on credit hours and lost my financial aid. I then had to get a job, and the only one I could find was as a night guard. I was so sleepy in the mornings that I slept through my classes, but I couldn't quit my job, even though I hated it. All in all, this has been a rotten term; everything has gone wrong for me.

- Does Mark seem in control? Explain your answer.

_____

_____

_____

_____

- What is Mark's attitude toward the things that happen to him?

_____

_____

_____

_____

- What advice could you give Mark?

_____

_____

_____

_____

_____

EXTERNAL LOCUS OF CONTROL

Mark has what can be called an **external locus of control**. He sees himself as a helpless pawn in life's game, being shoved here and there by forces beyond his control. He blames his lack of success on situations and events that are external to himself. He sees himself as a victim. This way of thinking has a negative effect on success.

Activity B: Thinking About Control and Success

Share with group members your thoughts on control and success. What are some areas of your life that you feel are beyond your control? How do they impact on your ability to succeed?

INTERNAL LOCUS OF CONTROL

When you see yourself as mainly responsible for the things that happen to you, you have an **internal locus of control**. This means you take responsibility not only for what has happened but for what *will* happen. You direct your energies and your skills toward achieving your goals. You make choices. You take action. You take control.

Activity C: Thinking About Responsibility and Control

Describe an area in your life in which you assume responsibility. How do you control what happens? How does your sense of responsibility contribute to your success in this area?

_____

_____

_____

_____

_____

Assignment 3:
Developing an Internal Locus of Control

Write an alternative script for Mark's story on page 30, assuming he has developed an internal locus of control. What choices could he make? Save this assignment in your portfolio.

WRAPPING IT UP

SUMMARY

- Motivation is the positive attitude that keeps you going when the going gets tough.

- Your motivation can come from several sources, including the desire for enjoying life, pleasing someone important, and doing something to help others.

- You have hidden resources that include strong motivations and skills. These resources can help you achieve your goals.

- Role models such as Winston Churchill and Michael Jordan overcame obstacles to become successful.

- Your self-esteem or self-concept is the way you feel about yourself. You can improve your self-esteem by thinking positively about yourself and concentrating on your strengths.

- You are in control when you take responsibility for what happens to you. People who have an external locus of control see themselves as victims of forces beyond their control. This attitude has a negative impact on success. People who have an internal locus of control take responsibility for what has happened and for what will happen. This attitude has a positive impact on success.

THINKING IT OVER

- What is the most important thing you learned in this chapter?

  _____

  _____

  _____

  _____

  _____

  _____

  _____

- How will you apply what you learned in this chapter to improving your motivation and self-esteem?

  _____

  _____

  _____

  _____

  _____

  _____

  _____

  _____

IN YOUR JOURNAL

Look back at the Self-Esteem Inventory on page 28. Now describe the progress you've made toward improving your motivation. Then write one or two affirmations that will help boost your self-esteem.

3

DEVELOPING ASSERTIVENESS

OBJECTIVES:

- To identify assertive behavior.

- To compare and contrast assertive behavior with aggressive or passive behavior.

- To practice expressing yourself assertively for greatest result.

- To use conflict resolution and self-advocacy techniques to maximum effect.

How Can I Communicate What I Want?

You've probably been in a situation where you know exactly what you want, but you're not getting it. In such situations some people just quietly accept what is available. Other people react differently. What do you think the young woman in the picture is saying to get the course she wants?

Nearly every day we have to make clear what we like or don't like about a situation and to tell how we would like that situation to change. For example, you might ask your supervisor for a raise or a new assignment. To succeed at these tasks, you have to be **assertive**—that is, identify and express to others what you need and want.

Assertiveness is much like other skills. It does not come naturally to everyone, but it can definitely be improved with practice. This chapter will help you learn about your assertiveness and use it effectively.

Being assertive can help you achieve the goals you set. Assertiveness can help keep you motivated to get what you want.

- Describe a recent situation in which you were assertive.

_____

_____

_____

To learn more about your assertiveness, respond to each statement by circling *A* for "always," *F* for "frequently," or *N* for "seldom or never."

1. I let other people know what I want and need.   A   F   N

2. I let other people's needs get in my way when I want something.   A   F   N

3. I am an ambitious person.   A   F   N

4. I let people use me.   A   F   N

5. No one can talk me into doing things I'd rather not do.   A   F   N

If you answered *A* to more than half the questions, you are rather assertive. Two or more *F* or *N* answers indicates that you can become more assertive.

IN YOUR JOURNAL

Identify some specific tasks you want to get done in the near future to work toward your long-term goals. Write whom you will contact and what you will say about your needs.

ANALYZING BEHAVIORS

GROUP ACTIVITY

In your group, discuss kinds of behavior that show assertiveness. Make a list of these behaviors. Analyze the descriptions in the excerpt for evidence of assertive and nonassertive behavior.

_____

_____

_____

_____

_____

_____

At the last moment Angela and Lavelle both decided to attend community college. Without comment, Angela took the courses her advisor suggested. Lavelle, however, pointed out to her advisor that she had completed her language requirement in high school and did not need to take the Spanish class that had been listed for her.

After meeting with her advisor, Lavelle went to the financial aid office to apply for assistance, though the deadline had passed. She told the administrator she really needed help and was willing to wait to see if there were any no-shows by students who had received grants. As Lavelle hoped, some grant recipients didn't register, and she received one of the grants.

Angela also went to the financial aid office but left discouraged after being told the deadline had passed to apply for a grant.

Lavelle went to every lecture class. Angela didn't like to get up early and missed several 8 A.M. history classes. When Lavelle got a low grade on a biology test, she made an appointment to see the instructor. The instructor looked at her class notes, made some suggestions, and helped her find a tutor.

Angela missed more classes and finally dropped history. She felt that everything had gone wrong during her first term, and she didn't know why.

SPEAKING UP FOR YOURSELF

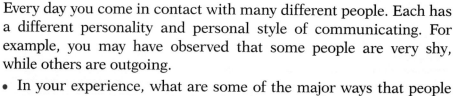

PERSONAL COMMUNICATION STYLES

Every day you come in contact with many different people. Each has a different personality and personal style of communicating. For example, you may have observed that some people are very shy, while others are outgoing.

DISCOVERY
ACTIVITY

- In your experience, what are some of the major ways that people differ in how they present their thoughts and needs to others when they speak?

  _____

  _____

  _____

  _____

  _____

Read this account of an incident that occurred in a small college in the Midwest. Describe any similarities between these students' styles and those you described from your experience.

> Frank, Melissa, and Murray failed to show up to give their oral reports, a requirement of Dr. Anderson-Barr's introductory political science class. Here is what each student did about the situation.
>
> Frank went to Dr. Anderson-Barr's office the day the report was due. He told her that his group had not done the work necessary for a good report, and he wanted nothing to do with it. He demanded an alternate assignment.
>
> Melissa was sick the day of the report. She brought a note from the student health center and asked Dr. Anderson-Barr to allow her to present on a different day.
>
> Murray decided to forget the whole thing because he had car trouble and nobody would believe that anyway.

GROUP
ACTIVITY

Activity A: Evaluating Behaviors

In your group, discuss whose approach—Frank's, Melissa's, or Murray's—you believe would stand the best chance of success. Why? Apply the ideas that you developed in the group activity on page 37. Then describe how you would respond to each student if you were the instructor. Pairs of students can role-play the dialogue between instructor and student.

DIFFERENT COMMUNICATION STYLES

You might have concluded from your experience and from the examples of Frank, Melissa, and Murray that people vary in the way they speak up for themselves. You can think of communication styles as a range of behavior from **passive** (someone who puts other people's needs first) to **aggressive** (someone who puts personal needs first without concern for other people).

Passivity

The passive person is basically saying to life and to others, "You win; I lose." Passive people are often those we describe as "nice," and for good reason. They always let others get their way and never stand up for what they want—and need! There is a price to pay for this kind of niceness. Passive people often feel "used" and "like a doormat." Beneath the niceness, they are often very frustrated and angry. Maybe you know someone like this.

Of course, many of us use passive behavior in certain situations, and sometimes it proves useful.

However, in college, passive behavior like Murray's seldom works to your advantage. You may expect that your college instructors—like your high school teachers, parents, or supervisors—will ask you what happened when you fail to do an assignment and will accept your explanation. Apparently Murray had that expectation. In college, however, instructors seldom ask for an explanation. They will just assign the grade you earn—in this case a 0—unless you come up with a well-stated, compelling reason for them to do otherwise, as Melissa did.

PORTFOLIO

Assignment 1:
Passive in Your Past

Write about two times when you used passive behavior. Describe one time when using passive behavior worked to your advantage and one time when it worked to your disadvantage. Save this assignment in your portfolio.

Aggressiveness

Aggressive behavior is exactly the opposite of passive behavior. The aggressive person says, in effect, "I win; you lose." An aggressive attitude is often encouraged in competitive areas such as sports. Some people see aggressiveness as an appropriate way to respond to problems. Aggressive people consider their needs to be more important than the needs of others and behave accordingly. In the example on page 38, Frank behaved in an aggressive manner toward his instructor by making demands rather than requests. He ignored the fact that the instructor has the right to set policy in her class. Aggressive behavior may bring success on the playing field. In the arena of college, however, and in day-to-day relationships generally, an aggressive communication style usually brings a negative response.

Assertiveness

The most productive communication style falls somewhere between aggressive and passive. Used effectively, assertive behavior can be seen as "I win, you win." This communication style requires careful thought to phrase statements and requests assertively. For example, you might have this thought about an instructor: "He just talks too fast in the lecture. No one can keep up." Such a statement does not express your needs. You could plan what to say to have the instructor slow down. You might phrase the idea this way: "I'm having a hard time keeping up in your lecture class. Would you please speak a little slower?"

- Which of the two ways to approach the instructor would be more effective? Why?

_____

_____

_____

_____

- In what other situations might the second approach work better? Explain.

_____

_____

Activity B: Claiming, Not Blaming

One strategy for using an assertive rather than an aggressive communication style is to change a "you" (blaming) statement into an "I" (claiming) statement.

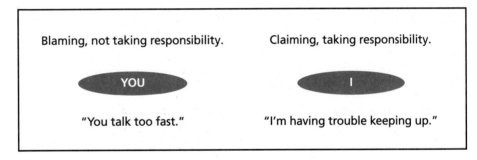

Blaming, not taking responsibility.	Claiming, taking responsibility.
YOU	I
"You talk too fast."	"I'm having trouble keeping up."

Practice, using the examples on the next page. Change the "you" statements to "I" statements.

IN YOUR JOURNAL

Think of a recent situation when you used either an aggressive or a passive communication style. Rewrite the situation in a way that shows how you might have achieved different results by acting assertively.

1. Your test covered things that were not covered in class.

   _____

   _____

2. You speak so softly; no one can hear you.

   _____

   _____

3. You financial aid advisors are always too busy talking on the phone to give me any help.

   _____

   _____

   _____

4. You talk so much you keep me from hearing the lecture.

   _____

   _____

   _____

5. Your assignments don't make sense.

   _____

   _____

6. You always keep me awake with your noisy phone calls.

   _____

   _____

   _____

7. You never keep the kids quiet when I am studying.

   _____

   _____

Assertive statements are most often made as "I" statements and tell the other person involved in a clear and nonthreatening way what your needs are. When you interact with others, you should take the time to make requests assertively, avoiding both passive and aggressive statements.

PORTFOLIO

Assignment 2:
Expressing Yourself

Write about a situation in which you need to be assertive. Describe the situation. Tell what your true feelings are and how you might express yourself to get what you want while still allowing the other person to win. Save this assignment in your portfolio.

SELF-ADVOCACY: PRACTICAL APPLICATIONS OF ASSERTIVENESS

Developing assertiveness enables you to be an advocate for the most important person in your life—you. As you probably know, one of the meanings of **advocate** is "an attorney." An attorney speaks up for, defends, and in general looks out for his or her client. When you are your own advocate—as you usually are in college, you must speak up for, defend, and look out for yourself.

Assertiveness enables you to go after what you want without stepping on the rights and feelings of others. You can see alternative ways to achieve your goals. You begin to advocate creatively for yourself. For example, if you get a "No" answer from someone at one level of an organization, you try someone else at a higher level of authority. Consider this exchange:

> LINDA: I have lost my student ID. I need a new one because I can't check out books in the library or use my meal plan . . .
>
> STUDENT WORKER: I'm new here. I don't know anything about replacing student IDs. I think you'll have to wait until after the weekend when the regular secretary comes back.
>
> LINDA: But I have to eat until then; I have to use the library and the gym. There must be some way. I'm sure this has happened before.
>
> STUDENT WORKER: I don't know. I guess you'll have to eat off campus.
>
> LINDA: Maybe your supervisor knows the answer. Where can I find that person?
>
> STUDENT WORKER: Well, you can ask, but I think she'll say the same thing. Go on back to the corner office.
>
> [5 minutes later]

SUPERVISOR TO STUDENT WORKER: She can go over to auxiliary services and pay $5 for a new ID. You can key a memo saying I authorized her to get a new ID.

STUDENT WORKER: No one told me that!

LINDA: (thinks to herself) Boy, I'm glad I didn't take "No" for an answer.

GROUP ACTIVITY

Activity C: Describing Linda's Style

Discuss these questions with your group, then write your responses.

How did Linda's behavior show self-advocacy?

_____

_____

_____

_____

What makes her advocacy assertive rather than aggressive?

_____

_____

_____

_____

_____

How might this encounter have ended differently if Linda hadn't been assertive?

_____

_____

_____

_____

_____

Based on Linda's experience and on your experiences, what conclusions can you draw about ways to deal with people in large organizations?

_____

_____

_____

_____

CONFLICT RESOLUTION

TECHNIQUES FOR RESOLVING CONFLICT

No matter how skilled you are at communicating, you will run into conflict from time to time. You've probably already had lots of experiences that involved tough choices, difficult decisions, and serious disagreements with other people.

DISCOVERY ACTIVITY

- What has your experience taught you about ways to deal with conflict? Give at least one specific example from your life.

_____

_____

_____

_____

_____

You can encounter conflict anywhere. In college, conflicts occur between instructors and students, between administrative personnel (financial aid, housing, and so on) and students, and between students themselves. Regardless of the kind of conflict, the techniques for resolving conflict are basically the same:

- **defuse**—to calm down or make less tense
- **negotiate**—to discuss and come to terms with others
- **mediate**—to act to settle differences between groups

Each technique applies to a different level of conflict, depending on how long the conflict has existed.

LEVEL ONE: DEFUSING CONFLICT

The best possible way to deal with conflict is to defuse the situation by keeping the lines of communication open. In other words, keep talking. Deal with an issue when it first occurs rather than allowing the conflict to build up into something explosive. At the early stages of a conflict, use these strategies to defuse the situation:

- Be calm and respectful of the other person.
- Politely persist in trying to get what you need.
- Try to see the situation from the other person's point of view. Consider what you can do or say that will make it easy for the other person to see your point of view and to meet your needs.

Suppose your academic advisor seems to rush through your meetings, not giving very much time or thought to your program of studies. This could begin to anger and annoy you if it happened several times. After several semesters of frustration on your part, a scene like this might occur:

> STUDENT: I think that I need to get my basic skills out of the way this term. I . . .
>
> ADVISOR: Sure, OK, let's just get these in the computer and get you on your way to registration. There's a line a mile long to see me. Here, see you next term.
>
> STUDENT: Wait a minute. I took that English class in summer school. Didn't you check the computer? You never listen to what I say! You just want to get me out of here as soon as possible! What's your problem? This is your job!
>
> ADVISOR: It's your responsibility to tell me these things. Don't get hostile with me, or I'll report you to the dean for disciplinary action! I'm not your mother; grow up!

Questions

1. What is the source of conflict in this scene?

_____

_____

_____

_____

2. Is the conflict resolved? Explain your answer.

_____

_____

_____

_____

_____

_____

3. How might the scene be different if both people tried to defuse the conflict?

_____

_____

_____

_____

_____

_____

_____

Activity D: Defusing a Conflict

Work with your group to recreate the scene between the student and the advisor so that the conflict is defused. You might first work together to outline a brief script. Then pairs of students can role-play the scene. As a group, discuss additional strategies for defusing a conflict.

LEVEL TWO: NEGOTIATION

Sometimes a conflict situation may get beyond Level One, making defusing difficult if not impossible. Tempers may have risen, and you and the other person (or persons) may have dug in your heels, unwilling to budge. In this kind of situation, you need strategies for negotiation. The most important thing to remember when negotiating is that both parties need to believe they've won _something_. Otherwise, resentment will prevent any lasting agreement. Here are some strategies for successful negotiation:

- Be a good listener, and think twice before you speak. Avoid speaking in anger. Listen to what the other person is saying and try to understand the needs behind the other person's words.
- Be clear about what you want, and have a clear understanding of what the other person wants. State your needs and feelings calmly and positively, using "I" statements. Avoid accusing the other person. If you're not sure what the other person wants, ask.
- Be willing to give up something, to compromise, so that no one has to be the loser.
- Keep your word. All the negotiations that you've gone through will be useless if one party or both parties do not live up to the agreement. Part of your success strategy must be to do what you say you will do. Be known as a person who keeps bargains.

Notice what has happened in this scene.

INSTRUCTOR: Maria, you are repeatedly late to class. I can't keep putting up with your lateness.

MARIA: I haven't been that late to class. You shouldn't be so strict. I would be on time if I could, but I've got problems at home.

INSTRUCTOR: I'm afraid that if you don't start coming on time, you'll have to drop the class.

Questions

1. What is the conflict? What does each side want?

_____

_____

_____

_____

_____

_____

_____

_____

_____

_____

_____

2. What are the instructor's needs?

_____

_____

_____

_____

3. What are Maria's needs?

_____

_____

_____

_____

_____

GROUP ACTIVITY

Activity E: Negotiating Strategies

Have pairs of students role-play the situation between Maria and her instructor. Negotiate the conflict using the strategies you've studied. As a group, discuss other possible strategies for negotiating this conflict.

LEVEL THREE: MEDIATION

When a conflict cannot be defused or successfully negotiated, a mediator may be necessary. A **mediator** is a person who does not take sides in the conflict. The mediator should be someone who is recognized and respected by both parties. The mediator's job is to sort out the problem, pose solutions, and help both sides work toward resolving the conflict. The key to the mediation process is convincing both sides to compromise on their demands. Both sides must be willing to give up something so that both sides can win.

The mediator tries to find answers to such questions as these:

- What does each side want?
- Where does each side seem to be stuck?
- What are some possible solutions?
- What is each side willing to give up?
- What is each side willing to accept as a compromise from the other?

The mediator's job is not to get the two parties to become friends. The goal is usually to settle the immediate conflict until a permanent solution can be reached.

Analyze this situation:

Audrey and Kim are roommates. Audrey has been allowing her boyfriend, Dion, to stay in their dorm room on weekends. Kim is upset about it and has complained to Audrey, but Dion is still there.

KIM: You and Dion are driving me out of my dorm room.

AUDREY: I have a right to have guests in my room if I like.

KIM: He's not just a guest. He's here *all* the time.

AUDREY: You're exaggerating. He visits only on the weekends.

The two women finally went to the school housing authority. The resident assistant, Gregory, was appointed as mediator.

Questions

1. What is the conflict? What does each person want?

_____

_____

_____

_____

_____

_____

2. What are some possible solutions Gregory might pose?

_____

_____

_____

_____

_____

_____

_____

_____

_____

_____

Activity F: Reaching a Compromise

Working with your group, choose teams of three classmates to role-play the situation. Kim and Audrey should each explain the situation to Gregory. Gregory should suggest possible solutions and discuss them with each woman. Kim and Audrey should then reach a compromise.

Assignment 3:
Writing About Conflict Resolution

PORTFOLIO

Write a few paragraphs describing a recent conflict situation. The situation might be one in which you were involved or one you know about. Recall the techniques you've studied in this chapter: defusing conflict, negotiating, and mediating. Which, if any, of these strategies were used in the conflict? What specific steps were taken to try to resolve the conflict? How did the conflict turn out? How might the conflict have turned out differently if some of the techniques in this chapter had been used? Save this assignment in your portfolio.

WRAPPING IT UP

SUMMARY

- Assertiveness is the ability to identify and communicate to others what we need and want.

- Evaluating your assertiveness can help you understand why you do or do not effectively achieve goals.

- People have different communication styles, ranging from passive to assertive to aggressive.

- One way to develop assertiveness is to claim (take responsibility) rather than blame (refuse responsibility).

- Self-advocacy is a key strategy in asserting yourself effectively, especially when dealing with organizations.

- You can be effective at conflict resolution by
  1. Defusing the conflict
  2. Negotiating
  3. Mediating or finding a mediator

- A mediator attempts to get two parties to settle their immediate conflict.

- Role-playing is a good tool for learning how to resolve conflicts and for improving your communication skills.

THINKING IT OVER

- What ideas, examples, and information did you find most useful in this chapter?

  _____

  _____

  _____

  _____

  _____

- How will you apply the strategies and techniques presented in this chapter to your short-term and long-term goals?

  _____

  _____

  _____

  _____

  _____

  _____

IN YOUR
JOURNAL

Describe your progress so far in achieving one of your goals. Focus on your use of assertiveness and its benefits as you move closer to achieving your goal.

4

DEALING WITH "THE SYSTEM"

OBJECTIVES:

- To develop skills for using an academic advisor effectively.

- To demonstrate how to use "the system" to meet your needs.

How Can the System
Work for Me?

Everyone knows the saying "You can't beat the system," and often enough it seems true. How do the scenes in the picture bear out this saying?

Bureaucracy is another term for "the system." It means all the rules and roles that together make the system work. Whatever you think of bureaucracies, like everyone else, you will have to deal with them. In this chapter you'll learn some techniques for getting what you want from bureaucracies, in particular the college system. You'll also learn that there's really no need to "beat the system." You need only to make the college system work for you.

GETTING STARTED

Think about systems or bureaucracies you have had experience with as you answer the questions below.

- When a bureaucrat, or representative of an organization, refuses your request, how do you usually react? Be specific.

  _____

  _____

  _____

  _____

- Did you ever decide not to go ahead with a project because you had difficulty with "the system"? How and why?

  _____

  _____

  _____

  _____

- Do you feel comfortable or uncomfortable making requests of people whom you don't know? Explain.

  _____

  _____

  _____

- Do you often ask others to advise you? Do you prefer to research or think through problems yourself, when possible?

  _____

  _____

  _____

IN YOUR JOURNAL

What goals of yours are likely to involve working with a bureaucracy? In your journal, describe some of the ways in which you plan to approach the bureaucracy.

APPROACHING THE SYSTEM

Dealing with bureaucracies is a necessary part of life.

GROUP ACTIVITY

A. What do you like or not like about dealing with officials, bureaucrats, or other representatives of large organizations? Discuss this question with your group. What are the most common complaints? What are the most common benefits?

_____

_____

_____

_____

_____

B. Choose two situations from the Data Bank that you have personally experienced. Describe the situations to your group, listening carefully as the others say what they admired in your handling of the situation or what they thought could be improved. What did you learn from the group's comments? What did you agree or disagree with?

_____

_____

_____

_____

_____

- Open account with a bank.
- Inquire into your child's school performance.
- Apply for college grant.
- Pick up package at post office.
- Appear in traffic court.
- Recover lost luggage on trip.

DATA BANK

- Fill out loan application form.
- Complete medical insurance claims.
- Transfer to new position.
- Return a faulty product.
- Have credit or other records corrected.

WHAT "SYSTEMS" DO YOU KNOW?

A bureaucracy or "system" can take many forms. The system might be a government agency, a corporation, or a college administration. The key elements in a bureaucracy are the set of rules and roles that make the system work.

DISCOVERY ACTIVITY

What system have you dealt with most recently? Describe the situation, and evaluate how the system worked.

_____

_____

_____

_____

_____

_____

Registration is part of the college "system" familiar to college students. For some students the process is complicated and frustrating but necessary.

THE COLLEGE SYSTEM

In the college arena, you will encounter people functioning in a different way from what you might be accustomed to. These people and the rules they follow make up the college system. As a student you face the challenge of learning to work within the traditions of the system to meet your academic needs.

"THE SYSTEM" IS PEOPLE

The heart of any system or bureaucracy is the people who run it. Remember this as you deal with the offices, agencies, and academic units within your college system. When you have a need that can be served by the system, sooner or later you're likely to be talking to someone—a real person—in the system.

Your best strategy is to try to work within the system rather than to challenge it. Know the rules, and follow them. The rules have been set up to serve as many people as possible. However, when you have a special need, don't feel that your situation is hopeless just because you have to deal with the system. Even when you are told that policies or regulations demand something, someone may—when your situation warrants—be able to bend or waive a rule for you. In many college units, that person is the college secretary—someone well worth having as an ally.

SOURCES OF INFORMATION ABOUT THE SYSTEM

Most colleges have information and media centers devoted exclusively to printing guides to the system. These guides include various catalogs, flyers, pamphlets, and manuals that list the course offerings, programs, regulations, and policies of the college. As a freshman you should become familiar with information sources at your school.

Activity A: Your School's Information Sources

- Which of your school's publications have you found useful so far? Describe how they have helped you.

_____

_____

_____

_____

_____

Catalog

The main sources of information about the college are the catalog, the student handbook, the schedule of classes, and the syllabus.

You received a catalog when you applied or when you arrived to register. This catalog is *the* most important source of information for your college years. Most catalogs list all or most of the following information:

- Departments, schools, and colleges within the institution
- Possible major courses of study
- Instructors' names with some information, such as where and when they received their degrees
- Course titles and requirements
- Basic skills and other institutional requirements
- Courses of study for each degree

The course of study lists all the courses you must complete successfully to earn your degree. You should always consult the course of study listing in your catalog before going to your advisor. Remember, in a very real sense, *you* are your advisor. You are the person most critically affected if you fail to take a required class or if you unnecessarily repeat classes.

Save the catalog that is in force when you start your program of studies. Sometimes requirements change during your course of study. When this change happens, you may—at most colleges—accept the new requirements or follow the requirements that were in force when you entered.

The following is a sample page from a college catalog.

ACADEMIC MAJORS AND MINORS

Academic Majors

A major is required for all baccalaureate degrees, except the Bachelor of Individualized Studies, and consists of at least 24 credits in the major field of which at least 18 credits must be upper-division courses.

Academic Minors

Students seeking a baccalaureate degree may elect to complete one or more minors from those available, and the minor will be designated on their transcripts. Minors will not be acknowledged after the degree has been conferred.

A minor consists of a minimum of 18 credits, at least 9 of which must be upper-division. The minor may be in a single department or may be inter-departmental. Specific requirements for these minors are available in printed form in departmental and deans' offices. Specific available minors are

College of Agriculture and Home Economics

Agricultural Business Management
Agricultural and Extension Education
Agronomy
Entomology
Family and Consumer Sciences
Fashion Merchandising
Food Service Administration
Home Economics
Horse Management
Horticulture
Hospitality and Tourism Services
Livestock Production
Natural Resource Economics
Nutrition
Plant Pathology
Soils

College of Arts and Sciences

American Government and Politics
Anthropology
Art
Art History
Biochemistry
Biology
Chemistry
City and Regional Planning
Communication Studies
Comparative Government
Computer Science
Creative Writing
Criminal Justice
Cultural Conservation
English
French
Geography
Geology
German
Government
History
International Relations
Journalism and Mass Communications
Linguistics
Mathematics
Music
Philosophy
Physics
Political Theory
Professional Writing
Psychology
Public Administration
Public Law
Russian
Sociology
Spanish
Theatre Arts
Women's Studies

College of Business Administration and Economics

Business Administration
Economics

College of Education

Counseling and Educational Psychology
Early Childhood Education

College of Engineering

Environmental Management

College of Human and Community Services

Community Health
Gerontology
Health Administration

Graduation Requirements

For the baccalaureate degree each student must complete a minimum of 128 credits including at least 55 credits numbered 300 or above. Program waivers require the approval of the Academic Deans' Council.

Each college has its own requirements for graduation listed under its curricula. However, there are certain graduation requirements common to all undergraduate colleges:

• A student must have an average of two grade points per credit in all courses taken at NMSU.

• The student will be required to show proficiency in written English in all class work of the university. Any instructor may remand a student to the English remedial laboratory for further training in written English. In each case, the student must complete the remedial laboratory work prior to submitting the application to graduate.

• Each student must complete at New Mexico State University the last 30 semester credits necessary for the baccalaureate degree (see exception under "Servicemen's Opportunity College" heading). Of these last 30 credits, the student not regularly enrolled at NMSU the previous year must complete a minimum of 20 credits in courses numbered 300 or above of which a minimum of 10 credits must be in the major field. The following may not be used toward these requirements: CLEP, USAFI/DANTES, and course challenge credits.

• Curricular requirements for a specific degree may be met by completing all of the course requirements for that degree as set forth in the catalog of matriculation provided that the selected catalog is not more than six years old when the requirements for graduation are met. This rule applies only to the course requirements and number of credits as specified for the degree. In all other cases, the current catalog is effective.

Upon completion of all requirements, multiple majors for a single degree (e.g., B.A.) will be noted on the academic record. A second bachelor's degree (e.g., B.S.) may be granted if all requirements for that degree have been completed. Two degrees may be granted at one commencement if the requirements for both have been met. The graduation fee must be paid for each degree.

Both designated and undesignated associate degree residency requirements vary with the college awarding the degree. Requirements for the two-year associate degrees and for the certificates are found in the section(s) concerning these degrees.

• Arts and Sciences, Engineering, Education, and Human and Community Services require that the last 15 credits be completed at NMSU or one of its branch campuses.

Academic Majors: This section gives you specifies about how many credits you need for your major.

Academic Minors: Note that you can have more than one minor at this institution. This section tells you how many credits you need for a minor and lists the fields you can choose from.

Graduation Requirements: This section lists the requirements for graduation. Note that your college may have other requirements in addition to the general ones listed.

Old Catalog requirements: At this institution you can use the old catalog requirements if you choose, for a period of six years.

Activity B: Your School's Catalog

- Describe how your current college catalog is organized.

  _____

  _____

  _____

  _____

  _____

- What sections of your college catalog seem to be most relevant to your situation?

  _____

  _____

  _____

  _____

  _____

Student Handbook

Most institutions publish a collection of the regulations that apply to students. This book includes topics such as dorm regulations, drug and alcohol policies, disciplinary procedures, student organizations and so on. Look through this document at the first opportunity to become familiar with the information it provides.

A sample from the table of contents of a student handbook is shown on the next page.

Activity C: Your School's Student Handbook

- Describe the main features of your school's student handbook.

  _____

  _____

  _____

  _____

  _____

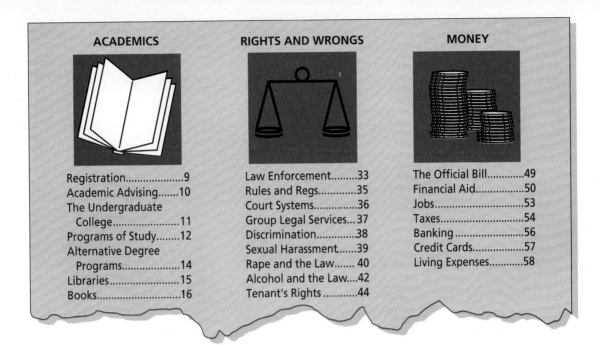

- What sections of your student handbook seem to be most relevant to your situation?

_____

_____

_____

_____

_____

_____

_____

Schedule of Classes

The schedule of classes is printed and distributed prior to each term. It lists class meeting times, instructors, and other information that is subject to change. The schedule booklet may include blank forms that you can use to plan your tentative class schedule.

The sample on the next page shows the kinds of information provided by a schedule of classes.

FALL SEMESTER 1993

DEPT NO SEC CRS	COURSE TITLE	TIME	DAY	PLACE	INSTRUCTOR

CHEMICAL ENGINEERING (CH E)

DEPT NO SEC CRS	COURSE TITLE	TIME	DAY	PLACE	INSTRUCTOR
CH E 150 1 3.0	INTRDN TO CHEMCL ENGR	1020-1135	TTH	JH283	HOLBROOK S T
	LABORATORY		TBA		HOLBROOK S T
CH E 150H 1 3.0	INTRDN TO CHEMCL ENGR	1020-1135	TTH	JH283	HOLBROOK S T
	LABORATORY		TBA		HOLBROOK S T
CH E 217 1 4.0	CHEMCL PROC CALCLTNS	0930-1020	MWF	JH209	PATTON J T
	LABORATORY	0230-0500	W	JH103	PATTON J T
CH E 217H 1 4.0	CHMCL PRC CLCLTNS-HON	0930-1020	MWF	JH209	PATTON J T
	LABORATORY	0230-0500	W	JH103	PATTON J T
CH E 300 1 1-3	SPECIAL PROJECTS		TBA		HOLBROOK S T
CH E 313 1 3.0	ENGINEERING MATERIALS	1030-1120	MWF	JH283	MUNSON-MCGEE S
CH E 313 2 3.0	ENGINEERING MATERIALS	0930-1020	MWF	GO201	MUNSON-MCGEE S
CH E 313H 1 3.0	ENGR MATERIALS-HON	1030-1120	MWF	JH283	MUNSON-MCGEE S
CH E 313H 2 3.0	ENGR MATERIALS-HON	0930-1020	MWF	GO201	MUNSON-MCGEE S
CH E 330 1 1.0	ENVNMTL MGT SEMINAR I	0330-0420PM	M	CE103	JACQUEZ R B
CH E 353 1 3.0	CHEML ENGRG THRMDYMCS	0130-0220	MWF	JH283	LONG R L

Activity D: Your Schedule of Classes

- What sections of the schedule booklet seem most relevant to your situation?

_____

_____

_____

_____

_____

_____

_____

_____

Syllabus

Each professor will probably give you a **syllabus** (plural: syllabi), a description of the course. The syllabus is a form of contract between the instructor and the student. The syllabus tells you the course content, the course requirements, the text and text readings, and grading policies. This document also provides information on tests, term papers, and topics to be covered.

Be sure to save all your syllabi. Some students tape them on the inside covers of their course notebooks. Syllabi are important enough for you to photocopy so that you can store a set each term.

The sample on the next page shows the kinds of information available in a syllabus.

Activity E: Your Course Syllabus

- Describe a syllabus from one of your courses. What important information does the syllabus contain?

_____

_____

_____

_____

_____

- How is this syllabus helpful?

_____

_____

_____

- What sections of the syllabus are most relevant to your situation?

_____

_____

_____

_____

_____

_____

_____

Office number:
Your instructor
may be found
at this location
during posted
office hours.

Office hours:
If you need
to see your
instructor, try
to arrange a
time during
these hours.

Prerequisite:
You need to
have taken this
earlier course
or have an
adequate score
(Math Placement
Exam) to
register for
this course.

Information Sheet - Math 142, Section 5
Applied Mathematics for the Biological and Social Sciences I
Fall 1994

Instructor
Office: SH 236 (Math Department Office)
Textbook: Goldstein, Lay, and Schneider, *Calculus and Its Applications,* Fifth Edition, Prentice-Hall, 1990.

Phone: 646-3901
Office Hours: 1:30-3:30 P.M. M-F

Prerequisite: C or better in Math 115, Intermediate Algebra, or adequate MPE score
Objectives: To understand some of the basic concepts of calculus; to appreciate the nature of its applications; to develop some facility in reading mathematics; to appreciate the importance of calculus to the development of science

Grading:
(15%) **Homework, quizzes, and log sheets**—At least one such assignment will be given each week.
(45%) **Tests**—Three 75-minute tests (15% each) will be given on the following dates:
Thursday, September 17
Thursday, October 15
Thursday, November 12
(10%) **Report**—A brief (3-5 typewritten pages) report on an approved topic related to the course will be required. It will be graded on writing as well as on expression of ideas. The topic must be approved by October 1; an abstract will be due on October 20; the paper is due on November 24.
(30%) **Final Exam**—A two-hour comprehensive final exam will be given Tuesday, December 15, from 8:00-10:00 A.M.

Course Grade: A 90% and above
B 80%-89%
C 70%-79%
D 60%-69%
F below 60%

Content: A tentative schedule of sections to be covered is:

8/25	0.1,0.2,1.1	10/1	2.6	11/5	4.5,4.6
8/27	0.3,0.4,0.5	10/6	2.7	11/10	review
9/1	1.2, 1.3	10/8	3.1	11/12	Test III
9/3	1.4,1.5	10/13	review	11/17	5.1,5.2
9/8	1.6,1.7	10/15	Test II	11/19	6.1
9/10	1.8	10/20	3.2	11/24	6.2
9/15	review	10/22	3.3	12/1	6.3
9/17	Test I	10/27	4.1,4.2	12/3	6.4,6.5
9/22	2.1,2.2	10/29	4.3	12/8	6.6
9/24	2.3,2.4	11/3	4.4	12/10	review
9/29	2.5			12/15	final exam

Make-up Work: Quizzes, homework, and log sheets cannot be made up. Tests can be made up provided the absence is excused (written documentation required).

Grading:
These tests and reports should
be entered on your calendar.
Note that the final exam
is worth 30% of your grade.

Content:
Note that the instructor gives
you a tentative schedule for topics,
tests, reviews. These are subject to change.

Make-up work:
Most institutions allow
individual instructors to
set their policy on
make-up work. Note
the specific definition
for excused absences.

HOLDING ON TO SOURCES

Develop the habit of saving all official documents—even flimsy ones like the carbons of drop/add slips—until you're sure they're no longer needed. Set up a file system or special loose-leaf folder in which to keep these documents. Remember, colleges live and die by the printed word, and they put great reliance on documentation.

PORTFOLIO

Assignment 1:
Designing a Better Booklet

Design a helpful college publication. It might be a new publication or an improvement on one of the sources described in this chapter. Explain how the publication would be helpful. Save this assignment in your portfolio.

YOUR ACADEMIC ADVISOR

In college your goals are usually connected with the process of taking the courses, gaining the knowledge, and earning the credits that will allow you to graduate. An important step in achieving these goals is taking the right sequence of courses. As you learned earlier, your college catalog almost always lists the courses required for your major. Be sure that you understand what courses you need for the major you've decided on.

• What might happen to students who are not aware of the correct courses for their major?

_____

_____

_____

_____

_____

_____

THE BEST ADVISOR

First and foremost, *you* are responsible for seeing that the courses you take are the right ones and that you take all the required courses necessary both for basic requirements and for your major.

There are dozens of students with the same sad story: They are staying extra terms in college because someone gave them incorrect information.

Here is the story of one such student.

> When I started college, I was assigned to Dr. Preston, a professor in the English department, because I was going to major in English. I thought that Dr. Preston was not very interested in advising me. He did not seem very interested in undergraduates at all.
>
> My first term, I asked Dr. Preston if I needed to start work on my language requirement. He replied, "Don't worry. They are going to do away with the language requirement."
>
> Great, I thought. Being young and foolish, I did what he advised. I didn't worry about it—until my senior year.
>
> When I applied to graduate, a clerk at the registrar's office said in reproving tones, "You can't graduate in the spring. You don't have the language requirement."
>
> "But...but...but...Dr. Preston said that the language requirement was being eliminated!" I protested.
>
> "Oh, they have been talking about that for years," the registrar said, rolling her eyes. "You still have to have it; nothing has changed."
>
> As it turned out, I was able to enter a fourth-term language class to satisfy the requirement but not without a great deal of cramming, pain, and tears. It had been four years since I had studied a second language in high school. If I had *not* had a language in high school, Dr. Preston's advice would have cost me *two extra years* in college. When I told him, he shrugged.

- What is the moral of this story?

_____

_____

_____

GOOD ADVISORS DO EXIST, BUT...

Despite the example of Dr. Preston, many advisors are professional, up-to-date on requirements, and good at what they do. Further, they are, for the most part, genuinely devoted to students. This is the case in departments that have advising centers with professional advisors.

Don't trust your luck, however. Know your course of study and question any course your advisor suggests that is not on the list. Be especially careful to check and double check if an advisor tells you that you don't need a course that is printed in the course of study. Check with another advisor and with the Dean's office.

HOW TO BE YOUR OWN ADVISOR

In addition to knowing your course of study and checking the advice you receive, you can ask yourself questions that will help you act as your own advisor. Here are some of those questions along with possible answers that can serve as guidelines.

- *How many courses can I take per term and still do well?* Choose fewer hours if your work schedule or home responsibilities are heavy or if you are a new student. Choose more hours only if the courses are relatively undemanding and your outside responsibilities are light.

- *At what hours should I schedule classes?* Consider what courses are available and when they are available. Consider your work and home schedule, your transportation arrangements, and the time of day you prefer. You may be forced to take classes at inconvenient times, but try to avoid this situation by registering early—before desirable sections are filled.

- *What courses can I take that will meet college-wide or basic skills requirements?* Most schools have specific requirements in math and English. They may also require you to choose courses from other disciplines, such as the social and physical sciences. Plan to take these courses in the early terms of your college years. In addition, if you decide to change majors, the requirements you've completed will apply to your new major. Here is an example.

Angelo decided to go into computer science when he started college. His advisor wanted him to take his English and math requirements, a general education science course, a social science course, and one computer science class. Instead, Angelo took his math class, his English class, and three different computer science classes.

At the end of the term, Angelo decided to switch his major to history. Unfortunately, only one of the computer science classes applied in his new major. If he had taken the general education science and social science, he could have applied all of these courses to his new major.

- *Are there any graduation requirements for courses that are offered only in a certain term sequence?* Language courses, for example, may be offered only in alternate terms. Here's what happened to one student.

Ruth knew that she would need Chemistry 101 as the first course of her major. Still, she decided to wait until the spring term. But in the spring only Chemistry 102 was offered. Ruth was forced to wait until the following fall to take Chemistry 101. During the summer session, she couldn't take any chemistry courses at all since 101 was a prerequisite for all of them.

- *Are there any other requirements I need to satisfy?* Athletes, for example, must meet standards set by national governing organizations. Some scholarships and grants specify certain courses, or, more often, course loads. Organizations such as fraternities, sororities, and marching bands may have requirements for members. Financial aid often depends on successfully completing a certain course load per term or per year. Check with the appropriate organization early in the year and avoid finding out at the last minute that you are missing a requirement and need to attend an extra summer session.

USING YOUR ADVISOR

Get to know your academic advisor at appropriate times. Slow times after registration, during the summer, or during breaks are best. Visit with your advisor. If you are undecided on a major, don't be embarrassed to say so. The freshman year is a time for trying out options. Work with your advisor to choose courses that can apply to almost any major, keeping your options open.

When you need to see your advisor, make an appointment and be prepared. Don't just show up with the crowd around registration time. Make a list of items to discuss with your advisor. Your list should include the following:

- Courses you've taken
- Courses you expect to take
- Alternative courses in case courses you want are not available
- Questions about the courses

If your advisor suggests you take courses outside the general education requirements and the requirements for your major, ask why you should take those courses. Ask in a tactful way so that you maintain a good working relationship with your advisor.

IF YOUR COLLEGE DOESN'T HAVE ACADEMIC ADVISORS

Remember: You are your own best advisor. So don't panic if you discover that your college doesn't have official academic advisors. Follow these two guidelines in this situation:

- Carefully read your printed course of study. Make sure the courses you choose are listed for your major.
- Faculty members or counselors often act as advisors in institutions without formal advisors. Ask around and see who can help you. If you can't find anyone to advise you, list the courses you think you need from your program of study. Then ask the head of the department in your major to review your choices.

CHANGING MAJORS

Yes, people do change majors, and you can, too, if you need to. Read Barry's story, which follows.

Ever since I was a kid, everyone—including me—assumed I would be an engineer like my dad. All my teachers encouraged me in math and science, and I always did well in those subjects, even throughout high school.

In college, I declared a major in electrical engineering. My first term, I took two engineering classes. I also took my required writing class and a sociology and a psychology class to meet general studies requirements. I took a photojournalism class just for fun. Over the term, I found my photography class much more exciting than my engineering class. In November, my journalism teacher told me that I had "an exceptionally artistic eye, a real talent." That really did it. I switched majors at the end of the year. I switched to art, though, rather than to journalism, because I'm best at artistic photography.

I have never been so happy now that I have switched. My advice to others is to try things out. You may find that you have talent in fields you don't even know about.

Like Barry, you may find yourself in a field that is wrong for you. Sometimes changing majors means that you need to spend more time in school before getting your degree, but the extra time may be worth it.

GROUP
ACTIVITY

Activity F: Advising Each Other

With your group, analyze each other's course selections in relation to your majors. Follow the guidelines under "How to Be Your Own Advisor" on pages 69-70. Write specific comments regarding your own course selections and major.

_____

_____

_____

_____

_____

_____

_____

_____

_____

_____

Assertiveness and the System

One key point to remember when dealing with any bureaucracy is to "persevere politely." Usually you can benefit from being persistent rather than throwing your hands up in disgust or losing your temper. If you get a "no" answer, try going up or around. You will not always be successful, but at least you'll have the satisfaction of trying. Often your persistence will be rewarded.

When you act assertively, remember to consider the needs of others, especially people who are representatives of the system. It's not necessary—and not smart—to humiliate or embarrass someone whom you might need to bypass. Remember Linda, who needed a new ID (see pages 43-44). She asked very politely to see the supervisor and did not try to portray the student worker as incompetent. Linda might have to deal with that worker again. She was wise not to alienate her.

FIGHTING THE SYSTEM

Fighting the system is not the same as being assertive within the system. Being assertive within the system is trying to make the existing rules work for you. When you fight the system, you're trying to make a permanent change in the rules of the system.

There is a good chance that you won't succeed in fighting the system. In many situations all you may learn is how much energy you need to accomplish change. Here's an example:

> Jay was an energetic freshman just out of the military. He was disgusted with the parking system at our college. He felt strongly that parking should not be on a designated Faculty/Student basis because he could never find a parking place in the student section before his 9:30 A.M. class. I suggested the practical solution: come at 8 A.M. when there are lots of spaces; study or do homework until class.
>
> But Jay was adamant. "The system must change," he demanded. "Students must have equal rights." He began a campaign for undesignated parking.
>
> He wrote to the college president. He circulated a petition. He contacted the student government, which eventually declined to take up his cause.
>
> After two terms, Jay estimated that he had spent twice as many hours on his campaign as he had on his schoolwork. His grades showed it; he was on academic probation. Jay finally got back on track and managed to graduate only one term later than expected. Five years later, the school still has designated parking.

This story is not meant to discourage you from trying to institute change in areas about which you feel strongly. It only suggests that the better choice is to work *with* rather than *against* the system.

PORTFOLIO

Assignment 2:
Writing a Letter

Think of a problem you've experienced at your school. Could the problem be solved by working within the system? If you feel the problem could be solved only by a change in the system, what change would you recommend? Who is the best person to make aware of the problem? Write a letter to that person describing the problem and your suggested solution. Save this assignment in your portfolio.

WRAPPING IT UP

SUMMARY

- The key elements of a bureaucracy, or "system," are the set of rules and roles that makes the system work.
- Colleges have information centers devoted to providing guides to the system, including catalogs, handbooks, flyers, and manuals.
- The guides list the course offerings and set forth the programs, regulations, and policies of the college.
- Each course has a syllabus that describes the course, course requirements, texts, and grading policies.
- The schedule of classes lists class meeting times, instructors, and other information that is subject to change.
- While first and foremost you are your own advisor, your academic advisor can also help you:
    1. Identify a major and its requirements.
    2. Comply with general education requirements.
    3. Select alternative courses.
- In dealing with the college system, positive results come from persevering politely rather than fighting the system or alienating its workers.

THINKING IT OVER

- What material from this chapter did you find most valuable? How?

_____

_____

_____

- How will you apply the information and ideas in this chapter to your short- and long-term goals?

  _____

  _____

  _____

  _____

  _____

  _____

IN YOUR
JOURNAL

Review the personal goal you identified that involves a bureaucracy. Describe your progress toward achieving this goal.

Analyzing Your Strengths

As you take charge of your college work, you bring with you all of the knowledge, skills, and habits that you've acquired. These strengths are enormously important to your success in college. When you become aware of your strengths—as you will in this section—you can then build on them and use them to maximum effect. Chapter 5 helps you develop an understanding of your learning style. This chapter will guide you to identify the circumstances in which you learn best. Chapter 6 leads you to recognize the status of your study skills. In this chapter you'll also learn about resources that can help you improve your study skills.

5

ASSESSING YOUR LEARNING STYLE

OBJECTIVES:

- To take inventory of your personal learning style.

- To identify strategies for effectively using your learning style.

What's My Learning Style?

What are some of the specific things the couple might be considering as they think about building a wall unit?

In reviewing their plans and their skills as builders, the couple aim to do the best job they can. As they begin to build, they will apply skills they already have and learn new ones.

As a student, you need to analyze the resources you bring with you to college. One of your most important resources is your learning style. Your **learning style** is the way you approach a learning task—the conditions and strategies that work best for you. This chapter will help you take inventory of your learning style and will suggest ways that you can use your learning style to achieve college success.

GETTING STARTED

Answer the questions below to find out what your general learning preferences are. In each question, circle the italicized word or phrase that best describes you. Save your results and compare them with the results of the checklist on page 101.

1. Are you a *day* or *night* person?

2. Do you rely more on *thoughts* or on *feelings* when you make decisions?

3. Do you prefer to *stick* to one thing until you finish, or do you prefer to *shift* among a few tasks?

4. In general, do you require *neatness*, or can you tolerate *disorder*?

5. Which three of your five senses—*touch, smell, sight, sound, taste*—are most important to you?

6. Are you more of a *people* person or a *loner*?

7. Do you tend to think in terms of *absolutes* (right or wrong), or are you more of a *relativist* (things are neither right nor wrong)?

8. Do you prefer to go from the *big picture to the details* or from the *details to the big picture*?

9. Do you learn better through *listening* or through *reading and writing*?

IN YOUR JOURNAL

Describe some of the problems you may be having or may have had in college. What role, if any, did your learning style play in these problems? What changes might help solve the problems?

LEARNING STYLE AND COLLEGE WORK

GROUP ACTIVITY

With your group, discuss learning style characteristics that will be important to success in college. Refer to the Data Bank for ideas. List the items the group agrees on.

_____

_____

_____

_____

_____

_____

_____

_____

_____

_____

_____

_____

_____

_____

_____

_____

- Feel energetic in the morning.
- Need to be in the mood to study.
- Can concentrate on only one thing at a time.
- Can concentrate anywhere.
- Need to have the right pen and paper.

DATA BANK

- Prefer being alone when studying.
- Strive to be perfect.
- Wait to gather facts before making a decision.
- Remember more from hearing than from taking notes.

Analyzing Your Learning Style

Pinpointing Your Preferences

People have different preferences about when, how, and under what conditions they learn. By completing the learning-style checklists that appear in this chapter, you can combine what you already know about your learning style with important factors you may not have considered.

DISCOVERY ACTIVITY

Describe something you've achieved recently in your college work or in your daily life. Your achievement can be something small or something major.

_____

_____

_____

_____

_____

_____

What were the conditions that enabled you to achieve? Describe your skills, your attitude, and the choices you made that contributed to your success.

_____

_____

_____

_____

The learning-style checklists examine nine areas in which you make choices that reflect your learning style. The nine areas are:

1. Time Preference—the time of day when you learn best.

2. Thoughts/Feelings Preference—whether you are a thinking person or are guided more by your feelings.

3. Pacing Preference—whether you do things one at a time or tend to juggle several things at once.

4. Aesthetic Preference—what kind of surroundings you prefer, such as formal and orderly or casual and disorderly.

5. Tactile Preference—whether the touch of certain items is important to you.

6. Introversion/Extroversion Preference—whether you are quiet and withdrawn or outgoing.

7. Relativism Preference—whether you see things in strict terms (like good and bad) or have a less strict view (seeing things as neither entirely good nor entirely bad).

8. Reasoning Preference—whether you like to go from the big picture to the details or from the details to the big picture.

9. Modality Preference—whether you learn new information better by hearing it or by seeing it in writing.

THE LEARNING-STYLE CHECKLISTS

Knowing your learning style can help you be more effective in making choices. You may be able to say to yourself, for example, "I have more energy in the evenings than in the mornings so I will schedule classes in the evenings."

After each checklist, you'll find strategies for the best way to work within your learning style. Ideally, you will be able to seek out situations that are compatible with your learning style. However, you may not always be able to work within your preferred style. People who are more visually oriented, for example, learn to cope with lecture classes.

Check one box after each statement, indicating whether the statement is true or not true for you most of the time.

TIME PREFERENCE

People respond in different ways to the cycle of daylight and darkness. This checklist helps you assess whether you have a preference for daytime or for night.

	TRUE FOR ME	NOT TRUE FOR ME
1. I have a hard time getting started in the morning.	☐	☐
2. I tend to be more alert after the sun goes down.	☐	☐
3. Even when I get enough sleep, my concentration in morning classes is not great.	☐	☐
4. It takes a while for me to wake up fully.	☐	☐
5. I do my best work at night.	☐	☐
6. I wake up full of energy.	☐	☐
7. I am not very alert at night.	☐	☐
8. When I work problems at night, I make more mistakes.	☐	☐
9. I prefer morning classes.	☐	☐
10. Sometimes, if I'm reading at night, I have to read something several times to understand it.	☐	☐

Scoring

To determine your time preference, count and record the number of "true" responses.

Items 1-5 _____   Items 6-10 _____

If you have more "true" responses for items 1-5, you are a **night person**. If you have more "true" responses for items 6-10, you are a **day person**. Record your time preference.

Time Preference _____

Making the Best of Day and Night Preferences

As you might guess, day people do best if they schedule demanding tasks or tough classes early in the day. One thing that day people often overlook is using the odd hours—for instance the hour between two classes—to do assigned readings and homework problems. The day people who attempt to do all their studying at night will probably spend much more time on each task than if they study during their "prime time." A better strategy is for a day person to go to sleep earlier and get up earlier in the morning to study before classes. A bonus of this plan is that the very early morning hours are often quiet, making concentration easier.

Night people have a harder time scheduling tough classes at their prime times. Most institutions schedule more morning classes than afternoon or evening classes. If you're a night person, afternoon classes are generally better for you than morning classes. Night persons find the quiet hours after others are in bed more productive for them. The only problem is that a night person who wants to sleep late often finds that most of the world wakes up early and quickly becomes noisy. Ear plugs and sleep masks may help. Some night persons even put on headphones and play soft music to lull themselves back to sleep when awakened.

THOUGHTS/FEELINGS PREFERENCE

This category helps you recognize whether your learning is guided more by your thoughts or by your feelings. Check one box after each statement, indicating whether the statement is true or not true for you most of the time.

	TRUE FOR ME	NOT TRUE FOR ME
1. I do much better in a class if I like the instructor, regardless of the subject matter.	☐	☐
2. When I feel "down," I can't concentrate on studying.	☐	☐
3. When I go to certain classes, or think about them, I get a strong emotional reaction (feel sick, feel thrilled, and so on).	☐	☐
4. I find it hard to study when I'm not in the mood.	☐	☐
5. I often make spur-of-the-moment decisions.	☐	☐
6. I like to analyze and weigh everything before making a decision.	☐	☐
7. If an instructor is knowledgeable, his or her personality isn't very important to me.	☐	☐
8. My background knowledge of a subject is the best predictor of how I'll do in a class.	☐	☐
9. When it's time to study, I just do it, no matter how I feel.	☐	☐
10. When I'm feeling "down," I can put that feeling aside if I need to do something.	☐	☐

Scoring

To determine your thoughts/feelings preference, count and record the number of "true" responses.

Items 1-5 _____   Items 6-10 _____

If you have more "true" responses for items 1-5, **feelings** have a strong effect on you. If you have more "true" responses for items 6-10, **thoughts** have a strong effect on you. Record your thoughts/feelings preference.

Thoughts/Feelings Preference _____

Making the Best of Thoughts and Feelings Preferences

Strong positive feelings about your instructors could motivate you to high achievement. Conversely, strong negative feelings could lead to academic disaster unless you find a way to deal with them.

Similarly, you'll need to find a way to deal with any negative feelings that come up during study times. For example, you might plan to reward yourself after studying by doing something pleasurable. Looking forward to your treat can help pull you out of a negative reaction to studying.

If you are strongly affected by thoughts, you probably will not often need to deal with negative feelings in academic situations. However, you may also be unable to benefit from the strong positive feelings that motivate a person who is more affected by feelings. You need to think ahead to the long-term outcomes of certain classes—good grades and graduating, for example—to make your study sessions more profitable.

IN YOUR JOURNAL

Write a letter to yourself, addressed to "Dear Thinker" or "Dear Feeler." Include your recommendations for ways to deal with instructors and studying.

PACING PREFERENCE

Pacing refers to the way you use time to get things done. Check one box after each statement, indicating whether the statement is true or not true for you most of the time.

	TRUE FOR ME	NOT TRUE FOR ME
1. When I'm "on a roll" on a project, I keep going until I'm done.	☐	☐
2. I do better work when I can concentrate totally on one thing.	☐	☐
3. Sometimes I lose track of time when I'm concentrating.	☐	☐
4. I push myself until something is completely done.	☐	☐
5. I throw myself totally into only one hobby or project at a time.	☐	☐
6. When I begin a project, I anticipate how much time it will take.	☐	☐
7. When I realize my concentration is slipping, I do something else.	☐	☐
8. I divide projects into parts and set time frames for the parts.	☐	☐
9. I reward myself when I complete part of a project.	☐	☐
10. I like to be doing several things— working on several projects or reading several books—at one time.	☐	☐

Scoring

To determine your pacing preference, count and record the number of "true" responses.

Items 1-5 _____   Items 6-10 _____

If you have more "true" responses for items 1-5, you have a **unitary style**—you like to concentrate on one thing at a time. If you have more "true" responses for items 6-10, you have a **spacing style**— you prefer to spread out a few tasks over time. Record your pacing preference.

Pacing Preference _____

Making the Best of Unitary and Spacing Style Preferences

If you have a unitary style preference, you probably have extraordinary powers of concentration. You are wonderfully productive when you are able to work single-mindedly on one project. The only problem comes when you need to deal with several tasks—tests, projects, papers—at the same time. One strategy that can work when you are faced with multiple tasks is to "blitz" each task one at a time. Focus your energy narrowly and at full force, completing one task after another. Be careful, however, to guard against driving yourself so hard early on that you do not have any energy left for later projects.

If you have a spacing style preference, you prefer to carefully schedule tasks, allowing time for breaks. Once you are aware that this is your preferred way of completing tasks, your strategy is simple. First you need to make accurate judgments about how long each task will take. Then you need to estimate the length of each work session, making sure you have time to complete each task before the deadline. Be sure to leave enough time for pleasant tasks among the more demanding ones, too.

PORTFOLIO

Assignment 1:
Write About Your Pacing Style

Describe one or more tasks you've completed recently. In what ways did your approach to the task or tasks show that you prefer to pace yourself in a unitary or spacing style? Make a plan for a new task or set of tasks based on your learning style preference for unitary or spacing. Save this assignment in your portfolio.

AESTHETIC PREFERENCE

The word **aesthetic** means "of or relating to the sense of beauty." Your aesthetic preference indicates how sensitive you are to your surroundings and to the way you present yourself to other people. Check one box after each statement, indicating whether the statement is true or not true for you most of the time.

	TRUE FOR ME	NOT TRUE FOR ME
1. I have a certain order for the things in my study place.	☐	☐
2. I am fairly neat.	☐	☐
3. If my study area is a mess, I can't concentrate.	☐	☐
4. I hate to turn in a messy paper.	☐	☐
5. How a study area looks has no effect on my ability to concentrate.	☐	☐
6. The top of my desk is a mess.	☐	☐
7. The content of a paper is more important than how it looks.	☐	☐
8. I can concentrate anywhere.	☐	☐

Scoring

To determine your aesthetic preference, count and record the number of "true" responses.

Items 1-4 _____   Items 5-8_____

If you have more "true" responses for items 1-4, you have a **high aesthetic preference**—aesthetics or visual appearance is important to you. If you have more "true" responses for items 5-8, you have a **low aesthetic preference**—the way something looks is not of great importance to you. Record your aesthetic preference.

Aesthetic Preference _____

Making the Best of High and Low Aesthetic Preferences

If you have a high interest in aesthetics, you are particular about how your living and study areas appear. You usually prefer a neat appearance, or at least one that is moderately orderly. If you start to study and have the nagging urge to reorganize things that don't look right around you, take a few minutes to arrange and stack things. Avoid becoming absorbed in the act of cleaning, however. Spending too much time cleaning is simply a way to avoid a task you don't want to do.

If your preference for aesthetics is low, appearances are not that important to you. This saves you the time of having to tidy areas before studying. However, you need to remember that appearance *does* count when you complete written assignments and turn them in for evaluation. A messy paper gives an instructor a negative impression of your work and will probably have a negative impact on your grade.

PORTFOLIO

Assignment 2:
Writing a Description

Write a one-paragraph description of your study area. Be specific about its appearance. What details indicate that aesthetics are, or are not, important to you? In another paragraph, describe the role that aesthetics plays in one of your course requirements. For example, what guidelines or rules has an instructor given for the appearance of a paper or project? Tell how you plan to meet those requirements. Save this assignment in your portfolio.

TACTILE PREFERENCE

Your **tactile** preference indicates how important the sense of touch is to you in your study habits. Check one box after each statement, indicating whether the statement is true or not true for you most of the time.

	TRUE FOR ME	NOT TRUE FOR ME
1. When I'm writing, I like to have several sheets of paper under the one I'm writing on.	☐	☐
2. I dislike reading books printed on cheap paper.	☐	☐
3. I have a favorite type of pen/pencil.	☐	☐
4. I always feel clothes before buying them.	☐	☐
5. I won't write on a surface that is uneven, dirty, or grooved.	☐	☐

Scoring

To determine your tactile preference, count and record the number of "true" responses.

True for Me _____   Not True for Me _____

If you have more "true" responses, you have a **high tactile preference**—tactility or sense of touch is important to you. If you have fewer "true" responses, you have a **low tactile preference**—this area is not so important to you. Record your tactile preference.

Tactile Preference_____

Making the Best of High and Low Tactile Preferences

If you are a highly tactile person, the feel of things is important to you. You should satisfy your need for writing materials and surfaces that feel good to you as you use them. If you're taking a test and find yourself sitting at a desk with a grooved top, for instance, try to get another desk, or ask to put something under your paper to provide a smooth writing surface. If you can't make changes, at least you'll be aware of why you're uncomfortable. The feel of your clothing is also important to you, and you should wear your most comfortable items in stressful situations such as tests.

If you are low in the tactile dimension, the feel of things does not play an important part in your learning style. The kinds of tools you use, therefore, will probably not have a major effect on what you do.

INTROVERSION/EXTROVERSION PREFERENCE

This checklist shows whether you prefer to be alone most of the time or would rather be among people most of the time. Check one box after each statement, indicating whether the statement is true or not true for you most of the time.

	TRUE FOR ME	NOT TRUE FOR ME
1. If I heard bad news, my first impulse would probably be to talk about it with a friend.	☐	☐
2. After I've been with people, I usually feel energized.	☐	☐
3. I usually like parties.	☐	☐
4. Studying with a group usually helps me learn better.	☐	☐
5. I don't like to be alone for very long.	☐	☐
6. If I heard bad news, my first impulse would probably be to go somewhere alone to think about it.	☐	☐
7. I usually dislike group work or study.	☐	☐
8. I usually feel drained after being with a group of people.	☐	☐
9. I generally dislike parties.	☐	☐
10. I am good company for myself and enjoy being alone.	☐	☐

Scoring

To determine your introversion/extroversion preference, count and record the number of "true" responses.

Items 1-5 _____   Items 6-10 _____

If you have more "true" responses for items 1-5, you tend to be more of an **extrovert**. If you have more "true" responses for items 6-10, you tend to be more of an **introvert**. Record your introversion/extroversion preference.

Introversion/Extroversion Preference _____

Making the Best of Introversion and Extroversion Preferences

In general, **extroverts** draw strength and energy from being with others. **Introverts** draw strength and energy from being alone. That is not to say that extroverts always like to be with people or that introverts always like to be alone. These are general preferences, and some people show the preference to a greater degree than others.

Usually, introverts prefer studying and doing other schoolwork alone. If this suits you, fine; but don't overlook the advantages of study groups for certain tasks, as described in Chapter 9. If you tend toward being an extrovert, you probably prefer group study. Beware, however, the tendency of groups to waste time socializing. Sometimes a mixed study group of extroverts and introverts works very well. The extroverts get things rolling and keep them going, and the introverts tend to keep the group focused.

PORTFOLIO

Assignment 3:
Writing a Personal Ad

Suppose you are writing a personal ad for yourself to meet a potential roommate, boyfriend, or girlfriend. Describe yourself as either an extrovert or introvert. Then describe some of the things you enjoy and prefer that reflect your type of personality. Be imaginative but honest. Don't forget humor. Save this assignment in your portfolio.

RELATIVISM PREFERENCE

Relativism is the way you view and judge events and people. Some people with low relativism tend to see events and people in clear-cut categories, such as "good" and "bad," "right" and "wrong." Their judgments are often made on the basis of very little evidence. Some people with high relativism tend not to make quick or clear-cut judgments. They are less concerned with categorizing events or people. Check one box after each statement, indicating whether the statement is true or not true for you most of the time.

	TRUE FOR ME	NOT TRUE FOR ME
1. People should know the difference between right and wrong.	☐	☐
2. Some people have ridiculous opinions.	☐	☐
3. I lose respect for a professor who doesn't know the answer to a question.	☐	☐
4. I don't like to do the wrong thing.	☐	☐
5. If you want the answer to something, ask someone who knows.	☐	☐
6. Opinions are just opinions; they're all equally valid.	☐	☐
7. Right or wrong depends on your point of view.	☐	☐
8. There are no good or evil people or actions.	☐	☐
9. When you scratch the surface, many "facts" taught in college are just the opinions of the professors.	☐	☐
10. There are no real answers, just more questions.	☐	☐

Scoring

To determine your relativism preference, count and record the number of "true" responses.

Items 1-5 _____   Items 6-10 _____

If you have more "true" responses for items 1-5, you are **low in relativism**. If you have more "true" responses for items 6-10, you are **high in relativism**. Record your relativism preference.

Relativism Preference _____

Making the Best of Low and High Relativism Preferences

If you are low in relativism, you may have a problem in classes that challenge some of your beliefs about what is right and wrong. If you find yourself becoming uncomfortable or angry over the content of a class, be aware that your feelings may result from your tendency to see things as either "black" or "white" or "good" or "bad." You need to be aware of the source of your feelings so that in your note taking you don't edit the things with which you disagree.

If you are high in relativism, you should be aware that in academic circles, not all opinions are equal. In almost all areas, opinions supported with data receive more respect. Suppose, for example, in an essay test, you want to make a point that you know is at odds with a position the instructor has taken. Your supporting data needs to be even stronger than if you agree with the instructor. Instructors will usually respect those who disagree with them *if* the assertions are well supported.

PORTFOLIO

Assignment 4:

Writing to Support a Viewpoint

Choose a controversial issue in your school or community or from the news. Write a letter to the editor of your school or community newspaper expressing your opinion on one side of the controversy. If you are low in relativism, make sure you understand and accurately describe the viewpoint with which you disagree. Then express your disagreement. If you are high in relativism, provide support for your opinion. Save this assignment in your portfolio.

REASONING PREFERENCE

The reasoning checklist helps you see whether you prefer deductive reasoning or inductive reasoning. In **deductive reasoning**, you move from general principles or ideas to specific cases. In **inductive reasoning**, you move from specific cases to general principles or ideas. Check one box after each statement, indicating whether the statement is true or not true for you most of the time.

	TRUE FOR ME	NOT TRUE FOR ME
1. I like to see the big picture before I get the details.	☐	☐
2. I wish textbooks would present the main ideas first instead of giving details and examples first.	☐	☐
3. When following directions, I read them through before starting.	☐	☐
4. People should get to the point and not digress when talking.	☐	☐
5. When I'm writing, I start my paragraphs with my main ideas.	☐	☐
6. I like to gather all the facts before making a decision.	☐	☐
7. I like for lecturers to begin with illustrations or examples, then make their point.	☐	☐
8. Textbooks are uninteresting because they tell you what to think instead of letting you draw your conclusions.	☐	☐
9. When I write, I like to begin by giving the readers facts that prove my main idea, which comes later.	☐	☐
10. I enjoy figuring something out when pieces are missing.	☐	☐

Scoring

To determine your reasoning preference, count and record the number of "true" responses.

Items 1-5 _____   Items 6-10 _____

If you have more "true" responses for items 1-5, you prefer **deductive reasoning**. If you have more "true" responses for items 6-10, you prefer **inductive reasoning**. Record your reasoning preference.

Reasoning Preference _____

Making the Best of Deductive and Inductive Reasoning Preferences

If you are a deductive reasoner, you prefer to know the main idea first and then get the supporting details or proofs. Most college texts and lectures are structured to favor deductive thinkers. As a deductive thinker, however, you may run into trouble with an instructor who uses an inductive approach. You may miss or ignore the supporting details that come before the main idea, thinking that they are introductory or irrelevant comments. Be attentive to see if a pattern exists in the way an instructor or text presents information.

Those who reason inductively are rare indeed and are supposedly the most creative thinkers. If you are one of them, you might have a problem staying tuned into a deductive presentation, such as a lecture, in which the main idea is presented first and is followed by numerous examples. This kind of presentation may seem dry and unchallenging to you. One technique is to let your creative mind come up with as many examples or details as you can that support the main idea of a deductive argument.

PORTFOLIO

Assignment 5:
Writing About Your Reasoning Approach

Think of a problem you solved recently. Was your approach deductive or inductive? In a paragraph or two describe what happened. Save this assignment in your portfolio.

MODALITY PREFERENCE

A **mode** is a way of doing something. Driving and flying, for example, are modes of travel. Speech is a mode of communication. Some people have a specific preference for the kind of mode in which they like to receive information. This checklist will help you recognize your preference. Check one box after each statement, indicating whether the statement is true or not true for you most of the time.

	TRUE FOR ME	NOT TRUE FOR ME
1. I dislike people reading to me.	☐	☐
2. I write down things I need to remember.	☐	☐
3. I take a lot of notes in lecture classes.	☐	☐
4. I prefer reading something to hearing it.	☐	☐
5. When someone uses a word I don't recognize, I sometimes ask the person to spell the word.	☐	☐
6. I prefer lecture classes.	☐	☐
7. Fairly often I remember things that I have only heard.	☐	☐
8. In lecture classes, I take fewer notes so that I can concentrate on listening.	☐	☐
9. I enjoy having someone read something interesting to me.	☐	☐
10. If someone wants me to read something, I might ask the person to tell me about it instead.	☐	☐

Scoring

To determine your modality preference, count and record the number of "true" responses.

Items 1-5 _____   Items 6-10 _____

If you have more "true" responses for items 1-5, you are probably a **visual** learner. If you have more "true" responses for items 6-10, you are probably an **auditory** learner. Record your modality preference.

Modality Preference _____

Making the Best of Visual and Auditory Modality Preferences

If you're a visual learner, you're probably already aware of it. You prefer to take in information through your eyes rather than through your ears. What do you do in a standard lecture class where the instructor talks? Use your visual preference by taking notes and later studying them.

    If you're an auditory learner, you tend to remember better what you hear than what you see. To do well on a test, however, your best strategy is to take notes in class. (Chapter 11 will deal with note-taking and note-studying strategies for those with different modality preferences.) Another helpful strategy for auditory learners is to read

Whether you're a visual learner or an auditory learner, taking notes during class is crucial to remembering information that will help you on tests.

aloud from your notes and from your textbook. You don't need to read every word, just key ideas and phrases that you need to remember. You can also make a tape and play it before you sleep, while you sleep, or on your car stereo if you commute.

PORTFOLIO

Assignment 6:
Describing Learning Techniques

Whether you are a visual learner or an auditory learner, you have probably developed techniques that help you remember things. For example, if you are visual, maybe you've developed a quick form of handwriting or have a knack for making diagrams. If you are more auditory, maybe you have memory tricks for remembering names and dates. In a paragraph, describe your most successful techniques. Save this assignment in your portfolio.

SUMMARY OF PREFERENCES

Briefly review each of the checklists. Write your preferences in the spaces below to get an overview of your learning style.

Time Preference _____

Thought/Feeling Preference _____

Pacing Preference _____

Aesthetic Preference _____

Tactile Preference _____

Introvert/Extrovert Preference _____

Relativism Preference _____

Reasoning Preference _____

Modality Preference _____

WRAPPING IT UP

SUMMARY

- Your learning style is the way you approach a learning task—the conditions and strategies that work best for you.

- Your learning style is reflected in nine specific preferences:

    1. Time Preference—the time of day when you learn best.

    2. Thoughts/Feelings Preference—whether you are a thinking person or are guided more by your feelings.

    3. Pacing Preference—whether you do things one at a time or tend to juggle several things at once.

    4. Aesthetic Preference—what kind of surroundings you prefer, such as formal and orderly or casual and disorderly.

    5. Tactile Preference—whether the touch of certain items is important to you.

    6. Introversion/Extroversion Preference—whether you are quiet and withdrawn or outgoing.

    7. Relativism Preference—whether you see things in strict terms (like good and bad) or have a less strict view (seeing things as neither entirely good nor entirely bad).

    8. Reasoning Preference—whether you like to go from the big picture to the details or from the details to the big picture.

    9. Modality Preference—whether you learn new information better by hearing it or by seeing it in writing.

THINKING IT OVER

- What ideas and information from this chapter did you find most helpful?

  _____

  _____

  _____

  _____

- How will you apply the ideas and information from this chapter in adjusting your college work to your learning style and your learning style to your college work?

  _____

  _____

  _____

  _____

IN YOUR
JOURNAL

Select your most difficult subject. Describe the problems you're having in this subject. According to your learning style preferences, what might be the cause of your difficulties? Describe the possible causes. Then, based on what you have learned about yourself, describe how you might improve your performance in this subject. Include specific examples of techniques that you might try.

ASSESSING YOUR STUDY SKILLS

OBJECTIVES:

- To evaluate your study skills.
- To develop a plan for strengthening study skills.

How Can I Assess My
Study Skills?

When you have a job to do, you need the right tools, and your tools need to be in good shape. What kinds of problems might occur if the people in the picture did not have the right tools or if their tools were not in excellent condition?

Another important tool or resource you need for successful college work is a set of study skills. These skills include your ability to concentrate, manage time, recognize and use a wide vocabulary, write English correctly, prepare for and take tests, and read and comprehend all kinds of written materials—especially textbook material.

In this chapter, you will evaluate your study skills and plan ways to improve them where necessary.

How confident are you about the study skills you've learned and used so far in your educational experience? For each study skill below, rate yourself on a scale of 1 through 3. Circle *1* for "below average," *2* for "average," or *3* for "above average."

1. Ability to concentrate   1   2   3

2. Ability to manage time   1   2   3

3. Ability to use a wide vocabulary   1   2   3

4. Ability to correctly use English grammar,
    mechanics, and spelling   1   2   3

5. Ability to prepare for and take tests   1   2   3

6. Ability to listen and take notes in a
    lecture   1   2   3

7. Ability to comprehend general
    materials   1   2   3

8. Ability to comprehend textbook
    material   1   2   3

Scoring

Add your points. A score of 16 or higher indicates that you think your study skills are in good shape. A score between 8 and 16 indicates that you think your skills need some work.

IN YOUR JOURNAL

Choose one or two skills for which you rated yourself 1 or 2. Change the skill or skills into goal statements. For example, if you gave yourself a low mark on Time Management, you might set a goal to make better use of your study time or to study for a specific amount of time each day.

WHICH SKILLS ARE IMPORTANT?

GROUP ACTIVITY

In your group, discuss some of the specific study skills and behaviors that are important for success in college. Refer to the Data Bank for ideas. List the items the group agrees on.

_____
_____
_____
_____
_____
_____
_____
_____
_____
_____
_____
_____
_____
_____
_____
_____
_____
_____
_____
_____
_____

DATA BANK

- Often become distracted when studying.
- Punctual.
- Well organized.
- Don't usually take time to look up unfamiliar words.
- Read text assignments more than once.
- Enjoy preparing for tests.
- Have a good system for taking notes.
- Read slowly and sound out unfamiliar words.
- Plunge right in and read a textbook chapter from beginning to end.

ANALYZING STUDY SKILLS

USING A STUDY SKILLS CHECKLIST

When most students think of college skills, they tend to think first of study skills, especially reading, writing, and test-taking skills. Often, students feel that their study skills are weak, since they may have been away from school for a while or have completed high school with only poorly developed study skills. Perhaps you feel anxious about your skills.

DISCOVERY ACTIVITY

• Briefly describe your recent history prior to attending college. Did you recently graduate from high school? Did you work?

_____

_____

_____

_____

• Describe the affect of your precollege experience on your study skills. For example, if you worked, did you learn new study skills or improve old ones?

_____

_____

_____

_____

By using the following study skills checklist, you will be able to see which study skills you need to brush up on or learn. You may also be pleasantly surprised to find that your skills are in better shape than you think. The checklist covers the following skill areas: Concentration; Time Management; Vocabulary; English Grammar, Mechanics, and Spelling; Test Preparation and Test Taking; Listening and Note Taking; Reading; and Text Reading.

Directions: Read each statement, then circle the letter that best describes you. Circle *3* for "always," *2* for "frequently," or *1* for "rarely or never."

Concentration

1. I am able to concentrate when I need to. 3 2 1

2. I can sit still when I need to. 3 2 1

3. I can bring my attention back to a task if I start to daydream. 3 2 1

4. I can concentrate on a subject even if I'm not very interested in it. 3 2 1

5. I can put personal worries or fears aside to concentrate on my studies. 3 2 1

6. I can prevent other people (roommate, family, friends) from distracting me while I study. 3 2 1

Concentration subscore: _____

Time Management

7. I follow a schedule. 3 2 1

8. I limit the number of commitments I make so that I am not pressed for time. 3 2 1

9. I pace my studying so that I have plenty of time. 3 2 1

10. I arrive on time for class, appointments, and other commitments. 3 2 1

11. I manage my time without being influenced by my friends. 3 2 1

12. I am prepared for class and hand in my assignments on time. 3 2 1

Time Management subscore: _____

Vocabulary

13. I use a dictionary to find definitions and pronunciations.   3 2 1

14. I figure out the meaning of an unfamiliar word by using other words around it.   3 2 1

15. I recognize most of the words I encounter in my daily reading.   3 2 1

16. I follow lectures easily.   3 2 1

17. I find just the right words to express myself.   3 2 1

18. I divide an unknown word into its root and prefix or suffix to discover its meaning.   3 2 1

Vocabulary subscore: _____

English Grammar, Mechanics, and Spelling

I feel confident in the following areas:

19. Punctuation   3 2 1

20. Capitalization   3 2 1

21. Expressing my thoughts in writing   3 2 1

22. Planning and writing a paper   3 2 1

23. Sentence structure   3 2 1

24. Paragraphing   3 2 1

25. Spelling   3 2 1

English Grammar, Mechanics, and Spelling subscore: _____

Test Preparation and Test Taking

26. I prepare well in advance for tests. 3 2 1

27. I feel calm when I take tests. 3 2 1

28. I remember what I really know when I take a test. 3 2 1

29. I complete exams in the time scheduled for them. 3 2 1

30. I know how to use my notes, textbooks, and handouts to prepare for tests. 3 2 1

31. After an exam, I go over the answers I got wrong and try to learn the right answers. 3 2 1

Test Preparation and Test Taking subscore: _____

Listening and Note Taking

32. While I listen to a lecture, I take notes. 3 2 1

33. I copy anything the instructor writes on the board. 3 2 1

34. When I listen, I have writing materials at hand to record the speaker's main ideas. 3 2 1

35. I use a system for taking notes. 3 2 1

36. My notes are good enough to use when I prepare for tests. 3 2 1

37. I feel that I record the main ideas when I take notes from a lecture. 3 2 1

Listening and Note Taking subscore: _____

Reading

38. I like reading.   3   2   1

39. I keep my place and don't skip lines or words when I'm reading.   3   2   1

40. I think I read as fast as most other students.   3   2   1

41. As I read, I don't sound words out by moving my lips.   3   2   1

42. I usually read groups of words at a time rather than one word at a time.   3   2   1

43. I am confident that I've understood most of what I've read.   3   2   1

44. I read well enough for most purposes.   3   2   1

Reading subscore: _____

Text Reading

45. I use a method, such as Survey-Question-Read-Recite-Review (SQ3R) or Preview-Read-Write-Recite (PRWR), to study textbook material.   3   2   1

46. I read textbooks at a different speed than I read fiction and magazine articles.   3   2   1

47. I preview a chapter before I begin to read it.   3   2   1

48. I read an assignment over many times as a way of learning the material.   3   2   1

49. The more I reread, the more I remember.   3   2   1

50. I am able to remember material regardless of whether the text interests me.   3   2   1

Text Reading subscore: _____

EVALUATING YOUR STUDY SKILLS

Add your subscores for each section of the study skills checklist. A total score of 90 to 150 indicates that your study skills are in top shape. If your score is between 60 and 90, your study skills are in good shape, but you need to work on specific areas where you scored low points (1 or 2 for a specific item or between 7 and 12 for a section). If your score is between 50 and 60, you will have to work hard to improve your study skills.

- What is your score?

  _____

- What are your three weakest study skill areas?

  _____

  _____

  _____

- What are your three strongest study skill areas?

  _____

  _____

  _____

- How did your score on checklist items 1 through 50 compare to your score on the self-assessment you took on page 106? Although the self-assessment had far fewer items, the scores of the two should correspond. In the self-assessment, a high score—meaning skill strength—in Test Taking, for example, should correspond to a high score on checklist items 26 through 31.

PORTFOLIO

Assignment:
Comparing Results

Describe how your results from the self-assessment and the checklist compare. What are your feelings about your skills now that you've used the checklist? Save this assignment in your portfolio.

IMPROVING YOUR STUDY SKILLS

You'll find help for improving your study skills in several chapters of this book. The study skill areas, chapters, and pages are listed below.

- Concentration: Chapter 19, pages 415–437
- Time Management: Chapter 7, pages 118–145
- Vocabulary: Chapter 13, pages 256–277
- English Grammar, Mechanics, and Spelling: Chapter 13, pages 256–277
- Test Preparation and Test Taking: Chapter 20, pages 438–475
- Listening and Note Taking: Chapters 10, 11, and 12, pages 194–254
- Reading: Chapters 13, 14, 15, 16, 17, and 18, pages 256–414
- Textbook Reading: Chapter 17, pages 346–375

Wrapping it up

Summary

Study skills include:

- Concentration
- Time Management
- Vocabulary
- English Grammar, Mechanics, and Spelling
- Test Preparation and Test Taking
- Listening and Note Taking
- Reading and Text Reading

These skills are necessary for success in college.

Thinking it Over

Now that you know more about study skills, review the list your group made on page 107.

- What potential problems do you see among the choices you listed?

  _____
  _____
  _____

- What additions or deletions would you make to the list?

  _____
  _____
  _____
  _____
  _____

- What have you learned by assessing your study skills through the material in this chapter?

  _____

  _____

  _____

  _____

  _____

- In your college work, how will you apply what you've learned in this chapter?

  _____

  _____

  _____

  _____

IN YOUR JOURNAL

Set goals for improving specific study skills. Notice the checklist statements on which you gave yourself low points. In your journal, turn those statements into goals. For example, suppose you scored low in Listening and Note Taking on item 33: "I copy anything the instructor writes on the board." You might set a goal to improve your note-taking skills by noticing what the instructor writes on the board and copying that information.

Managing Time and Resources

You've been managing time and resources most of your life, and you've probably done so with success in some areas. Effective time and resource management also enable you to take charge in achieving your academic goals. In this section, you'll learn strategies that will help you build on your strengths in managing time and other resources. Chapter 7 focuses on managing your time. This chapter will help you make planning and scheduling a daily habit and will introduce you to other important principles of time management. Chapter 8 focuses on your personal support system. This chapter will help you identify ways to obtain support from friends and family members and from community resources. Chapter 9 examines the resources of your college or university. This chapter will help you identify an array of resources to meet many of your needs, including financial aid, library research, and faculty recommendations.

7

MANAGING YOUR TIME

OBJECTIVES:

- To organize goals by using daily planning activities.

- To use a prioritizing system to plan and allocate time.

- To demonstrate the daily planning and check-off system of time planning.

- To investigate ways to deal with procrastination.

- To explain and apply principles of time management.

- To explain and apply the advantages of scheduling flexibility.

- To describe the time relationship between college study and on- or off-campus work.

Where Does the Time Go?

hat is the man in the picture experiencing? Think about similar experiences you have had. Many people today have the feeling that "there aren't enough hours in the day." Many people also have difficulty **setting priorities**—arranging tasks in order of importance from most to least. As a result, they try to do everything at once.

Most people feel the need to have more control of their time—to use time more efficiently. In this chapter, you will investigate how to successfully manage your time in relation to your goals.

The statements below will help you identify how well you manage your time. Circle *T* if the statement describes something that is true for you. Circle *F* if the statement describes something that is false for you.

1.	I follow a daily schedule.	T	F
2.	I don't procrastinate.	T	F
3.	I set priorities among the tasks that I schedule.	T	F
4.	I study in 20- to 30-minute time blocks.	T	F
5.	I have a specific place to study.	T	F
6.	When I study, I don't listen to my favorite music.	T	F
7.	I plan how I will complete a big assignment.	T	F
8.	I don't study similar subjects—like math and science—together.	T	F
9.	I couldn't work full-time and do well in college.	T	F
10.	I'd prefer an on-campus to an off-campus job.	T	F

If you're already an expert at managing your time, you should have answered True to all of the statements. As you read this chapter, you'll learn how to improve your least successful time-management habits and to develop more successful ones.

IN YOUR JOURNAL

Write a goal for improving your time management. You might, for example, want to learn to get started on things right away instead of procrastinating .

ANALYZING TIME USAGE

GROUP
ACTIVITY

Successful time management can offer positive results in all areas of your life.

A. With your group, discuss time-saving tips that you and other group members have used successfully. Make a list of the tips.

_____

_____

_____

_____

_____

_____

B. Brainstorm possible ways to improve your use of time. Begin by discussing the time-management problems in the Data Bank. Discuss other time-management problems and solutions.

_____

_____

_____

_____

_____

_____

_____

- Taking on too many things to do at once (overcommitment).
- Inability to arrange tasks in order of importance (lack of prioritizing).
- Not thinking ahead (lack of preplanning).

DATA
BANK

- Trying to avoid something unpleasant (procrastination).
- Inability to control yourself (emotional involvement).
- Positive and negative feelings about the same task (mixed motivation).

DAILY PLANNING AND GOALS

Many times in this book you have set goals for yourself. Some were specific goals, limited to the topic of the chapter. Others were long-term goals regarding your college, personal, and professional life. In earlier chapters you also made plans related to your goals.

Now that you've had some practice in setting goals and making plans, evaluate where you are with these skills.

DISCOVERY ACTIVITY

- What short-term or long-term goals have you accomplished recently?

  _____

  _____

  _____

  _____

  _____

  _____

- How did planning help you accomplish these goals?

  _____

  _____

  _____

  _____

  _____

- Do you see room for improvement in your ability to plan? What would you like to do better?

  _____

  _____

  _____

  _____

PLANNING: A DAILY HABIT

The best way to improve your planning skills and achieve your goals is to make planning a daily activity. Five to ten minutes daily is all the time you need to invest. The best times to plan are first thing in the morning or the last thing at night, depending on whether you are a day or a night person.

DECIDING WHAT TO PLAN

Begin by planning everything. Let's say you are a day planner. You're beginning your day with breakfast. Start by thinking about the things you have to do today. Write down all the items, not worrying about the order, just making sure you've included everything you know you have to do.

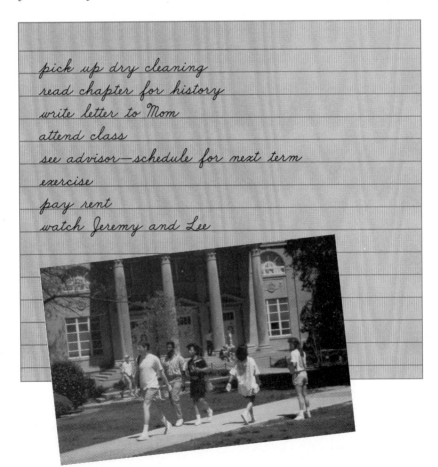

pick up dry cleaning
read chapter for history
write letter to Mom
attend class
see advisor—schedule for next term
exercise
pay rent
watch Jeremy and Lee

As a college student, you have many demands on your time. The best way to meet those demands—and manage your time—is to plan your time.

Activity A: List Tomorrow's Tasks

With your group, develop a reasonable "to do" list for tomorrow. The list can be based on one person's goals, or the list can reflect items from everyone's lives.

_____

_____

_____

_____

_____

_____

_____

_____

_____

_____

_____

_____

PRIORITIZING THE LIST

Once you have your complete list of tasks, you can begin to organize the items. Rearrange the items and list them according to times and their importance. You might want to do this in two stages. First, label each item A, B, or C, depending on whether the priority is high, not so high, or low. _You should give highest priority to the items that help you reach your goals_. Then arrange the items according to when you need to do them. For example, if you have to pick up your niece and nephew at 3:30 P.M. and watch them until 5:30 P.M., enter that event in the appropriate time slot. You might be able to do some items any time—or not at all—if they're low priority. Consider how much time each item will take and how important each is to your goals.

Be sure to label each item with its priority. The list on page 125 shows how you might label and place the items on a Daily Planning Form. If you prefer, you can also just arrange your list in time order (earliest to latest).

DAILY PLANNING FORM

Date _____

Hour		Item
7:00		
7:30	C	Pick up cleaning (Cleaner opens early and is near my home.)
8:00		
8:30	a	Read chapter for history (I study better in the morning.)
9:00		
9:30		
10:00	a	Attend class
10:30		↓
11:00		
11:30		
12:00		
12:30	B	See advisor—schedule for next term
1:00		
1:30		
2:00	C	Write a letter to Mom (Quick note during this afternoon break.)
2:30	a	Pay rent (office is near campus)
3:00		
3:30	a	Watch Wendy's kids until 5:30
4:00		
4:30		
5:00		
5:30		↓
6:00	a	Exercise
6:30		
7:00		
7:30		
8:00		

Activity B: Setting Priorities

Now prioritize the list your group made. Discuss which items are more important than others and why. Label each item *A*, *B*, or *C*, depending on its importance. Copy the list onto the Planning Form on the next page. List the activity at the time you think is reasonable.

USING THE DAY PLAN

After you complete a Daily Planning Form, keep it with you during the day. As you finish an item on your list, put a check beside it. If you have some spare time, do some of the low-priority items on your list.

MAKE PLANNING A DAILY HABIT

Pages 477-480 of the appendix contain Daily Planning Forms you can photocopy. Keep about a dozen copies in your notebook so that you can enter scheduled activities for the next week or two as they come up. Of course, if you prefer, you can buy a daily planner. Be sure you buy one that has enough space for your activities.

The important idea is to carry the forms with you as you go about your daily activities. When your English professor says, "A study session will be held on Wednesday before the midterm at 7:30 P.M. in EN 113," enter that information on your Wednesday page. Make a habit of looking ahead to the next day's schedule to see what you have to do. Write a reminder in your book a day *before* an event.

DAILY PLANNING: A RECAP

Follow these guidelines in your daily planning.
1. Do daily planning in a quiet environment, writing down everything to do for the day.
2. Assign priorities. The highest priorities go to items that are steps to your goals or commitments that you must complete.
3. Carry your day planner with you, and check off items as you do them. Do a final check at night. If you need to carry anything over to the next day, be sure to write it at the appropriate time slot.

DAILY PLANNING FORM

Date _____

Hour	Item
7:00	
7:30	
8:00	
8:30	
9:00	
9:30	
10:00	
10:30	
11:00	
11:30	
12:00	
12:30	
1:00	
1:30	
2:00	
2:30	
3:00	
3:30	
4:00	
4:30	
5:00	
5:30	
6:00	
6:30	
7:00	
7:30	
8:00	

PLANNING LONGER TASKS

In school you will often be dealing with long-term tasks such as individual and group reports, research papers, presentations, and projects. To cope with such challenges, use a four-part system:

1. Divide the task into sensible parts.

2. Estimate the time needed to do each part.

3. Count backward from the final deadline for the task, and assign intermediate deadlines. Enter the subdeadlines on the pages of your planner or on a calendar.

4. Keep track of your progress toward the deadlines.

GROUP
ACTIVITY

Activity C: Planning a Long-Term Assignment

Imagine that today is September 15 and that an instructor assigns a research paper due December 10. In your group, plan your steps for completing the paper.

A. Divide the task into sensible parts. Make a list of the steps of the project here:

_____

_____

_____

_____

_____

_____

_____

_____

_____

B. Estimate the time needed to do each part. On the list you made in item A, write the number of days or weeks. For instance, you might write "Select topic—1 week."

C. Count backward from the final deadline for the task, and assign intermediate deadlines. Write these deadlines on your list of steps, too. Use dates from the current year's calendar. You don't need to enter the dates in your planner for this group activity.

PORTFOLIO

Assignment 1:
Your Long-Term Plan

Now that you have completed the group activity, apply the process to a real long-term project. Choose a project you have been assigned for the current term. Enter the parts and dates in your planner or on a calendar. Save a photocopy of your planner or calendar in your portfolio.

DEALING WITH PROCRASTINATION

At times we all procrastinate. Often the longer we put an unpleasant task off, the bigger the task becomes in our minds.

DISCOVERY ACTIVITY

• In what types of situations do you procrastinate?

_____

_____

_____

_____

_____

_____

_____

• What specific activities or decisions do you tend to put off until "later"?

_____

_____

_____

_____

_____

_____

_____

_____

Felix's story is a typical one of procrastination, putting something off—and off.

If you looked in the dictionary under procrastination, you'd see my picture there. I was the worst! And the funny thing is, being lazy or avoiding work wasn't the cause. When I was putting something off, I would do anything—clean the house, change the oil in my car, change the oil in a friend's car, do laundry. Doing these things didn't help me when I was up at 5 a.m. the morning a project was due. When turning in a project, I was often tempted to slip it under the prof's door and run. I knew the quality was not very good—that I had not done my best.

Well, one day I was at a movie with Marisela, my girlfriend. Then I remembered for the twentieth time that I should have been working on my accounting project. I couldn't even enjoy the movie because I was feeling so guilty. When we stopped for food afterward, I told Marisela how I felt about ruining another good time by feeling guilty.

"Felix," she said, "just doing the project would be easier than suffering all the guilt. So, do it." She was right.

The next day she helped me list all the parts of the project and when I should complete each part to finish the project on time. After that, everything changed. I developed the habit of making schedules and sticking to them. When I was on schedule or even ahead of schedule, I could say, "You're right where you should be." The guilt was gone.

- What do you do when you're procrastinating?

  _____

  _____

  _____

  _____

- How do you feel when you know you've avoided something for a long time?

  _____

  _____

  _____

  _____

HOW TO GUARD AGAINST PROCRASTINATING

If you are a procrastinator, now is the time to make changes in your behavior. Here are some strategies you can try.

Strategy 1. List benefits procrastination has given you. Some people get a thrill out of the last-minute pressure. The tension makes them feel energized. Others find satisfaction in complaining about all they have to do. They feel more important. The following questions will help you identify factors that have made procrastination attractive for you.

- What benefits, if any, did you receive from procrastinating?

  _____

  _____

  _____

  _____

- What other way might you get the same feelings or benefits?

  _____

  _____

  _____

  _____

  _____

  _____

Strategy 2. Review your goals daily so that you can keep them firmly in mind. Use your planner and develop the habit of writing things down. You may want to add a page for long-term assignments with the specific steps you need to complete the work. Record all deadlines—both intermediate and final—on the regular pages of your planner.

Strategy 3. Be wary of the tendency to say, "Oh, forget it. I'll do it later." When you sense this tendency, do something to move ahead on the very thing you want to forget. Getting started is always the hardest task, but it is also the most critical. If you delay getting started, the task will assume larger-than-life proportions in your mind. Just do something—any part of the task. After starting, don't let too many days go by without adding to your progress.

Strategy 4. Divide a project into chunks, and set deadlines for each part. You've already explored this technique. Follow your planner for getting work done. When you are on schedule, take pride in your accomplishment.

Strategy 5. Reward yourself for progress you make along the way. After you take the first step to avoid procrastination, do something nice for yourself. Rewards don't have to be big ones. Small things count—like reading a letter you've received or taking a hot bath. These little pleasures can become a strong reason to break your old habit of procrastination.

Activity D: Rewards

Share with other group members some rewards you use when you have accomplished a task. List some common rewards among your group.

GROUP
ACTIVITY

_____

_____

_____

_____

_____

_____

_____

_____

GUIDELINES FOR TIME MANAGEMENT

Managing time effectively is a challenging and very rewarding task. By following the guidelines provided in this part of the chapter, you should be able to assume greater control over how you use your time. With practice, you should soon be able to accomplish your most important tasks on time and without feeling overwhelmed or pressured.

There are basic guidelines for effective time management.

- Schedule your time.
- Set realistic goals for work time.
- Set realistic goals for your study time.
- Set realistic goals for your personal time.

DISCOVERY
ACTIVITY

Before looking at the guidelines, write your response to each of the following questions, describing your current knowledge and habits.

- Why should you schedule your time?

  _____

  _____

  _____

- What is a realistic goal for work time?

  _____

  _____

  _____

- What is a realistic amount of study time for a subject, compared to the amount of class time you spend on that subject?

  _____

  _____

  _____

- Why should you schedule personal time?

  _____

  _____

  _____

THE BENEFITS OF SCHEDULING

Preparing and following a schedule brings several benefits.

- A schedule gets you started—gives you a direction.
- A schedule helps you accomplish unpleasant but necessary duties.
- A schedule keeps a check on the natural tendency to relax the pressure before a task is completed.
- Difficult tasks and long-term projects can be enjoyable when not done under time pressure.
- A schedule helps free your mind. Writing and organizing tasks on paper or on a computer lessens the burden of thinking about the tasks all the time. This allows you to actually enjoy your personal time.
- A schedule keeps you aware of the importance of working toward your goals.
- A schedule organizes your daily living and helps your days run more smoothly.

SUGGESTIONS FOR SCHEDULING

Now that you see the benefits of scheduling, you'll want to make your own schedule, using the Weekly Schedule Form on page 136. A schedule is somewhat different from the planner you made earlier in this chapter. On your planner you organized daily tasks by priority and time. A schedule covers a full week and should include all regular school-related tasks and employment as well as family responsibilities and household chores.

Use the following suggestions to complete your weekly schedule.

1. Make *your* schedule fit *your* needs. A friend may have a wonderful weekly schedule. Your friend's schedule, however, won't be *your* schedule and won't work so wonderfully for you.

2. Leave some flexibility in your schedule. The first people to throw away their schedules are those who schedule every minute and then go crazy trying to keep up the pace.

3. Schedule time for exercise and recreation. Without these activities you will not be efficient in your job or schoolwork.

4. Experiment to find your best study times. You may study best during a long block of time at night. You may study productively during the odd hours between classes.

5. If you are studying two similar subjects—math and statistics, for example—study a different type of subject between them, like history. You may confuse similar subjects if you study them close together.

6. Allow 5 to 10 minutes to prepare before each class. Reread the lecture notes from the previous lecture to put your mind back into the subject and flow of the class.

7. Schedule a weekly review time to read through all your notes and quiz yourself. Many people choose Sunday afternoon or evening to get back into the rhythm for the week.

8. Color code your schedule. Use green for classes, pink for study time, or whatever color combinations you like. Color coding helps you tell at a glance where you are and how you've balanced your daily or weekly activities.

9. Allow an average of two hours of study for each hour you are in class.

- Which of the guidelines on pages 133 to 135 are most helpful for your current situation? Why?

_____

_____

_____

_____

_____

WEEKLY SCHEDULE

Week of _____

Time	Sunday	Monday	Tuesday	Wednesday	Thursday	Friday	Saturday
5:30-6:00							
6:00-6:30							
6:30-7:00							
7:00-7:30							
7:30-8:00							
8:00-8:30							
8:30-9:00							
9:00-9:30							
9:30-10:00							
10:00-10:30							
10:30-11:00							
11:00-11:30							
11:30-12:00							
12:00-12:30							
12:30-1:00							
1:00-1:30							
1:30-2:00							
2:00-2:30							
2:30-3:00							
3:00-3:30							
3:30-4:00							
4:00-4:30							
4:30-5:00							
5:00-5:30							
5:30-6:00							
6:00-6:30							
6:30-7:00							
7:00-7:30							
7:30-8:00							
8:00-8:30							
8:30-9:00							
9:00-9:30							

For many students, on- or off-campus employment is a source of income. A weekly schedule should reflect work hours, plus the time required to get to and from work.

Employment On or Off Campus?

Should you work on campus or off campus? On-campus employment often means work-study. If you qualify for work-study, pursue the on-campus job. Keep the following information in mind:

- A recent study done at a western university revealed that students who work on campus graduate at a higher rate than students who don't work at all.

- On-campus employers will usually schedule your work hours around your classes. Off-campus employers may pressure you to skip a class or give up studying for a test to help out.

- In on-campus employment you can work a maximum of 20 hours, according to federal government guidelines. Your work-study money is budgeted to cover the term. If you choose to work off campus, be realistic regarding the number of hours you agree to work. Off-campus employers may pressure you to work overtime.

- Working on campus puts you nearer to your classes than off-campus work.

- At an on-campus job, education is valued and encouraged. Coworkers in an off-campus job may be less supportive of your educational goals.

Attending College Part-Time

When you have many responsibilities or must work full-time, you may consider attending college part-time. Part-time attendance is also a good way to ease back into the school environment if you've been away from studying for a while. After attending college part-time, many students find ways to reduce their home or work pressures and become full-time students.

A drawback to part-time status is that most financial aid is available only to full-time students. Still, being a part-time student can have certain advantages. As a part-time student you can concentrate on a few basic courses to develop a strong foundation for taking advanced courses. Part-time study may also allow you more time to make up your mind about a major before making a formal commitment. As a part-time student you may also have more time to develop and refine the study skills, scheduling habits, and self-discipline you need for academic success.

SUGGESTIONS FOR STUDY MANAGEMENT

To make the most effective use of your study time, use the following guidelines:

1. Study in short bursts of 20 to 30 minutes with a 5-minute break after each study period. During your breaks, move around, stretch, massage your neck, exercise, eat, or drink a nonalcoholic beverage. Make your break a total change from your studying.

2. Experiment to find positions in which you study best. Studying doesn't have to be a sit-at-the-desk activity—unless that position works well for you. You can pick up your book or notes, walk around, stand at a table, hold your book up on a shelf.

3. Schedule study time when you are not overly tired. If you try to study when you are tired, you will read a page of your text, probably remember nothing, and have to go back. If this happens, get up, get a drink of water, walk around, change positions. If your tiredness continues, go to bed.

4. Assemble all of your materials before you start to study. Try to complete each task the first time, unless the task is long-term.

5. If you have only an hour or two between classes, go to the library or find an empty classroom, and use the time to study.

6. Avoid temptations. Stay away from people and places that always take more of your time than you want to spend.

7. If you have many distractions at home or in your room, get out and study somewhere else.

- Which of these guidelines are most useful in your current situation? Why?

_____

_____

_____

_____

_____

_____

_____

_____

_____

_____

_____

_____

_____

_____

_____

_____

Assignment 2:
Analyzing Someone's Schedule

PORTFOLIO

Carolyn is a freshman majoring in computer technology at a large community college. On pages 140 and 141 you'll find a page from her daily planner and a copy of her weekly schedule. She is living at home several miles from the college. What hints can you give Carolyn, based on what you see in these two documents? Save this assignment in your portfolio.

CAROLYN'S DAILY PLANNING FORM

Date *November 30, 199—* _____

Hour	Item
7:00	
7:30	
8:00	
8:30	
9:00	C Call Marie
9:30	
10:00	A Go to English class
10:30	
11:00	A Go to Comp class
11:30	
12:00	
12:30	
1:00	
1:30	
2:00	A Go to Sociology class
2:30	
3:00	
3:30	A See eye doctor
4:00	
4:30	B Get new tire
5:00	C Shopping
5:30	
6:00	
6:30	
7:00	
7:30	
8:00	
8:30	

CAROLYN'S WEEKLY SCHEDULE

Week of _November 28, 199—_

Time	Sunday	Monday	Tuesday	Wednesday	Thursday	Friday	Saturday
5:30-6:00							
6:00-6:30			Get up		Get up		Get up
6:30-7:00	Wake up	Get up	B'fast	Get up	B-fast	Get up	B fast
7:00-7:30	← Breakfast	Breakfast	Dress	B'fast	Dress	B fast	Dress
7:30-8:00	Dress	Dress	Drive to work—	Dress	Drive to work	Dress	Dress—Drive to work
8:00-8:30	Read paper	Drive to class		Drive to class		Drive to class	
8:30-9:00	Church	ENG 100		ENG 100		ENG 100	
9:00-9:30		↓		↓		↓	
9:30-10:00	Read	↓		↓		↓	
10:00-10:30	paper						
10:30-11:00	Do CT 115	CT 115		CT 115		CT 115	
11:00-11:30	↓	↓		↓		↓	
11:30-12:00	Drive to work	Eat	K-Mart 8-5	Eat	K-Mart 8-5	Eat	K-Mart 8-5
12:00-12:30		↓		↓		↓	
12:30-1:00		SOC 201		SOC 201		SOC 201	
1:00-1:30		↓		↓		↓	
1:30-2:00	K-Mart 12-9	PSYCH 110		PSYCH 110		PSYCH 110	
2:00-2:30		↓		↓		↓	
2:30-3:00		Go home		Go home		Go home	
3:00-3:30		Back to class		Back to class		Back to class	
3:30-4:00		CT 201		CT 201		CT 201	
4:00-4:30		↓		↓		↓	
4:30-5:00		Drive home →		Drive home →		Drive home	
5:00-5:30		Relax—Eat →		Relax-Eat →		Relax-Eat	Drive home
5:30-6:00		TV →		TV →		TV	Relax-Eat
6:00-6:30		TV →		TV →		TV	TV
6:30-7:00		TV →		TV →		TV	TV
7:00-7:30	Job at K-Mart	TV		TV		TV	TV
7:30-8:00		Study Psych →				→	TV
8:00-8:30						→	TV
8:30-9:00		Study Soc →				→	TV
9:00-9:30	Study Soc	Study Soc →				→	TV
9:30-10:00	↓	Study CT 115 →				→	TV

SETTING UP YOUR STUDY AREA

To maximize the effectiveness of your study time, create a study area that supports good study habits. The essential features of a supportive study area are good lighting and desk or counter space for organizing your materials.

DISCOVERY
ACTIVITY

Describe the place where you do most of your studying.

• Where is your study area located?

_____

_____

_____

_____

• What items does the area contain?

_____

_____

_____

• Is your study area well suited for studying, in your opinion? Why?

_____

_____

_____

If you are living in a dorm, you probably have a desk. This might work as your study area. The problem with many dorm desks is that the lighting is poor. Experiment with ways to improve the lighting—adding an extra lamp or higher wattage bulb, for example. Good lighting prevents eyestrain and reduces fatigue.

If you are living at home, you must also find a place with good lighting. The kitchen table is usually not a good study place.

The lighting is probably poor, and the area may be too busy. If you have a family, you will probably need to set up a place somewhere else. A closed door should signal to others that you are studying and are not to be disturbed. If you need to, make a "Do not disturb" or a "Quiet time!" sign.

SHOULDN'T I MAKE MY STUDY AREA LOOK NICE?

Yes, you should, especially if the appearance of things is important to you. Your study area should be uncluttered, however, so that you won't be distracted. For example, you might need to move a desk that's facing a window if you gaze out that window too often. In addition, avoid the following items in your study area:

- A picture of your boyfriend/girlfriend
- A wonderful picture or photograph, which always catches your eye
- Letters you need to answer
- Your favorite music

NO MUSIC WHILE I'M STUDYING?

The answer to this one is yes and no. Dead silence makes some people so nervous that they can't concentrate. Yes, you can have music, but probably not your favorite music or music with words. Music with lyrics causes people to think the words in their mind.

One interesting note: When the former Soviet Union trained cosmonauts, officials researched every kind of music from every time period and every part of the world. They found that one specific type of music *improved* learning if played during studying. The music was that of the seventeenth- and eighteenth-century European period called the Baroque. Bach and Vivaldi are two of the most famous composers from that period. Try playing music by those composers to see if it helps you.

WRAPPING IT UP

SUMMARY

- To improve your planning skills and achieve your goals, make planning a daily activity.

- Prioritize your tasks, giving the highest priority to items that help you reach your goals.

- Use a day planner and carry it with you. Arrange your tasks according to the best time to do each task and the amount of time required for each task.

- To manage long-term projects, use a four-part system:
  1. Divide the task into sensible parts.
  2. Estimate the time needed to do each part.
  3. Count backward from the final deadline for the task, and assign intermediate deadlines. Enter the subdeadlines on the pages of your planner or on a calendar.
  4. Keep track of your progress toward the deadlines.

- To avoid procrastinating, examine any benefits you get from procrastinating, review your goals daily, do something to get started on your task.

- The basic guidelines for effective time management are to schedule your time, set realistic goals for work time, set realistic goals for study time, and set realistic goals for personal time.

- To improve your studying, study in 20- to 30-minute segments with a 5-minute break between. Make sure your study area has adequate lighting and is free of distractions.

THINKING IT OVER

- What ideas or guidelines in this chapter are most useful?

  _____
  _____
  _____
  _____
  _____
  _____
  _____
  _____
  _____

- How will you apply what you learned in this chapter to improving your time-management skills?

  _____
  _____
  _____
  _____
  _____

IN YOUR
JOURNAL

Review the goal you set at the beginning of this chapter. Describe the progress you've made toward achieving that goal. Based on what you've learned in this chapter, what new goals will you set for managing your time? Describe the goals and what steps you plan to take to achieve them.

8

DEVELOPING YOUR PERSONAL SUPPORT SYSTEM

OBJECTIVES:

- To identify people who can provide personal support.
- To investigate community agencies that provide support.
- To analyze causes of stress.
- To reduce stress by using stress-reduction techniques.

Who Can
Help Me?

One of your greatest resources is your system of personal support—the people you count on when you need help. How does the person in the picture seem to be getting support?

Developing a personal support system is an extremely important task. You can't assume that you have a support system just because you have family and friends. You know you have support only when you ask for and receive it. This chapter will help you identify ways to get the support you need.

Getting Started

A larger version of this questionnaire, known as "The Perceived Social Support Scale," has been used by researchers to identify the quality of people's support systems.

Check one box after each statement, indicating whether the statement is true or not true for you most of the time.

	TRUE FOR ME	NOT TRUE FOR ME
1. There is a special person who is around when I am in need.	☐	☐
2. I get the emotional help and support I need from my family.	☐	☐
3. I can count on my friends when things go wrong.	☐	☐
4. I can talk about my problems with my family.	☐	☐
5. I have friends with whom I can share my joys and sorrows.	☐	☐
6. There is a special person in my life who cares about my feelings.	☐	☐

Scoring

If you have more "true" responses, you have a high level of social support. If you have more "not true" responses, you have a low level of social support. If you have the same number of "true" and "not true" responses, you have a medium level of social support.

(Adapted from Blumenthal, et al. *Psychosomatic Medicine* 49:339-40, 1987. Reprinted by permission of Williams & Wilkins.)

IN YOUR JOURNAL

Set one or more goals that you would like to achieve in the area of personal support. For example, you might want to have more people in your life who can help you.

WHAT IS SUPPORT?

GROUP ACTIVITY

In your group, discuss support—what it is, who gives it, when you need it, and when you give it. In addition to your discussion, analyze the scenario in the Data Bank. Develop your own definition of support, and write it in the space provided.

_____

_____

_____

_____

_____

_____

_____

_____

_____

_____

_____

_____

_____

There are a couple of things I always do when I start one of my engineering classes. First, I go and talk to the instructor, tell him or her about myself, how I'm working most nights as a janitor. If the instructor seems interested, I explain about how I used to be a high-altitude welder but quit to get an engineering degree when I saw my brother paralyzed after a fall. That way, when they see my name on the roll, they know

DATA BANK

I'm no goof-off kid. After all, I'm twenty-eight with a wife and two children. Next, I talk to Janna. We set up a family schedule for work time, school and study time, and family time. Each of us has responsibilities to the kids during the week. If we see a conflict, I start looking for help. Mrs. Lyons is usually available to babysit since I help her out with fix-it chores when I can.

IDENTIFYING YOUR SUPPORT

FRIENDS AND FAMILY

Your personal resources can provide you with a wide range of valuable support. To get that support, however, you usually have to ask for help.

Recall times in your life when you needed support.

DISCOVERY
ACTIVITY

• How did you try to get the support you needed?

_____

_____

_____

_____

_____

_____

_____

_____

• Were your methods of getting support successful? Describe what you said or did.

_____

_____

_____

_____

_____

_____

_____

_____

_____

_____

You might find asking for help hard to do. You might feel too proud, or you might be embarrassed to share a personal problem. The fact is, however, that if you ask, most people who are close to you are willing to help you. The key is to ask. Try approaches such as the following:

- I'd really like to talk to you about something important that's going on with me.
- Could I ask you to help me sort through a problem?
- There's something on my mind, and I'd like you to listen and tell me what you think.
- May I tell you something and ask you not to tell anyone else about it?

Confidentiality is very important. The person you ask to help you should be trustworthy. That's why friends and family members are personal resources—they know you best and care about you more than anyone else. Of course, friends and family members are not all saints! Use your judgment when reaching out to others, but be willing to take some risks too. Asking for help is a way of asserting that you have a right to receive help. Don't forget that you can also *give* support when others ask you. Support is a reciprocal process—when you receive help, be willing to give help in return.

OTHER SOURCES OF PERSONAL SUPPORT

Support groups, religious leaders, counselors, "hot lines," and therapists are other sources of personal support. If you are unable to reach out to friends or family, private sources of support are widely available, both on and off campus. (On-campus support services are discussed in Chapter 9.) You'll find listings for various support services in telephone books, local newspapers, and special-interest magazines and newsletters.

Some sources of personal support are only a phone call away. Before you call, prepare a list of questions to ask. Keep pen and paper handy for copying information.

THE "SAFETY NET"

In every community, agencies and bureaus exist whose sole purpose is to help people in distress. As a group, these services are often called the "safety net" because they are a means of last resort for people who have no other support. Some of these services are funded by the federal government, others by state governments, and still others by county or city governments.

You can usually find listings of such services in your phone book. Look under state government listings—*Florida, State Government* or *Florida, State of*, for example. From there, look for a listing such as "Human Services" or "Human Resources." When you speak to a representative, be clear about what you need. Identify your situation specifically—single unemployed parent with two children under 12 years of age, for example. Also be prepared to answer other specific questions the representative may ask. That agency may be able to help you directly, or it may refer you to another agency.

PORTFOLIO

Assignment 1:
Charting Your Resources

Make a chart of your personal resources. Begin the chart by including the friends or relatives you feel you might be able to call on for support. List other support groups that you are personally familiar with. Include a column for the kind of support the friend, group, or organization offers. Include a column for phone numbers, addresses, and available times. Make whatever personal notes you might want to include about each resource. Be sure to allow room on the chart for additional assignments. Save this assignment in your portfolio.

Even though you are a student, you may be eligible for many of the services provided in the community. Among the most common community services are food stamps, Aid to Families With Dependent Children, Medicaid, Child Support Enforcement, Social Services, and Public Health Services.

Food Stamps

The food stamps program is a federal food supplement plan. This plan is intended to guarantee that families can obtain basic nutrition.

Single students may also be eligible if they are working at least 20 hours per week. Under this program, you receive food stamps to use in place of money at the grocery store. You may purchase only food products with food stamps; you are not allowed to purchase alcohol or soap products, for example.

Aid to Families With Dependent Children (AFDC)

Aid to Families With Dependent Children is a financial assistance program primarily for single parents with little or no income. AFDC is usually funded by the states, using federal subsidies. If eligible, you receive money to pay rent, utilities, and other basic expenses.

Medicaid

Medicaid provides medical care and medication for heads of households with children. Most of those receiving Medicaid must also be eligible for AFDC, but exceptions are made.

Child Support Enforcement

State governments include child support enforcement agencies that provide help when a noncustodial parent fails to pay child support. These agencies find the parent in default and force the person to pay.

Social Services

Social services agencies provide protective services to both children and adults. They handle cases of child abuse and child neglect as well as other services for preserving the family, such as counseling. Social services agencies in most cities also provide shelters for abused women and children. These shelters provide a temporary safe haven until permanent accommodations can be arranged.

Public Health Services

State governments provide most public health services. The services include immunization and medical testing for **AIDS** and other sexually transmitted diseases. Some also have food supplement programs for pregnant and nursing women and for young children.

Activity A: Identifying Community Resources

With your group, identify safety net resources within your community. Use the telephone directory to find the names, addresses, and telephone numbers of agencies that provide support. List several of these resources in the space provided.

_____

_____

_____

_____

_____

_____

_____

_____

_____

_____

_____

_____

_____

Assignment 2:
Completing Your Resources Chart

Retrieve the chart of your personal resources you began for Assignment 1. Add community, state, or federal government support groups that you feel may be of value in your situation. Include a note on the kind of support the group or organization offers. Include phone numbers, addresses, and available times. Make whatever personal notes you might want to include about each resource. Save this assignment in your portfolio.

RECOGNIZING STRESS

A broad definition of **stress** is "the body's general response to any situation." In other words, just about anything you do is likely to be stressful. There's good stress and bad stress. **Good stress** includes events you find interesting and exciting, such as watching your home team win a game. **Bad stress** includes events and situations that cause pain or worry, such as an upcoming midterm test or a breakup with a close friend. Of course, good stress for one person may be bad stress for someone else. In fact, the same event that seems good to you at one time may seem bad at another time. Most people, however, know what kinds of things generally make them feel relaxed or positively excited and what things make them feel pain, sadness, or anxiety.

DISCOVERY
ACTIVITY

- Identify some sources of good stress in your life.

  _____

  _____

  _____

  _____

  _____

- Identify some sources of bad stress in your life.

  _____

  _____

  _____

  _____

  _____

- Do you have a method for handling bad stress? If you do, how does it work?

  _____

  _____

  _____

  _____

  _____

  _____

  _____

HANDLING STRESS

Because almost any activity, event, or situation can cause stress, you're unlikely to get rid of all causes of stress. You can, however, reduce the harmful effects of stress on your mind and body. First you need to recognize when you are under stress. Some people are so accustomed to feeling pained, worried, or depressed that they don't even realize they're experiencing stress. At several times during the day, take a moment to ask yourself "How do I feel?" Notice your mental state and your body language. Here are just a few of the signs that indicate stress.

- Clenching jaw or grinding teeth
- Shaking hands
- Clenching fists
- Sweating with worry
- Aching head
- Trouble concentrating
- Rapid and shallow breathing
- Feeling as if you want to scream
- Feeling as if you want to hit something or someone

- Can you tell when you're under stress? What signs do you look for in yourself?

_____

_____

_____

_____

_____

_____

_____

Recognizing that you are under stress is a big step toward reducing the effect of that stress on your mind and body. Exercise and relaxation are two proven methods for further reducing stress.

Method 1: Exercise

One of the best stress reducers is exercise—regular exercise. Aerobic activities such as running, swimming, jogging, jumping rope, calisthenics, and fast walking are good forms of exercise. Exercise helps you reduce stress by strengthening your muscles (including your heart) and brings more oxygen into your body. These processes help your body resist the harmful effects of stress.

Now for the "regular" part. You don't need to be a professional athlete to benefit from exercise. Just 20 to 30 minutes a day, three days a week, is enough to build up your physical resistance to stress. You should, however, exercise according to a regular pattern—every day or every other day.

- What kind(s) of exercise do you prefer?

  _____

  _____

  _____

  _____

- Do you exercise regularly? What is your pattern?

  _____

  _____

  _____

  _____

- How could you improve your exercise plan?

  _____

  _____

  _____

  _____

  _____

  _____

  _____

  _____

  _____

Method 2: Relaxation Techniques

Another way to reduce the effects of stress is through progressive relaxation techniques. You can buy a commercial tape that will guide you through a relaxation process. Most of them present a similar series of steps involving **visualization** (seeing your body, a place, or some object in your mind), paying attention to your breathing, and relaxing your muscles. Here is a progressive relaxation sequence you can follow:

1. Sit or lie in a quiet room with your eyes closed. If you're sitting, your feet should be flat on the floor, and your hands should lie loosely in your lap. If you're lying on your back, your feet should be about an arm's length apart and your hands palm down at your sides. Focus your attention on your breathing, noticing its rhythm—in and out.

2. Start with your feet. Tighten the muscles of your feet by curling your toes and holding the tension for a few seconds. Be careful not to cramp your instep. Then suddenly release all the tension. Notice the good feeling that accompanies the release of tension.

3. Now tighten your calf muscles, holding the tension briefly then releasing it. Concentrate on the feeling in your muscles when you release the tension.

4. Continue tensing and releasing parts of your body: your buttocks, your stomach, and your arms and hands. Tighten the muscles of your shoulders by bringing them up toward your neck, holding the tension, and releasing it. Again, notice the relaxed feeling after you release the tension.

5. Squeeze your face muscles, "making a face," then release the tension. If you're lying on your back, roll your head from side to side to release tension. If you're sitting, slowly rotate your head a few times first clockwise, then counterclockwise.

6. Be sure to maintain relaxation in the parts of your body that you've already relaxed.

7. After you've progressively tightened and relaxed all the major muscle groups in your body, sit or lie quietly with your eyes still closed, and notice the way your body feels when it is relaxed. Focus your attention on your breathing. Count from one to ten each time you exhale. Try to maintain this relaxed state for at least 15 minutes.

You can make your own tape of these steps and use it to guide you through the relaxation process. With practice, you'll soon be able to do the steps from memory. Then you'll be able to achieve relaxation almost instantly, even in very stressful situations.

PORTFOLIO

Assignment 3:
Expanding Your Resource Listings

Create a new chart to complement your personal resource chart. List your exercise routines and relaxation techniques. Include a column to list the times you feel more comfortable using each stress reducer. List whatever equipment or materials you might need for each. Include a column identifying what kind of stress each technique or exercise seems to work best for. Save this assignment in your portfolio.

SUMMARY

- Your system of personal support includes the people you count on when you need help.
- Friends and family members are the main elements of your personal support system.
- The key to getting the help you need is to ask for it.
- Support groups, religious leaders, counselors, "hot lines," and therapists are other sources of personal support.
- The "safety net" is a group of community agencies and bureaus that help people who have no other means of support.
- Stress is the body's general response to any situation. There is good stress and bad stress.
- The first step in reducing the harmful effects of stress is to recognize that you are under stress.
- Exercise and relaxation are two proven methods of reducing the harmful effects of stress.

THINKING IT OVER

- What is the most important thing you learned in this chapter?

  _____

  _____

  _____

  _____

  _____

  _____

- How will you apply what you learned in this chapter to improving your personal support system and reducing the effects of stress in your life?

_____

_____

_____

_____

_____

_____

_____

IN YOUR JOURNAL

Take a look at the goals you set at the beginning of the chapter. What progress have you made toward achieving them? What new goals do you now have regarding support and stress reduction? How will you achieve them?

9

USING INSTITUTIONAL SUPPORT

OBJECTIVES:

- To investigate services provided by campus offices.

- To identify and use the resources of the campus library.

- To formulate reasons to obtain faculty support.

- To use peer study groups.

Where Can I Find
Support?

Needing help and getting help are two common human experiences. How is the person in the picture getting help?

Whenever you have problems in college, remember that resources are available to help you deal with them. Many of those resources are available on your college campus, through campus offices, faculty, and other staff members. As you work through this chapter, you will discover sources of support that can make your college experience more productive and satisfying.

GETTING STARTED

Our society is composed, in part, of many different kinds of institutions—organizations with specific purposes. Examples of these institutions are banks, schools, hospitals, insurance companies, libraries, and government agencies. These institutions provide many different kinds of services that enable our society to function. At some time or another, everyone gets services or support from one or more of these institutions.

Think back on your own experiences of needing and getting support from an institution.

- Describe a situation in which you needed and received help from an institution.

  _____

  _____

  _____

  _____

  _____

- What help have you needed in relation to your college enrollment and course work? Were you able to find the help you needed?

  _____

  _____

  _____

  _____

IN YOUR JOURNAL

In what areas of your life do you need more support or a different kind of support from an institution? Set a related personal goal. An example might be, "I'd like to learn how to use the campus offices that deal with student finances so that I can improve my financial situation."

EXPLORING SUPPORT SOURCES

Some kinds of support can come only from offices or departments within your college or university.

GROUP
ACTIVITY

A. In your group, discuss kinds of problems you and other students typically have in college. Organize the problems into categories, such as money, time, motivation, and other people. Make a list of general advice and sources of help.

_____

_____

_____

_____

_____

_____

_____

B. Within your group, role-play at least two of the situations in the Data Bank. Then analyze the situations you role-played, and try to develop a set of guidelines for dealing effectively with faculty. In the space provided, list the guidelines your group develops.

_____

_____

_____

_____

- Your paper will be late.
- You need help with a concept.
- You need advice on your major.
- The bookstore is out of text-books for your class.
- You need to make up a test.

DATA
BANK

- You can't understand the instructor's accent.
- You think you should drop the class.
- You need a reference.
- You want to change your lab sections.

USING INSTITUTIONAL RESOURCES

Your college or university is an **institution**—an organization with a specific purpose. To carry out its purpose—education—your school provides support services designed to meet a variety of student needs.

DISCOVERY ACTIVITY

- Check which support services are available on your campus and whether you have used them.

	ON CAMPUS		USED	
	YES	NO	YES	NO
• Counseling Services	☐	☐	☐	☐
• Activities/Fitness Centers	☐	☐	☐	☐
• Student Center/Union	☐	☐	☐	☐
• Financial Aid Services	☐	☐	☐	☐
• Career/Placement Services	☐	☐	☐	☐
• Learning Assistance/Resource Center	☐	☐	☐	☐
• Library	☐	☐	☐	☐

- Which of these services successfully met your needs?

_____

_____

_____

- Which of these services did not meet your needs?

_____

_____

_____

_____

PROVIDING SUPPORT

Although your institution is unique in the student support services it offers, most institutions offer some form of the following services:

- Counseling services
- Activities/fitness centers
- Student center/union
- Financial aid services
- Career/placement service
- Learning assistance/resource center
- Library

Counseling Services

Counselors are usually available to help students deal with personal problems, including adjusting to college life. Problems with roommates, relationships, personal habits (eating disorders, drug problems, and so on), are commonly handled by counseling services. Any information you share with a counselor is kept *absolutely* confidential. Some counseling units also provide personal-growth seminars and other services such as stress management or workshops to help people stop smoking.

- What counseling services does your institution provide?

  _____

  _____

  _____

  _____

- Where are the counseling services located at your institution?

  _____

  _____

  _____

  _____

  _____

- What steps should a student take to use the counseling services at your institution?

_____

_____

_____

Activities/Fitness Centers

Access to swimming pools, tennis courts, weight-lifting and aerobic exercise facilities, and jogging paths and tracks may be covered by your activities fees.

- Where is the fitness center on your campus?

_____

_____

- What equipment and activities are available at your campus fitness center?

_____

_____

_____

_____

- What are the hours of operation and basic rules for using the fitness center?

_____

_____

_____

_____

Student Center/Union

The student center or student union usually contains recreational facilities—eating facilities, lounges, places for study, and other services. Sometimes the student center also includes word processing services, tutoring, student book exchanges, and a student bulletin board. Check the directory the next time you visit this building to find out the range of services offered.

- Where is your student center or union located?

  _____

  _____

- What specific services are available at your student center?

  _____

  _____

  _____

  _____

- What are the hours of operation and basic rules for using the student center?

  _____

  _____

  _____

  _____

Financial Aid Services

In this office counselors and printed information will help you determine whether you are eligible for financial assistance. Before you visit this often busy office, prepare a list of questions to make your visit more efficient.

- Where is the financial aid service located on your campus?

  _____

  _____

- What are the specific services your financial aid center provides?

  _____

  _____

  _____

  _____

• What are its hours of operation and rules?

_____

_____

_____

_____

Career/Placement Service

Your school's career office can help you write your résumé and make you aware of various job opportunities. If you haven't yet decided on a career, the office can give you screening tests to help you make that decision. In addition, the office can help you start a file of recommendations to use when you apply for jobs.

• Where is your school's career/placement service located?

_____

_____

• What are the hours of operation for the career/placement service?

_____

_____

• What are some of the specific services offered at the career/placement service?

_____

_____

_____

_____

Learning Assistance/Resource Center

Learning centers offer a variety of services. Some teach study skills through individual or group classes and seminars. Others offer tutoring or computer-aided instruction. If you are having an academic problem—not doing well in a particular course, for example—the learning center is a good place to look for help. The staff should be aware of the options for academic help on campus.

- Where is your campus learning assistance or resource center located?

_____

_____

- What are the hours of operation of the learning/resource center?

_____

_____

_____

- What are some of the specific kinds of help your campus learning center offers?

_____

_____

_____

_____

PORTFOLIO

Assignment 1:
Describing a Campus Resource

Visit at least one of the campus resources described in this section. Prepare a list of questions before your visit. During your visit, be courteous to the staff, treating them as you would expect to be treated if you had their job. Obtain as much information about the resource as you can, including any brochures or other handouts. Then write a two- or three-paragraph description of each resource you visited, identifying important features. This description should be aimed at incoming first-year college students, such as your peers, who may be unaware of the resource. Save this assignment in your portfolio.

The Library: The Prime Campus Resource

On most campuses the library is a hub of activity. Because the library contains more information than any other campus facility, it naturally is the place where most people go to do research, study, and read.

The information center of the library provides directions for using the wide range of library resources.

- How many libraries does your campus have? Does each one have a special subject area? If so, identify the subject areas.

  _____

  _____

  _____

  _____

- What are the operating hours of the library?

  _____

  _____

- What kind of index system does the library have—card catalog, computerized index, or both?

  _____

  _____

USING THE LIBRARY

The library is traditionally the place to find books on all subjects; however, books are only one resource in a modern library. Your library also probably contains periodicals (journals, magazines, and newspapers), microfilm and microfiche collections, a photocopying service, and areas for quiet as well as group study. Today's libraries are multipurpose and multimedia resources.

Here is a brief description of resources commonly found in college libraries. In your research you will undoubtedly find other valuable features in your library.

The Key Resource: The Reference Librarian ≈

By far, the reference librarian is your most valuable resource to successful use of the library. All libraries have at least one librarian. Some libraries employ many professionally trained librarians who do specialized tasks such as ordering and cataloging books, keeping track of checkouts and returns, and overseeing the day-to-day operations.

The reference librarian has one purpose only: to help people find resources in the library. You can usually find the reference librarian at a desk near the reference section or the library catalog section.

Until you become familiar with your own campus library, don't be afraid to use the librarian to help you find what you need. Don't worry about asking "dumb" or "stupid" questions—the librarian has heard them all. You can even be as honest as this: I have to write a term paper, and I don't know where to start.

Activity A: Consulting the Librarian

Prepare a list of questions you have about the library. Then go to the library, and find the librarian. Some librarians will give you a tour of the library or show you the major sections on a library map. Some libraries also have a handbook, a copy of which the librarian may give you.

Computerized Catalogs and Indexes ≈≈≈

To keep up-to-date with the information explosion, most libraries now use computer catalogs in place of the old card catalogs.

A major advantage of the electronic catalog is that it can make the same information available at many workstations—even in different buildings—simultaneously. An electronic system is also fast, easy to use, and easy to update.

From Computerized Catalog

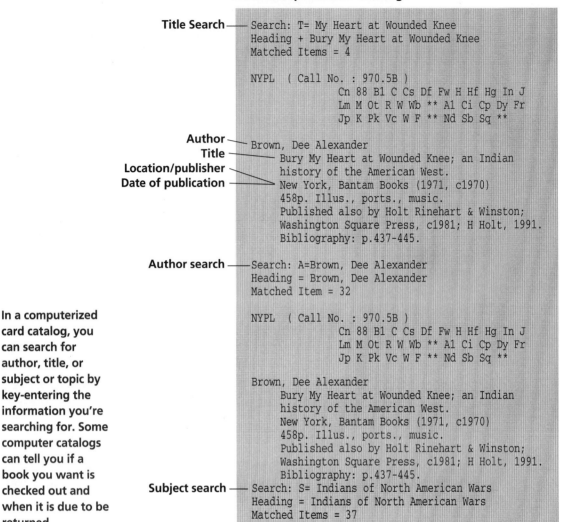

Title Search — Search: T= My Heart at Wounded Knee
Heading + Bury My Heart at Wounded Knee
Matched Items = 4

NYPL (Call No. : 970.5B)
Cn 88 B1 C Cs Df Fw H Hf Hg In J
Lm M Ot R W Wb ** A1 Ci Cp Dy Fr
Jp K Pk Vc W F ** Nd Sb Sq **

Author — Brown, Dee Alexander
Title — Bury My Heart at Wounded Knee; an Indian
Location/publisher — history of the American West.
Date of publication — New York, Bantam Books (1971, c1970)
458p. Illus., ports., music.
Published also by Holt Rinehart & Winston;
Washington Square Press, c1981; H Holt, 1991.
Bibliography: p.437-445.

Author search — Search: A=Brown, Dee Alexander
Heading = Brown, Dee Alexander
Matched Item = 32

NYPL (Call No. : 970.5B)
Cn 88 B1 C Cs Df Fw H Hf Hg In J
Lm M Ot R W Wb ** A1 Ci Cp Dy Fr
Jp K Pk Vc W F ** Nd Sb Sq **

Brown, Dee Alexander
Bury My Heart at Wounded Knee; an Indian
history of the American West.
New York, Bantam Books (1971, c1970)
458p. Illus., ports., music.
Published also by Holt Rinehart & Winston;
Washington Square Press, c1981; H Holt, 1991.
Bibliography: p.437-445.

Subject search — Search: S= Indians of North American Wars
Heading = Indians of North American Wars
Matched Items = 37

In a computerized card catalog, you can search for author, title, or subject or topic by key-entering the information you're searching for. Some computer catalogs can tell you if a book you want is checked out and when it is due to be returned.

If you are researching **AIDS**, for instance, you would not want to limit yourself to information from a book that was published in 1986—too much new information has been uncovered since then. A computer catalog lists recent sources of information published in journals and other periodicals as well as in recently published books. Suppose you find a citation for a recent source of information, but your library does not have the source. You can usually get the source from another library, through the interlibrary loan service.

In addition to computer catalogs, libraries also have electronic indexes or data bases. These provide you with current articles on a variety of subjects. The indexes are specialized, such as *Psychlit* (Psychology) and *ERIC* (Education), and are constantly being updated. Use them if your library subscribes to them. If computer indexes are not available, use the bound-book form of the index.

With the computer index, you key your topic and the computer searches for the information. If you use an index in book form, you simply select your topic alphabetically. You may need help from the reference librarian if you can't find anything using your wording of the topic. For example, if you were researching female members of adolescent gangs, this topic might be listed under something like *juvenile delinquency* or *offenders, youthful*. Usually a reference librarian can suggest other possible wordings to help you locate the information you need. The librarian can also help you log onto the computer index.

In evaluating student research papers, college instructors usually give more importance to citations from current journals than from published books. This is a good reason to use the systems that give you the most recent information.

```
077 BOBST LIBRARY GEAC LIBRARY SYSTEM- ALL*CHOOSE SEARCH
What type of search do you wish to do?
    1.  TIL - Title, journal title, series title, etc.
    2.  AtT - Author, illustrator, editor, organization, etc.
    3.  A-T - Combination of authors and title.
    4.  SUB - Subject heading assigned by library.
    5.  NUM - Call number, ISBN, ISSN, etc.
    6.  BOL - Boolean search on title, author and subject.
    7.  LIM - Limit your search to a portion of the catalog.
  Enter number or code:          Then press SEND


077 BOBST LIBRARY GEAC LIBRARY SYSTEM- ALL*CHOOSE SEARCH
    Start at the beginning of the subject and enter as
    many words on the subject as you know below.
    When you can, be specific.
        Ex:  Molecular biology     (Not biology)
```

Electronic catalog systems are user-friendly. They provide clear, simple directions for finding the information you want.

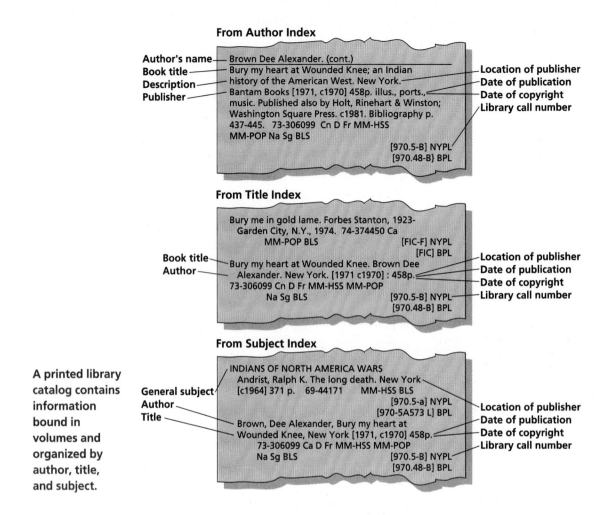

From Author Index

Author's name — Brown Dee Alexander. (cont.)
Book title — Bury my heart at Wounded Knee; an Indian
Description — history of the American West. New York. — Location of publisher
Publisher — Bantam Books [1971, c1970] 458p. illus., ports., — Date of publication
music. Published also by Holt, Rinehart & Winston; — Date of copyright
Washington Square Press. c1981. Bibliography p. — Library call number
437-445.   73-306099 Cn D Fr MM-HSS
MM-POP Na Sg BLS

[970.5-B] NYPL
[970.48-B} BPL

From Title Index

Bury me in gold lame. Forbes Stanton, 1923-
Garden City, N.Y., 1974. 74-374450 Ca
MM-POP BLS   [FIC-F] NYPL
[FIC] BPL

Book title — Bury my heart at Wounded Knee. Brown Dee — Location of publisher
Author — Alexander. New York. [1971 c1970] : 458p. — Date of publication
73-306099 Cn D Fr MM-HSS MM-POP — Date of copyright
Na Sg BLS   [970.5-B] NYPL — Library call number
[970.48-B] BPL

From Subject Index

INDIANS OF NORTH AMERICA WARS
Andrist, Ralph K. The long death. New York
General subject — [c1964] 371 p.   69-44171   MM-HSS BLS
Author — [970.5-a] NYPL
Title — [970-5A573 L] BPL — Location of publisher
Brown, Dee Alexander, Bury my heart at — Date of publication
Wounded Knee, New York [1971, c1970] 458p. — Date of copyright
73-306099 Ca D Fr MM-HSS MM-POP — Library call number
Na Sg BLS   [970.5-B] NYPL
[970.48-B] BPL

A printed library catalog contains information bound in volumes and organized by author, title, and subject.

Printed Catalogs

In this system, the library catalog consists of two or three multi-volume sets containing information on the books in the library. One set of volumes includes information arranged alphabetically by the last names of the authors; a second set includes information arranged alphabetically by the titles of the books; a third set contains information arranged alphabetically by subject.

In some libraries catalog information is contained on 3-inch × 5-inch cards, with three cards for each book: author, title, and subject. On the author card, the author's name appears first, and the card is filed alphabetically by the last name of the author. On the title card, the title of the book appears first, and the card is filed alphabetically by the first word of the title. On the subject card, the subject or topic of the book apears first, and the card is filed alphabetically by the first word of the topic.

The Shelf Location of a Book

A card catalog or computer catalog will tell you where to find the book in the library. The location of the book is indicated by a call number. The call number gives the general category or classification of the information the book contains plus a designation for the specific book. Libraries use one of two classification systems, the Dewey decimal system or the Library of Congress system. These are the broad categories of each system.

The Dewey Decimal System

000-099—General Works
100-199—Philosophy
200-299—Religion
300-399—Social Sciences
400-499—Language

500-599—Pure Science
600-699—Technology
700-799—The Arts
800-899—Literature
900-999—History

Library of Congress System

A— General Works, Polygraphy
B— Philosophy, Religion
C— History
D— History and Topography
E-F— America
G— Geography, Anthropology
H— Social Science, Political Science
K— Law
L— Education
M— Music

N— Fine Arts
P— Language and Literature
Q— Science
R— Medicine
S— Agriculture, Plant and Industry
T— Technology
U— Military Science
V— Naval Science
Z— Bibliography and Library Science

Each system includes numerous subdivisions for each class of information. Under the Dewey decimal system, for example, History is further divided into American History (973), which in turn includes such subcategories as the American Revolution (973.3) and the American Civil War (973.7).

Activity B: Using the Catalog System

Select a topic you're interested in. The topic might be one you need to research for a course. Use the catalog system of your library to find three books on the topic. List the information the catalog gives you about each book, including author, title, place of publication and copyright date, and a brief description of the book. If the computer catalog allows you to do so, print out the information on each book.

_____

_____

_____

_____

_____

_____

_____

_____

_____

_____

_____

_____

_____

_____

_____

_____

_____

_____

_____

Periodicals

Journals, magazines, and newspapers are published at regular time intervals—daily, weekly, monthly, or quarterly. That's why they're called **periodicals**. All periodicals are usually located in the same section of the library. The most recent issues are usually loose on shelves, organized alphabetically by title. The past issues are bound into book format or are put on microfiche or microfilm. A special device is used to read periodicals on microfiche or microfilm.

Periodicals are indexed and cataloged separately from books. The main catalog for periodicals is *The Reader's Guide to Periodical Literature* (often called *Reader's Guide*). This is a general index of all sorts of magazine and journal articles on a wide range of topics. Under the name of a specific topic, you'll find the names of periodicals, the dates of the periodicals, and the titles of the articles relating to that topic.

The *Reader's Guide* is fairly easy to use. If you're unfamiliar with it, however, ask a reference librarian to help you get started. When you find an article you need, note all the identifying information, including the page number on which the article begins.

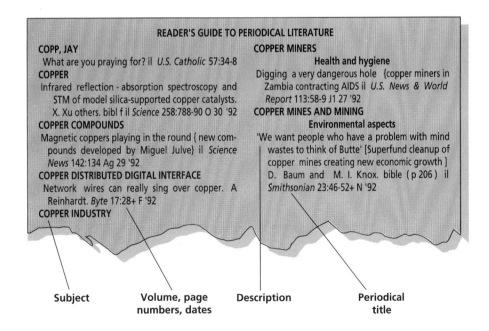

READER'S GUIDE TO PERIODICAL LITERATURE

COPP, JAY
What are you praying for? il *U.S. Catholic* 57:34-8
COPPER
Infrared reflection - absorption spectroscopy and STM of model silica-supported copper catalysts. X. Xu others. bibl f il *Science* 258:788-90 O 30 '92
COPPER COMPOUNDS
Magnetic coppers playing in the round { new compounds developed by Miguel Julve} il *Science News* 142:134 Ag 29 '92
COPPER DISTRIBUTED DIGITAL INTERFACE
Network wires can really sing over copper. A. Reinhardt. *Byte* 17:28+ F '92
COPPER INDUSTRY

COPPER MINERS
Health and hygiene
Digging a very dangerous hole {copper miners in Zambia contracting AIDS il *U.S. News & World Report* 113:58-9 Jl 27 '92
COPPER MINES AND MINING
Environmental aspects
'We want people who have a problem with mind wastes to think of Butte' [Superfund cleanup of copper mines creating new economic growth] D. Baum and M. I. Knox. bible (p 206) il *Smithsonian* 23:46-52+ N '92

Subject   Volume, page   Description   Periodical
               numbers, dates   title

Activity C: Using the **Reader's Guide**

Using the same topic you chose for the activity on page 178 or another topic, find citations for at least three articles related to the topic in the *Reader's Guide*.

_____

_____

_____

_____

_____

_____

_____

_____

_____

_____

_____

_____

_____

_____

_____

_____

_____

_____

_____

_____

Reference Books

Most libraries have a large collection of books that readers can use only in the library. These are called reference books. You're probably already familiar with some of these books, such as the dictionary and general encyclopedia. Other reference sources, such as specialty dictionaries and subject encyclopedias, may be new to you. These reference materials are expensive or popular and, for these reasons, are not available for circulation outside of the library.

General References

Multivolume encyclopedias and one-volume dictionaries are organized alphabetically by subject or word. Encyclopedia articles often have cross-indexing and bibliographic information that can steer you toward other resources when you're researching a topic.

In procedures called behavior modifications, therapists use positive reinforcers to shape behavior in desired ways. For example, behavior modification has been used to help retarted children learn basic school subjects. The children may receive smiles, hugs, or food for doing their schoolwork and behaving properly. In other behavior modification programs, children work for tokens or points. Later they can exchange the tokens for candy, toys or other rewards. Such programs have also proven effective with children of normal intelligence and with juvenile delinquents. Edwin B. Fisher, Jr.

Related articles in *World Book* Include:

Alienation	Emotion	Mental illness
Child	Etiquette	Motivation
Developmental	Habit	Pavlov, Ivan P.
psychology	Instinct	Personality
Displacement	Kinesics	Skinner, B. F.
behavior	Learning	Watson, John B.
	Learning	
	disabilities	

Additional resources

Hall, Elizabeth. *From Pigeons to People: A Look at Behavior Shaping*. Houghton, 1975
Manning, Aubrey. An Introduction to Animal Behavior. 3rd ed. Addison-Wesley, 1979.
The Natural History Reader in Animal Behavior. Ed. by Howard Topoff. Columbia Univ. Pr., 1987.

(Excerpt from *The World Book Encyclopedia*)

Specialized Reference

After doing your general research and picking up cues to pursue, you can move to more specific or specialized materials. Your library probably contains a few of these specialty books called **subject encyclopedias** or **dictionaries**. Almost every field of study has a subject encyclopedia or dictionary, including ones for music, education, philosophy, and sociology. The reference librarian can help you locate these specialized resources.

Using References

Assume that you've found a book or periodical with the information you want to use. What do you do next? If the book is a reference book or a periodical, you can't check it out. You'll need to take notes in the library. If the book is available for check-out, you can take notes later in your study area. Once again, remember to copy the full citation with all information: author, title, date, journal, issue, page numbers, publisher, city of publication, and copyright date. This way you will avoid having to make return trips to the library to get the information for the reference notes or bibliography section of your paper.

Circulating Books

Circulating books are books that you can check out of the library. You can find them by using the computer catalog or card catalog. When using the catalog, be sure to make note of all information you'll need to find the book: call number, author, or title. You also need the publishing and copyright information to list the book as a source for your research. You can take this information from the catalog and double-check it on the copyright page of the book (the page immediately following the title page).

Be aware that, in general, the information you find in circulating books may not be absolutely current. This is true especially if you are researching a topic such as "space exploration" or "genetic engineering" in which new information develops all the time. If your subject is "the history of space exploration during the 1970s," however, timeliness is not an issue. Any book published after 1980 is likely to be as up to date as you need for that topic.

Activity D: Finding Circulating Books

Go to the circulating stacks and find the books you looked up in the card or computer catalog in the activity on page 178. If these books were not circulating books, look up three or more books that are circulating and find them on the shelves. Describe the process of locating the books. What was easy? What was hard? What surprised you?

_____

_____

_____

_____

_____

_____

_____

_____

_____

_____

_____

_____

_____

_____

_____

_____

_____

_____

_____

Miscellaneous Resources

Some libraries have other services and offerings that may be available to you. Many libraries have videotapes of documentaries, art performances, and classic films. Some libraries have various kinds of information available on CD-ROM (Read-Only Memory). The music sections of some libraries have audiotapes, records, and CDs of musical performances, plays, and poetry. Some libraries even have prints of famous artwork that you may borrow to hang in your room. These items may be important parts of your research or your relaxation. For a complete list of resources available through your library, ask your librarian.

PORTFOLIO

Assignment 2: ~~~~~~
Describing the Campus Library

From your research, you should be ready to develop a guide for specific parts of the campus library. Combine your information into a written document that describes the features of the library resource(s) you explored. Save this assignment in your portfolio.

GAINING FACULTY SUPPORT

You've no doubt had the opportunity to introduce yourself to someone. The person was a stranger but some circumstance brought you together. Maybe he or she repaired your car, installed your phone, sold you a camera, or was a new neighbor. Maybe you did not *have* to introduce yourself to the person, but you did so anyway.

DISCOVERY ACTIVITY

• How did introducing yourself change the situation for you?

_____

_____

_____

_____

• How did introducing yourself change the situation for the other person?

_____

_____

_____

_____

Many college instructors are warm, willing to help, and have great concern for their students' progress. They're also very busy people. This means *you* are responsible for becoming known to your instructors.

- What are some reasons you would want to make yourself known to a faculty member?

  _____

  _____

  _____

  _____

- What might be a good way to get a faculty member to know who you are?

  _____

  _____

  _____

  _____

Based on your own experiences and observations, what suggestions do you have for the two students presented in the following description? Read each situation, then respond to the questions after each one.

> Martha is a 23-year-old single parent. She went from high school to a job as an admitting clerk at a large hospital where she remained for five years. Martha wants to be a nurse, but to be admitted to the nursing program, she needs the recommendations of her instructors. She is not sure how to make herself better known to them. In her biology class, she has considered just going up before class, introducing herself, and telling her instructor, Dr. Ramirez, about her hospital experience. She's uncertain because this is a large class.

- What do you think of Martha's plan?

  _____

  _____

  _____

Elva is also starting the application process for the nursing program. She, too, is in Dr. Ramirez's introductory class. She is just out of high school and works part-time at a fast food restaurant. Her plan for introducing herself to Dr. Ramirez is to go to the instructor's office during the posted office hours to ask a question about the lecture.

• What do you think of Elva's plan?

_____

_____

_____

_____

_____

• Suppose Keith, another student, did not need a recommendation from a faculty member. What benefits might he gain from having an instructor get to know him?

_____

_____

_____

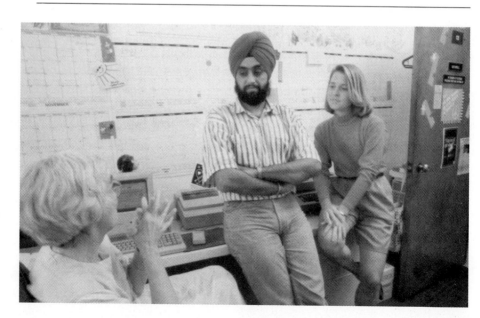

The two students, center and right, are meeting with their instructor during her office hours.

WHY MAKE YOURSELF KNOWN?

You can gain several benefits from making yourself known to your instructors. Here are some examples.

- Personal interaction can help motivate you in a difficult subject.
- You may have special needs that instructors can accommodate if they know about them—vision or hearing problems, for example.
- If you're especially interested in a subject, your instructors might be able to make suggestions to help you explore the subject in greater depth. They may recommend books, journal articles, or other resources.
- You feel more involved, and your involvement helps you learn.
- If instructors know you care about doing well in their classes, they can help you achieve your goal.

MAKING CONTACT

Most instructors post hours during which they are available in their offices to meet with students. You are responsible for making arrangements to meet with instructors during their office hours. Don't let shyness hold you back. A meeting with an instructor can be a valuable experience. If you do poorly on a test, for example, talking with your instructor about what went wrong and what you should do next can have a positive effect on your attitude as well as on your grade.

Guidelines for Making Contact

Faculty members welcome your visits if you observe the following guidelines:

1. Be respectful of what's going on in the instructor's office. If the instructor is rushing around madly or working furiously at a computer, you may have chosen a bad time. Just say "Hello" and ask to schedule an appointment.
2. When you miss a class, don't ask the instructor to recap the lecture or class for you. Instead, get notes from another student.

3. When you've missed a test or are late with an assignment, take responsibility for your actions. Don't make excuses. Admit your shortcoming and present your plan for meeting the instructor's requirements.

Instructors Are People Too

The words may sound trite, but instructors are just human beings like everyone else. If you're considerate, interested, and hardworking, you'll make a positive impression. This positive contact between you and your instructors will increase your chances of succeeding in college. You'll find the effort worthwhile.

You may also gain different insights into the subject of the class. For example, your instructor may share his or her motivation for following a career in that area of knowledge. You may become aware of practical applications for the subject—even job possibilities. You may even develop a greater personal interest in the work you are doing for the class.

Activity E: Role-Playing

With a partner, role-play a meeting between a student and an instructor. Decide what kind of problem or situation the student will present to the instructor. Decide whether the instructor will be busy. After role-playing the scene, ask for feedback from the group on how effective the presentation was.

IN YOUR JOURNAL

Describe a problem or situation you would like to present as a way of letting an instructor get to know you. Make a plan for making contact with the instructor. When you are ready, introduce yourself. Afterward, jot down in your journal how the meeting went. Include what went well, what went wrong, and how you might do better next time.

PEER RESOURCES: STUDY GROUPS

Help with studying is not limited to instructors, paid assistants, and tutors.

DISCOVERY
ACTIVITY

- When have you worked with a group to solve a problem? Describe the problem and what happened.

  _____

  _____

- What was the advantage to working with a group?

  _____

  _____

Guidelines for Study Groups

Joining a study group is an effective way to work on class problems and prepare for tests. You may have worked in groups to study for tests, taking turns asking possible test questions. A regular study group that meets weekly to go over lecture and textbook notes can add greatly to your academic success.

Each member of a study group should participate actively to obtain the greatest benefit from the study group.

1. The ideal size for a study group is three people. Side conversations and time wasting become issues when more than three are in the group. Two people can study together, but when doing problems, a third person can "break the tie" if answers differ.

2. Finding times to meet is sometimes difficult. For most courses, a block of one to one-and-a-half hours is necessary. Plan on two hours or more to prepare for a test. Choose a quiet, neutral place such as a room in the student union or the library. A vacant classroom is another possibility.

3. If your group meets to go over problems, you should each do the problems independently first. Doing the problems for the first time in the group might give you the impression that you know how to work a problem when you really don't. Then, in the group, compare your results. If one result differs from the other two, try to figure out where the process differs. Remember, the idea is to understand the process, not just to get the right answer.

4. If your group meets to go over lecture or textbook notes, use your notes to quiz each other, following the self-test guidelines in the note-taking chapter, Chapter 12, pages 250–254.

5. A regular working group should meet at least once a week. A group that meets only to prepare for an exam may meet once or twice before the exam. Use the guidelines for group study before a test in Chapter 20, pages 438–475.

6. Group interaction is crucial. When you talk and ask questions, you learn. If you're quiet and just listen, you tend not to learn as much and may be mistaken about how much you really know. You can't learn by just being there; you must participate.

PORTFOLIO

Assignment 3:
Forming a Study Group

Form a study group in one of your most difficult classes as early in the term as you can. What two people in your class could you work well with? Approach one of the people. If he or she says yes, the two of you can approach the third person. If someone says no, try someone else. In the first meeting, collaborate on a plan for studying. Write out your plan and make sure the other two members agree to it. Save this assignment in your portfolio.

WRAPPING IT UP

SUMMARY

- Most colleges and universities provide the following support services:

Counseling Services	Career/Placement Service
Activities/Fitness Centers	Learning Assistance/Resource Center
Student Center/Union	Library
Financial Aid Services	

- A library is a multipurpose and multimedia center, containing the following resources: computer catalogs, indexes, and data bases; books; periodicals; microfilm and microfiche collections; audio and video recordings; and photocopying services.

- The reference librarian is the key library resource.

- The library computer catalog or card catalog system contains author, title, and subject listings for all materials in the library.

- Books are located on library shelves by call number, reflecting either the Dewey decimal system or the Library of Congress system.

- *The Readers' Guide to Periodical Literature* is a general index of many magazines and journal articles on a wide range of topics.

- You may want to make yourself known to an instructor to increase your motivation, get help with a special problem, get help exploring a subject, get a recommendation for a job or special college program.

- A peer study group that meets weekly can help you work on class problems and prepare for tests. The group should include three people, meet for one to two hours, and be interactive.

THINKING IT OVER

- What ideas and information in this chapter did you find most useful?

  _____

  _____

  _____

  _____

  _____

  _____

  _____

- How will you apply the ideas and information from this chapter in taking advantage of support services offered by your school?

  _____

  _____

  _____

  _____

  _____

  _____

IN YOUR JOURNAL

Refer to the goal you set in the journal activity on page 164 at the beginning of this chapter. What progress have you made toward that goal? What new goals will you set based on what you've learned in this chapter?

Note Taking

How successful would doctors be without access to notes on patients' medical charts? You can easily see that without patient notes, medical care would not be very effective. Those notes enable doctors to take charge of a patient's illness. In the same way, taking notes in your college courses enables you to take charge of new and important information that you need to remember. Chapter 10 focuses on preclass note-taking strategies. This chapter will demonstrate the importance of sharpening your listening skills and introduce some techniques for preparing for lectures. Chapter 11 presents strategies for effective note taking in class. This chapter will provide specific techniques for listening actively and taking notes effectively. Chapter 12 describes ways to use lecture notes after class. In this chapter you will learn to use your notes as a cumulative study aid and test-preparation guide.

LEARNING PRECLASS NOTE-TAKING STRATEGIES

OBJECTIVES:

- To analyze ways in which listening skills are useful for taking notes.

- To apply preclass preparation strategies for taking notes.

- To demonstrate note taking as a three-part process that begins before class.

How Can I Best Prepare Myself?

The recent college graduate on the left is shopping for a used car and is asking the sales representative some questions. What steps could the student have taken earlier to make sure he makes the most of his discussion with the sales representative?

Just as you prepare for an important purchase, interview, or meeting, there is a great deal you can do to prepare for lectures and classes in which you need to record significant information. In this chapter you will learn techniques for listening and note taking.

Knowing how to listen and take good notes is essential to your success as a student. Rate your abilities for each statement that follows. Circle *A* for "always," *F* for "frequently," or *N* for "seldom or never."

1. I give speakers my complete attention. A F N

2. I can refocus my mind when it wanders. A F N

3. I have an idea of what information
I am listening for. A F N

4. I am able to recognize and write down the
most important points. A F N

5. I ask questions to clarify what I don't
understand. A F N

6. I make sure I can hear the instructor. A F N

7. I listen for key words or phrases. A F N

8. My notes are brief and to the point. A F N

Scoring

If you circled *A* for all eight statements, your listening skills are in good shape. If you circled *F* for more than four statements, your skills may need just a little work in those areas. If you circled *N* for more than four statements, you think you need work in these areas.

IN YOUR JOURNAL

Set a goal for improving your listening and note-taking skills. Choose a statement from the questionnaire that you responded to with an *F* or *N*. Change this statement into a goal. For example, you might set a goal such as "I'll try to improve my ability to give speakers my full attention." Then describe what you think you might do to achieve that goal.

WHAT KIND OF NOTE TAKER ARE YOU?

GROUP ACTIVITY

From telephone messages to college lectures, many everyday situations require note-taking skills.

A. To find out more about your note-taking ability, work with a partner. While one partner describes a process, place, person, or situation, the other partner takes notes. Select a topic from the Data Bank, or develop a different idea of your own. Choose topics that are not familiar to the note taker. Then switch roles.

B. Discuss these questions in your group:

• What problems did note takers have? Did the problems have anything to do with the interest level of the topic or its vocabulary?

_____

_____

• How was the process of note taking affected by the partner who did the describing?

_____

_____

• How accurate were your notes compared to the original information the partner gave?

_____

• What was most difficult about taking notes—listening to the information or writing the information?

_____

• How to develop black-and-white photographs.
• How to reach a location.
• How to repair a bicycle (appliance, crockery, and so on).

DATA BANK

• How to make a quilt (kite, model, and so on).
• How to build a collection of stamps (dolls, coins, and so on).
• How to play a game or sport.

CHAPTER 10: LEARNING PRECLASS NOTE-TAKING STRATEGIES **197**

THE PROCESS OF NOTE TAKING

LEARNING TO LISTEN

DISCOVERY ACTIVITY

Listening is a concentrated mental effort to take in and process information you hear. Draw upon your own experience and knowledge to complete the following statements:

• Listening is an important skill in daily life because

_____

_____

• Listening is an important skill in school because

_____

_____

• Two important benefits of listening well in daily life are

_____

_____

• Two important benefits of listening well in school are

_____

_____

_____

IMPROVING LISTENING SKILLS

Wouldn't it be wonderful if you could listen to a lecture and remember every word the instructor says? Unfortunately, such an experience is rare. Studies show that after 24 hours you forget half of what you heard. After two weeks you're likely to have forgotten 80 percent of what you heard. For these reasons, improving your listening skills is a worthwhile activity.

These are some of the ways to improve your listening skills:

- Identify the topic of the information you're listening to.

- Identify information you already know about the topic.

- Listen for clues the speaker gives about important ideas—such as, "the most important point is...," "the key points are...," and "chief among these reasons is...," "the three causes are...."

- Quickly and silently repeat to yourself the information you hear.

To prepare for a lecture, identify the topic and read related information about the topic. Prepare a list of questions you expect to be answered during the lecture. Even if the lecture does not answer some of your questions, the act of preparing questions will help you listen attentively.

PORTFOLIO

Assignment 1:
Practicing Your Listening Skills

Practice your listening skills by listening to a radio or television documentary. Afterward, describe what you learned to someone, using your words. Try to recall as many main ideas and details as you can. In writing, describe how effective you think your listening was. What information was new to you? What information did you feel you understood well? What information did you not understand very well? Save this assignment in your portfolio.

BEGINNING THE NOTE-TAKING PROCESS

Although many students view note taking as an isolated act, it isn't—or should not be. Taking notes is part of a process that begins before class, goes on during class, and continues after class. By applying certain preclass preparation strategies, you maximize your ability to absorb and record information *in* class, as well as to reinforce and study the information after class.

PRECLASS STRATEGIES

Most activities benefit from advance preparation. Before preparing a meal, you choose a recipe and gather your ingredients and utensils. Before taking a trip, you plan a route and estimate expenses. Yes, you can cook a meal or go on a trip without bothering to prepare in advance. Chances are, though, that the meal or the trip will work out better if you do plan.

- Before class, do you prepare yourself specifically to take notes? If so, how? If not, can you think of any ways in which you could prepare yourself?

_____

_____

_____

_____

_____

_____

_____

Like most other activities, note taking is an activity that benefits from advance preparation. The more background you have for the subject matter of a lecture, the more easily you will be able to hang new pieces of information on the hooks of what you already know. For example, a student who comes to class understanding the difference between protons and electrons will have an easier time following a lecture on atomic theory than a student who knows nothing about the structure of atoms.

Here are eight strategies for preparing to take notes:

1. *Before class, read in advance the textbook pages that relate to the lecture topic.* Develop a basic understanding of the main ideas. If you're not sure which pages to read, check with your instructor beforehand.

2. *Make note of questions that occur to you as you read.* If the lecture does not provide answers for your questions, you can pose the questions to your instructor during or after class.

3. *Familiarize yourself with important terms.* Knowing the vocabulary of the lecture will help you understand the subject matter. You will also be better prepared to take notes. Before a lecture, you can also decide on abbreviations you want to use for long or hard-to-spell terms —"HRE" for Holy Roman Empire, "sczo" for schizophrenia, "meta" for metaphorical, for example.

4. *Complete reading and written assignments when they are due.* If an instructor bases part of a lecture on previously assigned work, you will be better able to follow the presentation if you are up to date on your assignments.

5. *Review your notes from the previous session.* The current lecture will often build on ideas from earlier classes. Also, flag any points in your notes that are unclear or incomplete. Discuss your questions with the instructor, with another student, or in your study group.

6. *Come to class on time, and bring any materials you need.* By catching the very start of the lecture, you will follow the instructor's flow of ideas. Remember your notebook, glasses, pen, and so on.

7. *Take a seat near the front, away from windows and away from students who might distract you.* Be sure you have a clear view of the instructor. Some students feel safer "hiding" in the back or to the side. However, taking a front seat helps you stay connected with the instructor and the lecture and will keep you alert.

8. *Assume your responsibilities as a student, and recognize those of the instructor.* As a student you are expected to perform certain duties:

- Attend classes regularly.
- Prepare by reading about the lecture topic before class.
- Take part in class discussion and group work with peers.
- Give your full attention during lectures.
- Take complete notes, including main ideas and details, as well as notes on multimedia presentations by the instructor.
- Complete assignments on time and to the best of your ability.
- Meet periodically with the instructor to discuss your progress.

Instructors are expected to:

- Attend classes regularly.
- Inform students of the course requirements.
- Provide instruction and guidance in the course content.
- Offer a variety of instructional activities to address students' different learning styles and goals.
- Provide grades, feedback, and guidance on students' work and participation.

Activity A: Evaluating Your Preclass Note-Taking Process

How effectively do you prepare for taking notes? For each statement, evaluate yourself by circling *A* for "always," *F* for "frequently," or *N* for "seldom or never."

1. I read the textbook pages that relate to the lecture topic before class.   A   F   N

2. I make note of questions that occur to me as I read.   A   F   N

3. I familiarize myself with important terms.   A   F   N

4. I complete readings and written assignments when they are due.   A   F   N

5. I review my notes from the previous session.   A   F   N

6. I come to class on time with all materials I need.   A   F   N

7. I take a seat near the front, away from distractions.   A   F   N

8. I assume my responsibilities as a student and recognize these of the instructor.   A   F   N

Scoring

If you circled *A* for all eight statements, your preclass note-taking processes are in decent shape. If you circled *N* for more than four statements, you think you could improve your skills. If you circled *F* for more than four statements, your skills may need just a little polishing.

PORTFOLIO

Assignment 2:
Writing Your Plans for Improving

In Activity A, notice the statements for which you circled *N* (sometimes or never). Rewrite these statements as goals. For example:

> GOAL: I'll make a habit of reading the textbook pages that relate to lectures before class.

Then write a paragraph that outlines your plans for improving your performance. For example, from now on you might write reminders on your calendar to read certain chapters before class. You might decide to get up earlier to make time for reading your notes. Save this assignment in your portfolio.

Advantages of Listening and Note Taking

Improving your listening skills and note-taking skills will help you take full advantage of the information provided in lectures. Here are some of the main reasons to improve your skills.

- *Lectures combine information from a variety of sources.* Successful study requires more than reading the textbook. Even if a lecture is on a topic covered in the textbook, you usually need to take notes. One textbook, no matter how heavy (or expensive), cannot cover all the material needed for a college course. In lectures instructors can share the benefit of many other books they've read in their field. They can also cover up-to-date information, such as research studies, discoveries, and events that took place after the course books were written.

Lectures often provide information that is not contained in your textbooks. Taking notes is the best way to remember information provided in a lecture.

- *Lectures highlight significant points.* In choosing which information to discuss in a lecture, instructors are telling you what they consider most important. Not surprisingly, they may later ask test questions abut this information. Be sure to listen for key words and phrases.

- *Your instructor's explanations are helpful.* Your instructor's explanations of concepts may be better suited to your particular learning style than the textbook version. Occasionally, a textbook passage may not make sense to you. In class, however, the instructor can explain the same concept in different ways or offer additional examples to help clarify a point. The instructor may also provide an opportunity for you to ask questions or discuss difficult subject matter.

- *Listening and note taking keep you involved.* The more different ways you're involved in the learning process, the more likely you are to understand and remember what is being taught. In class, you become engaged in multiple ways—thinking, looking, listening, writing, and discussing. As you use these different modes, you are also analyzing and organizing information, which helps you make sense of it.

Activity B: How Listening and Note Taking Are Connected

- Look back at the notes you took in your group activity on page 197 at the beginning of this chapter. How could you benefit from the above ideas on listening and profiting from lectures if you were to take those notes again?

_____

_____

_____

_____

_____

_____

_____

_____

_____

_____

WRAPPING IT UP

SUMMARY

- Listening is an important skill that can be improved with practice, both in and outside the classroom.

- You can improve your note taking by:

    1. Reading the related textbook passages.

    2. Jotting down questions to ask in class.

    3. Getting to know unfamiliar terms.

    4. Completing assignments.

    5. Reviewing notes from previous sessions.

    6. Coming to class on time and with needed materials.

    7. Sitting near the front and away from distractions.

    8. Assuming your responsibilities as a student and recognizing those of the instructor.

- Be sure to attend classes regularly and avoid distractions.

THINKING IT OVER

- Which ideas and information from this chapter did you find most useful?

    _____

    _____

    _____

    _____

- How can you apply the strategies from this chapter to improve your preclass preparations?

_____

_____

_____

_____

_____

_____

_____

_____

_____

_____

IN YOUR
JOURNAL

Choose two strategies that you recorded in your journal for improving your listening and note-taking skills (page 196). Describe your success in using these strategies, any problems you had, and your plan for using new strategies from this chapter.

11

IN-CLASS NOTE-TAKING STRATEGIES

OBJECTIVES:

- To apply strategies for active listening and for processing what you hear.
- To apply specific methods and techniques for taking notes.
- To demonstrate note taking as a three-part process.

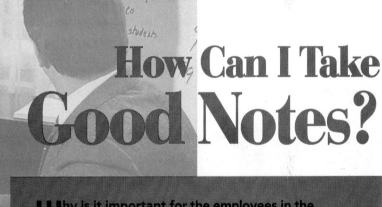

How Can I Take Good Notes?

Why is it important for the employees in the picture to have good note-taking skills? What everyday situations can you identify that require note taking?

Whether you're at work listening to your supervisor describe a new system, at home having a friend explain how to program a VCR, or at a classroom lecture on psychology, you need to concentrate on what the speaker is saying and to take careful notes.

Taking notes means more than just sitting in the classroom and "writing stuff down." As you'll learn in this chapter, taking notes is a process that requires active involvement.

GETTING STARTED

Getting the most out of classes and lectures is an important step toward accomplishing your academic goals. To really understand the presentation and effectively review the material later, you need to become an *active* participant in class.

Are you ready to actively listen and take notes in class? To find out, use the following checklist. For each statement, circle *A* for "always," *F* for "frequently," and *N* for "seldom or never."

1. I listen carefully to the instructor.   A   F   N

2. If my mind wanders during a lecture, I'm able to refocus my attention on the instructor.   A   F   N

3. I listen not just for facts but for ideas and connections between ideas.   A   F   N

4. Rather than prejudge the material or the instructor and tune out, I encourage myself to stay focused on the lecture.   A   F   N

5. I concentrate my attention on the instructor, picking up both verbal and nonverbal clues.   A   F   N

6. When I get lost or confused during a lecture, I continue to make an effort to reconnect with the instructor's train of thought.   A   F   N

7. I avoid letting my own thoughts or feelings interfere with my ability to listen.   A   F   N

8. I ask questions when I don't understand something.   A   F   N

9. As I take notes, I make an effort to distinguish the speaker's main ideas from secondary ideas and details.   A   F   N

10. I make my notes accurate by including detailed information and examples that support broad ideas.   A   F   N

11. My notes are organized to show the speaker's logic and reasoning. For example, I record cause and effect relationships, conclusions, contrasts, and summaries.   A   F   N

12. My notes include vocabulary words and phrases that are characteristic of the course topic.   A   F   N

13. When appropriate I use diagrams, graphs, and other visual ways of recording information.   A   F   N

14. I take notes quickly and neatly enough to record all the facts that I consider important and to make them easy to review.   A   F   N

Scoring

If you circled *A* for eight or more statements, your listening and note-taking skills are in good shape. If you circled *N* for eight or more statements, you believe that your skills need some improvement. If you circled *F* for eight or more statements, your skills may need just a little development or polishing.

IN YOUR JOURNAL

Look at the statements in the inventory for which you gave yourself a rating of *N*. In your journal, change these statements into specific personal goals. For example, if you circled *N* for the statement number 4, you might write a goal like this:

PERSONAL GOAL: "I've often been annoyed with my sociology professor's opinions. From now on I'm going to try not to prejudge her or tune out but to focus on the lecture topic."

After a few classes, describe how you're progressing toward your goal and why.

WHAT IS "TAKING GOOD NOTES"?

Note taking is more than just writing words on paper.

A. With your group, create a set of four specific guidelines for judging the quality of notes. For example, you might evaluate notes on the basis of accuracy, completeness, orderliness, and legibility.

B. Read the following portion of a lecture that an instructor gave in an English class. Then use the guidelines your group developed to compare and evaluate the two sets of student notes that follow the lecture.

_____

_____

_____

_____

_____

_____

_____

_____

Readers may make two kinds of identification with characters in a story. First, readers may recognize in a story character a more or less realistic representation of themselves. For example, if the character is shown as misunderstood by his or her parents, some readers, because of the vividness of the narrative, may recognize their own experiences in those of the character.

Second, readers may find, by identifying with the story character, the fulfillment of their own desires. For example, a reader may be poor, not very attractive, or not popular, but find symbolic satisfaction in identifying with a character who is represented as rich, gorgeous, and madly sought after for dates.

Drawing hard-and-fast lines between these two kinds of identification is not easy. Basically the former kind—which we may call "identification by self-recognition"—rests upon the *similarity* of the reader's experiences with those of the story character, while the latter kind—"identification for wish-fulfill-ment"—rests upon the *dissimilarity* between the reader's life and the character's life. Many (perhaps most) stories engage, or seek to engage, the reader's attention by *both* means.

Kareem English 60 11/15/93	Stephanie English 60 11/15/93
2 kinds of reader ID w/story chars:	Two kinds of identification: reader recognizes self, reader identifies with character to fulfill own desires — ugly reader identifies with beautiful char.
1R sees self in char Ex: char misunderstood by parents — R IDs fm personal experience	
2R ids w/character to fulfill- ing own desires. Ex: R is poor, 0 attractive 0 popular IDs w/ rich, attractive, popular char.	"ID by self-recognition"— similarity of experience "ID for wish fulfillment"— dissimilarity — uninteresting vs. interesting life
Dif btween 2 types not always clear or big.	Stories use *both* means.
#1 = "ID by self-recognition" — based on similarity of R's and char's experiences.	
#2 = "ID by wish fulfillment" — based on dissimilarity btween R's dull life and char's interesting life. Many stories try to engage R's ID both ways.	

IN-CLASS STRATEGIES

LISTENING AND NOTE TAKING

In Chapter 10 you learned what you can do *before* class to prepare yourself for listening effectively and taking good notes *during* class. In this chapter you'll learn strategies that will help you listen actively and take better notes.

Of course, listening and note taking are not new skills to you; you've had experience with both these skills at other times in your life.

Based on your past experiences, answer these questions about listening and note taking.

DISCOVERY ACTIVITY

• Why does concentrating help you during lectures?

_____

_____

_____

• Why do you listen carefully and take notes during lectures?

_____

_____

_____

• Why should you improve your ability to listen and take notes?

_____

_____

_____

_____

Three goals of a good listener and note taker are:

1. To listen actively.
2. To **process**—analyze, organize, and classify—what you hear, identifying important information.
3. To take notes quickly, accurately, and in an organized way.

How do these goals compare to your own goals for listening and note taking?

_____

_____

_____

_____

_____

Listening and note taking are two ways to actively participate in lectures. Through active participation you remember more of the information contained in a lecture.

The strategies that follow will help you accomplish the three goals listed on page 214. As you read, remember that listening and taking notes at the same time can be a challenge—particularly when instructors race through material or pack many facts into their sentences. Note taking becomes easier, however, with practice and experience.

ACTIVE LISTENING

Hearing and listening are not the same. Hearing is often passive and automatic, while listening requires active involvement. Listening is a concentrated mental effort to take in and process information you hear. To listen effectively, follow these tips:

- *Concentrate.* Make a conscious decision to listen and focus on the topic by not letting your thoughts wander. Then hold to your decision. Concentrating is especially important if the subject matter is difficult or dry, if the instructor talks too slowly or gives a disorganized lecture, or if you have personal matters on your mind. If you find your mind wandering, try a technique called **shadowing**. When you notice your mind drifting, return your attention to the instructor. In your mind, repeat or *shadow* the instructor's last sentence or two until you're focused on the lecture again.

- *Focus on what's important.* Listen for main ideas, connections between ideas, and important details. Listen for answers to these questions related to the topic: Who? What? When? Where? Why? How?

- *Have a positive attitude.* A positive attitude toward your course means assuming that the material is worth learning and not prejudging the material or the instructor. Convincing yourself in advance that organic chemistry is tedious or impossible to understand serves no purpose. Indeed, such judgments are self-defeating. Rather than tuning out, encourage yourself with positive messages such as: *Learning as much as I can from this lecture will help me understand the subject.*

- *Look and listen.* Focus your attention on the instructor. Listen for both verbal and nonverbal clues. Watch facial expressions and listen to tone of voice. Often these will give you clues as to what instructors think is important—and what they will probably include on an exam. If an instructor repeats the same point, suddenly slows in speaking, or pauses deliberately to allow you time to write, the instructor is sending you a message: "This point is important."

- *Stay connected.* At times you won't grasp an instructor's point, or the pace of the lecture will be too fast for you to process all the information. Don't give up. Stay focused, and try to reconnect with the speaker's train of thought. Keep track of the ideas and details that seem important to you. Even if you pick up only 20 percent of what the instructor is trying to communicate, that's still 20 percent more than you'll get if you tune out. That's also 20 percent that you won't need to catch up on after class.

- *Keep your mind focused.* Avoid letting your mind get stuck on one point. If your instructor makes a statement to which you passionately object, don't let your thoughts or feelings cause you to stop listening. Instead, make a note to discuss the point with another student or the instructor, and keep focusing your attention on the lecture.

- *If you don't know, ask.* Active listening means asking questions. Ask for clarification when you don't understand a point. If interrupting with a question seems inappropriate to you, write down your question and ask it later.

- *Provide feedback.* Finally, remember that communication flows in two directions. Let your instructor know that you *are* actively involved. Answer questions, participate in discussions, nod your head, and offer other forms of verbal and nonverbal feedback. Giving feedback not only helps to maintain your own interest level but may also energize an instructor who has probably covered the same subject matter numerous times before.

PORTFOLIO

Assignment 1:
Taking Notes

During the next lecture you attend, remember the strategies for active listening. You might want to copy the list of strategies or make notes based on them. Then, after the lecture, take time to evaluate your lecture notes. For each of the following questions, write a paragraph that describes your experience.

- Overall, how would you rate your success in putting the active-listening strategies into practice: excellent, pretty good, or could be better? Explain why.

- What specific difficulties did you encounter while trying to apply the strategies?

- How might you overcome these difficulties in the future?

Save this assignment in your portfolio.

IDENTIFYING IMPORTANT INFORMATION

When you're listening actively, your brain is rapidly analyzing, organizing, and classifying information. One important purpose of these processes is to identify the important information in what you're hearing—the main ideas, supporting information, organization, and special language.

Main Ideas

What are the speaker's main ideas? When you write a paragraph, you usually express your main idea in a sentence at the beginning or end of the paragraph. You then support that idea with facts, examples, and details. Similarly, when you listen, you need to distinguish the speaker's main ideas from secondary ideas and supporting details.

Sometimes instructors clearly identify their main ideas by repeating them, writing them on the board, or displaying them via an overhead projector. Often, instructors will raise their voices or use a phrase that, in effect, announces KEY POINT COMING! Phrases like the ones below, for example, signal that the information that follows will usually be important enough for you to write down:

the most important	the underlying cause
the principal reason	the main effect
another key factor	as a result
the greatest problem	the basic idea

Supporting Information

What supporting information does the speaker provide? Listen for clues from the speaker that indicate supporting details. Often, instructors simplify matters by *enumerating* supporting facts, that is, naming or listing them one by one. They often give a lead-in sentence that specifies the number of supporting facts:

The outcome of the election had two immediate effects. . . .

Four factors brought an end to the crisis. . . .

The insect progresses through three stages of development. . . .

Statements like these will alert you to the instructor's main idea as well as to the facts that support or develop the idea.

Similarly, instructors will sometimes introduce examples or other supporting details by using phrases such as "for example" or "for instance." Listening carefully for such clues will help you process and organize what you're hearing.

Organization

How is the information organized? Read the following sentence:

Alit tlel earni ngisada ng ero usth ing.

Gibberish? Not at all. The letters just need a little regrouping:

A little learning is a dangerous thing.

The point, of course, is that you'll more easily understand information if you recognize how it is structured. Use verbal clues to help you. Here are some examples:

CLUE	MEANING
therefore as a result consequently	signals a cause-effect relationship
in conclusion the point of this is	indicates that the instructor is about to summarize material
in contrast to by comparison unlike	signals that the instructor is comparing two people or things

Tuning in to such verbal clues is similar to reading road signs that tell you what's ahead.

Special Language

What is the language of the lecture? Most subjects have their own vocabulary. For example, you probably recognize that words such as *parallelogram* and *diagonal* are used in mathematics; words such as *alliteration* and *personification* are used in literature; and phrases such as *the law of supply and demand* and *gross domestic product* are used in economics.

Usually, the instructor explains or defines such key terminology and provides helpful examples during the lecture. By listening actively, you will become familiar with the specific vocabulary of the lecture. Knowing the vocabulary will help you understand the main ideas.

Activity A: Listening Practice

Lecture A: You are about to hear someone read aloud a lecture excerpt from page 481 of the appendix. In the lecture, two main ideas are presented. Listen for the ideas and for the phrases that are clues to those ideas. Then answer the questions without looking at the printed lecture.

Questions

1. What two main ideas did the speaker present?

_____

_____

_____

_____

_____

2. What phrases did the speaker use to introduce the ideas?

_____

_____

_____

3. How were the two main ideas related?

_____

_____

_____

_____

_____

Lecture B: Listen for the facts, examples, and details that support the main idea of this excerpt from page 481 of the appendix.

Questions

1. What is the main idea of the lecture excerpt?

_____

_____

_____

_____

_____

2. How did the speaker use facts, examples, and details to support and develop the main idea?

_____

_____

_____

_____

3. Which statements give clues to what and where the supporting information is?

_____

_____

_____

_____

Lecture C: Listen for "the language of the lecture" in this lecture excerpt from page 482 of the appendix. "The language of the lecture" is the key words and phrases the speaker uses to present the main ideas.

Questions

1. What are the main ideas of the lecture excerpt?

_____

_____

_____

_____

2. What key words and phrases do you need to understand to grasp the main ideas?

_____

_____

_____

3. How are the main ideas related?

_____

_____

_____

Assignment 2:
Describing the Active Listening Process

During the next lecture you attend, practice listening actively to answer these questions.

- What are the speaker's main ideas?
- What facts, examples, and details does the speaker use to support or develop the main ideas?
- How is the information organized?
- What vocabulary is special to the lecture?

After the lecture, write a paragraph describing how answering the four questions helped you process and record what you heard. Save this assignment in your portfolio.

RECORDING THE INFORMATION YOU NEED

There is no one correct way to take notes. There are, however, a number of specific note-taking methods and techniques you may use to record information.

Use the note-taking methods that work best for *you*. Don't be afraid to experiment. Combine or adapt methods to suit your purposes.

Remember: You'll be using your notes to study for tests. Therefore, your goal is to organize and record the information you need in a manner that is clear, complete, and easy to understand.

DISCOVERY
ACTIVITY

Describe your own note-taking style.

- What kind of notebook do you use? Spiral bound? Ring binder? What size paper does it have?

_____

_____

_____

- Do you normally write on every line?

_____

_____

- How much room do you leave for adding comments later?

_____

_____

- What kind of pen or pencil do you use?

_____

_____

- Are your notes messy or neat? How would you direct a classmate to use your notes for study purposes?

_____

_____

_____

_____

_____

_____

_____

_____

_____

PREPARATION

The nine strategies that follow will help you in your note taking.

1. Use a loose-leaf binder to store your notes; a spiral notebook doesn't allow you to insert lecture handouts. Write on 8½- by 11-inch lined paper; a small memo pad might force you to cram your notes.

2. In your binder, set up a separate loose-leaf section for each course. This will allow you to access course materials easily and quickly.

3. Write on one side of the paper only.

4. Leave a wide left margin and top and bottom margins. Later you'll be able to use the margins to annotate your notes with questions that will help you study for a test.

5. Begin each note-taking session on a clean sheet of paper. Write the date at the top of the page, and number the pages.

6. Write in pen. Unlike pencil notes, ink will not smear or dull quickly.

7. Write neatly. Choose the form of writing, cursive or printing, that is neater and faster for *you*. To speed up your writing, avoid fancy capital letters and other flourishes.

8. Write your name, address, and phone number in the front of your binder. If lost or misplaced, your valuable notes are more likely to be returned.

9. Don't use a tape recorder, except perhaps as a backup device. Recorded notes are difficult and time-consuming for most people to study, although they may be used for a very thorough review of certain parts of lectures.

SPACE FOR STUDY NOTES

Leave a margin of at least 1½ inches on each page of notes. Don't use the margin for notes. Save the margin space for key words and phrases, questions, and comments that you will add *after* the lecture. An example follows.

Boer War (History 201)   Oct. 14, 1993
         Boers vs. Bantu (Zulu) genocidal struggle
         Boers won - echoes still felt today
                  (Rose?)
         1870-1880 Cecil Rhodes carved out his fortune
              at Cape. His dream was Cape to Egypt RR.
              Rhodes exploited political—social situation.
         1880s Gold discovered in Dutch Transvaal—Orange
              Europeans. Americans flooded in. Boers did not like
                  Diamonds discovered. Boers becoming more
                  antagonistic - taxing heavily
         1880 Rhodes tried coup d'etat
              Jameson raid - allegedly to aid settlers in
                  Orange Free state
                  While Gladstone was in. British backed off
         1899 Boer War
              dirty war:
              Boers were good fighters - fought guerilla war
              British started concentration camps - families
              World opinion against British
              Kaiser sent arms to Boers - support indicated
              antagonism of Germany - Brits
         British had been allies of Germans - many upper class
         educated in Germany.
         Germans' animosity a shock to Brits.
         British barely win.

USING PAGES CREATIVELY

For some subjects you may need to include diagrams, sample problems, charts, graphs, or other visual information in your notes. You may want to divide the page in half vertically and use one side for notes while reserving the other side for visual information only. Here's an example:

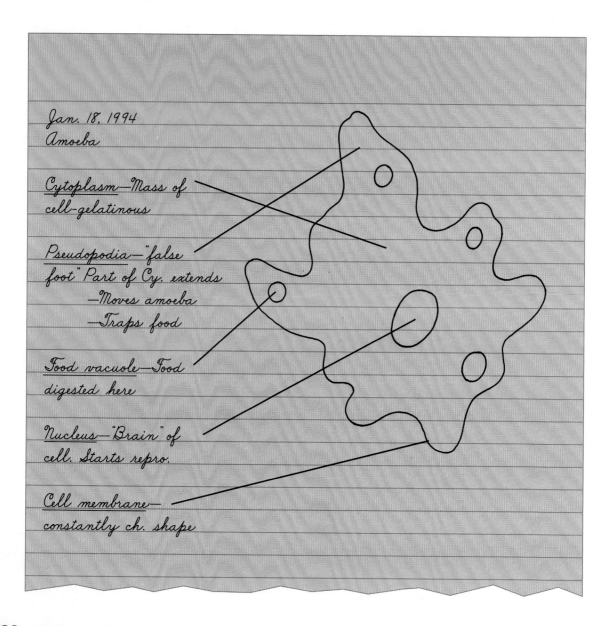

Jan. 18, 1994
Amoeba

Cytoplasm—Mass of
cell-gelatinous

Pseudopodia—"false
foot" Part of Cy. extends
  —Moves amoeba
  —Traps food

Food vacuole—Food
digested here

Nucleus—"Brain" of
cell. Starts repro.

Cell membrane—
constantly ch. shape

CONDENSING AND SUMMARIZING

If possible, get the essential information down on paper in carefully chosen words and phrases. Complete sentences are often unnecessary and take up valuable time. Take care, however, to record in such a way that your notes are thorough, accurate, and legible.

Here's an example of how a speaker's words might be effectively condensed and summarized on paper:

COMPUTER MONITORS: FRIEND OR FOE?

The computer monitor has become a commonplace and familiar object in both offices and homes. But some researchers are suggesting that commonplace and familiar does not necessarily mean safe.

Computer monitors emit a steady stream of electromagnetic radiation. Millions of office workers, professionals, and students sit in front of monitors, often for eight or more hours a day, absorbing some of that radiation. Does this make the ubiquitous computer monitor something of a Trojan Horse, entering our lives under the guise of a useful tool, only to emit invisible but destructive radiation?

Research studies have produced contradictory results. A 1988 study of environmental hazards in Oakland, California, found that women who used video display terminals (VDTs) had a higher rate of miscarriages. However, follow-up studies failed to duplicate those findings. In fact, some scientists argue that stress is the culprit, not radiation. It seems that people who work at VDTs all day usually have high stress jobs, and the miscarriages could be stress related.

Another issue which makes it difficult to reach a conclusion is that monitors emit two kinds of electromagnetic radiation, very low frequency (VLF) and extremely low fre-

CM common-offices & homes
Some research. say maybe not safe

CM emit elec. mag. radiation: millions
sit 8+ hrs before CM

Is this dangerous?

Research-contradict results
1988. Oakland Study - more miscarr.
Other studies said No
Some say stress not CM culprit

Complicates:
　　CM　2 kinds elect mag. rad.
　　VLF (very low freq.)
　　ELF (extrem. "　")
Researchers only VLF
ELF may be bad - not studied yet
ELF - back of CM

Confusion - no one knows - so
Manufact. building low. emiss. CM
　　Safe: from Sweden
　　still Swed. not sure

quency (ELF). So far, researchers have investigated only the effects of VLF radiation. ELF radiation has already been found to cause problems for people who live near power lines (and, possibly, for people who use electric blankets). But researchers have not studied the effects of ELF radiation on computer users. And to complicate matters further, ELF radiation is emitted from the back of computer monitors.

If you're confused about how seriously to take all this, you're not alone. Nobody really knows yet whether a problem even exists. Still, operating on the assumption that it's better to be safe than sorry, manufacturers are taking the initiative and building a new generation of low-emission monitors. Their low-emission levels meet safety standards developed in 1986. Keep in mind, though, that these "Swedish standards" are not based on any conclusive medical evidence that monitors are dangerous. Rather, they are based on the premise that "the less radiation, the better."

Meanwhile, the *University of California at Berkeley Wellness Letter* recommends the following precautions: Sit at least an arm's length from your computer screen, sit at least 4 feet from your co-workers' monitors and turn your monitor off when you are not using it—don't just dim it.

Finally, if you're about to buy a monitor, there's some good news—you won't have to pay extra; low-emission monitors cost the same as their "high"-emission counterparts.

[Scientists don't know for sure if the rays emitted by computer monitors are harmful.]

"Less rad. is better"
UC Berke Well. Letter - precautions
1. Sit arms length from CM
2. Sit 4' from coworkers' CM
3. Turn off CM when not using

Good news new low emissions CM—
no more $

(Marjorie Leeson, from *Computing Fundamentals*)

WRITING SHORTCUTS

A speaker commonly talks about five times faster than a listener can write. As a result, students sometimes have a hard time taking notes at the same speed that an instructor lectures.

These writing shortcuts can help you keep up with the flow of ideas by helping you write faster.

- Use abbreviations and symbols.
- Write numerals instead of spelling out numbers.

For example, compare these two samples. What words were omitted in the second sample? What abbreviations and symbols were used?

The wagons traveled more than five hundred miles before finally arriving in Oregon on October 12.

Wagons traveled 500+mi. → Oreg., 10/12

Use as many abbreviations and symbols as you feel comfortable with. In addition to standard abbreviations and symbols, you can also make up your own. However, in the front or back of your binder, be sure to keep a running list of the abbreviations and symbols you use—and what they mean!

Here are some commonly used abbreviations and symbols to get you started:

p., pp.	page, pages	#	number
ch.	chapter	$	money
e.g.	for example	%	percent
i.e.	that is	& *or* +	and
cf.	compare	>	greater than
ex.	example	<	less than
a.m.	morning	. . .	therefore
p.m.	afternoon	w/	with
info	information	w/o	without
thru	through	B4	before

ORGANIZING NOTES

Organize your notes in a way that allows you to use them effectively for review and self-testing. Consider using an outline form or other visual organizers such as charts or maps.

Outlines

An efficient way to take notes is to use outline form, writing the main idea on one line, then indenting and writing the supporting ideas underneath. Outlines not only record information but also help you remember how the information is organized and how ideas relate to one another. Here's an example:

Feb. 8, 1994

Blood Corpuscles differ in characteristics, function, effects of deficiency
  I. Red blood cells
      A. Characteristics
          1. shape-tiny round discs, indented centers
          2. color-pale pink (millions make dk. red)
      B. Function-increase blood's O² carrying capacity
      C. Deficiency-anemia (lack of hemoglobin)
  II. White blood cells
      A. Characteristics
          1. colorless cytoplasm
          2. ability to leave blood stream
      B. Function-fight infection (digests bacteria)
      C. Deficiency-lessens body's defense against infect.

(Pauk, Salamanca, et al., Ed., from *Listen and Read*)

Visual Organizers

Leaf through a textbook, and you're likely to see many different tables and diagrams. Such visual devices help you grasp not just facts but also connections between facts.

When you take notes, use similar visual organizers to help you understand and remember information. Visual organizers can take many different forms, such as charts, time lines, Venn diagrams, or concept maps. Study the examples that follow.

Chart
In a chart, information is organized in columns.

Psychologists & Their Theories		
Name	**Theory**	**Characteristics**
Sigmund Freud	Psychoanalytic	1. Sexual origin of problems
		2. Long-term therapy
		3. Unconscious components: ego-id-superego
		4. Defense mechanisms
Carl Jung	Psychoanalytic (later Jungian)	1. Followed, then broke w/F
		2. Collective unconscious
		3. Archetypes
Alfred Adler	Psychoanalytic (later Adlerian)	1. Followed, then broke w/F
		2. Inferiority complex
B. F. Skinner	Behaviorism	1. Treat behavior—not cause
		2. Reinforcement theory
		3. All behavior predictable

(Mark Garrison, from *Introduction to Psychology*)

Time Line

In a time line, information is organized according to dates in chronological order.

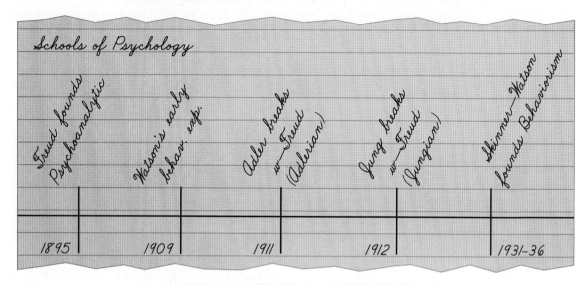

Schools of Psychology

| 1895 | 1909 | 1911 | 1912 | 1931–36 |

Freud founds Psychoanalytic — Watson's early behav. exp. — Adler breaks w/ Freud (Adlerian) — Jung breaks w/ Freud (Jungian) — Skinner—Watson founds Behaviorism

Venn Diagram

In a Venn diagram each circle represents a category of information. Information shared by two or more categories is shown in the area where the circles overlap.

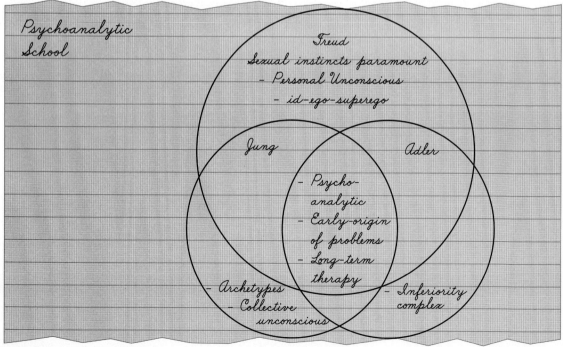

Psychoanalytic School

Freud
Sexual instincts paramount
- Personal Unconscious
- id-ego-superego

Jung

Adler

- Psycho-analytic
- Early-origin of problems
- Long-term therapy

- Archetypes
- Collective unconscious

- Inferiority complex

Concept Map

In a concept map, information is organized to show the relationships among facts and ideas.

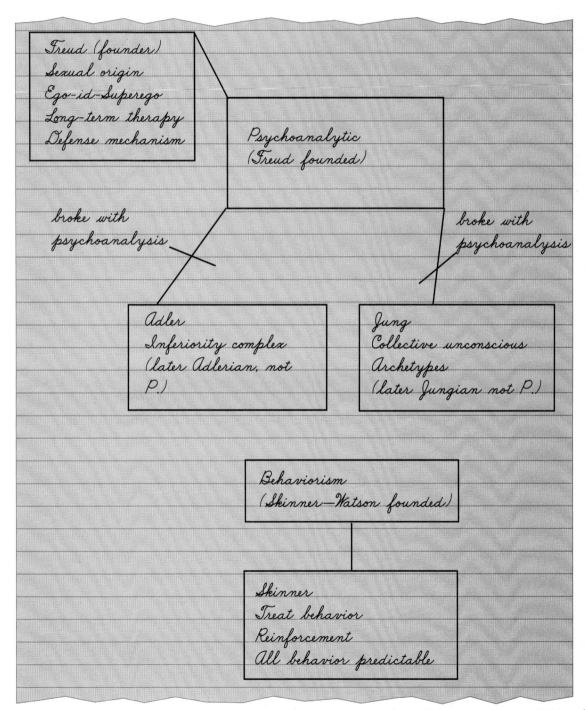

Freud (founder)
Sexual origin
Ego-id-Superego
Long-term therapy
Defense mechanism

Psychoanalytic
(Freud founded)

broke with
psychoanalysis

broke with
psychoanalysis

Adler
Inferiority complex
(later Adlerian, not P.)

Jung
Collective unconscious
Archetypes
(later Jungian not P.)

Behaviorism
(Skinner—Watson founded)

Skinner
Treat behavior
Reinforcement
All behavior predictable

HIGHLIGHTING

For quick reference, highlight important points in your notes. Consider these methods:

- Print key terms in capital letters.
- Underline definitions.
- Put an asterisk (*) beside points your instructor stresses.
- Write "COPY" or "C" beside information that you copy down.
- Bracket content or write "TEST" next to material that will appear on the next test.
- Use the margin space to emphasize key points (as you'll read about on page 245).
- Use a highlighter only on key terms. Avoid overusing highlighting since this will make everything in your notes seem important.

TAKING COMPLETE NOTES

When the time comes to study your notes for an exam, you want to find complete notes. Follow these six tips to ensure that your notes are complete.

1. Take as many notes as appropriate. Too many notes are better than too few. You can always ignore notes that prove unnecessary or repetitious. If you omit information that turns out to be significant, you have no way of studying it. So when you're not sure if something is important, write it down and decide later.

2. Copy information that your instructor displays, projects, or writes on the chalkboard or displays on the overhead projector. If something is important enough for your instructor to put in written form, it's important enough for you to record in your notes.

3. When your instructor defines or explains a term, include the definition in your notes. Underline, circle, or otherwise highlight the term and its definition.

4. Include specific examples that your instructor shares. Reviewing and studying concepts and terms becomes easier if you've recorded examples in your notes. Often, a well-chosen example or two can cause a meaning to "click" in your mind.

5. Continue listening and taking notes until the end of the class. Don't "turn off" as the end of class approaches. Keep your books open and your thoughts on the subject. An instructor may cram important information into the last few minutes of class. An instructor may also use the final minutes to summarize key points of the lecture.

6. Verify material you may have missed or not understood. When your notes are incomplete, mark your notes with a question mark, circle, or blank space. After class, check with another student or with the instructor to fill in any gaps.

IN YOUR JOURNAL

Review the tips for recording information beginning on page 234. Choose three tips that you are most likely to use or that you would like to master. In your journal, explain why these tips will be especially helpful to you. Describe how you might practice them to improve your note taking.

Activity B: More Practice in Note Taking

Listen with your book closed as one of your classmates or your instructor reads the excerpt from Lecture D, "Mood and Memory," from page 483 of the appendix. Take notes in your binder as you listen, using as many of the tips described on page 234 and this page as you comfortably can. Save your notes for later use (see Assignment 1 of Chapter 12 on page 248).

After you've finished taking notes on the lecture excerpt, answer the following questions.

Questions

1. What is the main idea of the excerpt?

_____

_____

_____

_____

_____

2. What example illustrates the main idea?

_____

_____

_____

_____

_____

_____

_____

_____

3. What is one explanation of mood-dependent recall?

_____

_____

_____

_____

_____

_____

_____

4. How might mood-dependent recall affect your test-taking abilities?

_____

_____

_____

_____

_____

_____

_____

_____

Compare your notes against the printed text. Are they as clear, complete, and easy to understand as they could be? Rate them on a scale of 1 to 3, with *1* meaning "excellent," *2* meaning "good," and *3* meaning "could be better."

Clear _____   Complete _____   Easy to understand _____

- For any 2 or 3 ratings: How could your notes be improved? Be specific.

  _____

  _____

  _____

  _____

  _____

- Are your notes well organized? If not, how could you improve the organization?

  _____

  _____

  _____

  _____

  _____

- Could you have recorded essentially the same information in less space or less time? How?

  _____

  _____

  _____

  _____

  _____

IN YOUR JOURNAL

Based on what you've learned in this chapter, write two or more paragraphs in your journal discussing the following points:

- Your greatest strengths in listening and note taking.
- Your weaknesses in listening and note taking.
- Which specific listening and note-taking strategies will prove most useful to you.

WRAPPING IT UP

SUMMARY

- Good note taking requires attention to proper materials such as binders, paper, and pens.
- Listening is a concentrated mental effort to take in and process information you hear.
- Goals of a good listener and note taker include:
    1. Listening actively.
    2. Processing what you hear.
    3. Taking quick, accurate, organized notes.
- Active listening techniques include:
    1. Concentrating.
    2. Identifying important ideas, connections between ideas, and supporting information.
    3. Having a positive attitude.
    4. Focusing on the instructor and the instructor's train of thought.
    5. Asking questions.
- To benefit from classwork, process and record information by:
    1. Organizing your notes well.
    2. Learning and using the language of the lecture.
    3. Using proper materials such as binders, paper, and pens.
    4. Using diagrams, graphs, and other visual information.
    5. Condensing and summarizing.
    6. Using shortcuts like abbreviations and symbols.
    7. Outlining and highlighting.

THINKING IT OVER

- What ideas in this chapter did you find most useful?

  _____

  _____

  _____

  _____

  _____

- How will you apply the ideas and techniques given in this chapter to improving your listening and note-taking skills?

  _____

  _____

  _____

  _____

IN YOUR JOURNAL

Look again at the inventory you took on pages 210–211. In your journal, decide how you have improved your listening and note-taking skills. Are there any skills that you could still improve? Write about your plans to sharpen these skills.

CHAPTER

12

USING
NOTES
AFTER
CLASS

OBJECTIVES:

- To effectively review notes after class.

- To create meaningful marginal notes using recall questions, key words, and phrases.

- To use rapid review, marginal notes, and self-testing in preparing for tests.

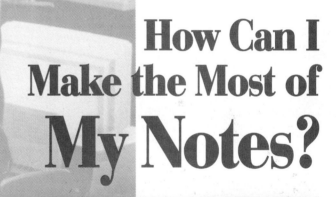

How Can I Make the Most of My Notes?

The woman in the picture has completed a computer course and is showing other students and her teacher what she learned. During the course the woman took notes. How did her notes help her reach the situation shown in the picture?

We benefit in many ways from recording events in the form of pictures, letters, and notes. In this chapter you will learn how to use classroom "records"— that is, your lecture notes—to maximum effect for success in college.

GETTING STARTED

After you've taken notes on a lecture, how will you use those notes? After class your notes will help you remember new material, especially when you need to prepare for tests.

Use the following checklist to rate yourself on the way you use your notes after class. Circle *A* for "always," *O* for "often," *R* for "rarely," or *N* for "never."

1. I review my notes within 24 hours
after class.   A   O   R   N

2. I write key words and questions in
the margins of my notes.   A   O   R   N

3. I review my notes every week or
two.   A   O   R   N

4. I use my notes for self-testing.   A   O   R   N

Scoring

Review the ratings you gave yourself. If most or all of your answers were *A* or *O*, you are already using good after-class strategies regarding your notes. If you answered *R* or *N* to most of the questions, you need to improve the way you use your notes after class.

IN YOUR JOURNAL

Choose one of the after-class strategies from the inventory for which you rated yourself "rarely" or "never." Set a goal for improvement in using this strategy. For example, if you rarely or never write key words and questions in the margins of your notes, set a goal to make your notes more useful by adding margin notes.

YOUR AFTER-CLASS STRATEGIES

GROUP ACTIVITY

Class notes are helpful only if you use them.

A. In your group, discuss the ways in which class notes are helpful to you *after* class. Include a discussion of items from the Data Bank as well as ideas of your own.

_____

_____

_____

_____

B. Choose a partner with whom you share a class. Exchange notes that you each took for a class two to five days ago. Read each other's notes, and evaluate how useful the notes would be in preparing for a test. Identify whether the notes have key words, phrases, and questions in the margins. Are answers to questions complete? Then describe how you could improve the notes.

_____

_____

_____

_____

_____

DATA BANK

- Notes help you remember important points and details.
- Notes are easy to read.
- Notes help you prepare for tests.
- Notes help you understand difficult ideas.
- Notes are a good way to review.

- Notes help you organize the topic in your mind.
- Notes enable you to compare material from lectures with material from textbooks.
- Notes from previous classes help you understand the material.

HOW TO USE NOTES AFTER CLASS

Using NOTES TO SELF-TEST

As the weeks of a term pass, you'll accumulate notes in the various courses you're taking. How can these notes be useful to you?

DISCOVERY
ACTIVITY

• Describe how you currently use your notes after class.

_____

_____

_____

• Describe problems you have in using your notes after class.

_____

_____

_____

_____

To get maximum benefit from your notes, actively review them, recalling important points, filling in any gaps, and resolving any questions. Apply these strategies:

• Rapid review

• Making marginal notes

• Self-testing

• Periodic review

RAPID REVIEW

Go over each day's notes within 24 hours after taking them. During the first 24-hour period, you forget the greatest amount of what you heard and saw. The sooner you reread your notes, the easier it will be for you to fill in missing words and details, rewrite illegible words, and clarify any confusing phrases or incomplete ideas.

Reviewing and "cleaning up" your notes while they are fresh in your mind won't take more than a few minutes. These few minutes will save you much more time and effort later. Further, as you review the ideas and information presented in class, you will reinforce your learning. You'll also begin to prepare for tests. As you reread your notes, also write any questions you want to ask in the next class session.

MAKING MARGINAL NOTES

During your rapid review, add marginal study notes to your class notes. These notes include recall questions, key words, and phrases, as shown in the example on page 246.

What information should you write in the margin? That depends on what *you* decide will be most helpful. Typically, the information you write in the margin will include the following:

- Important concepts, definitions, and examples.
- Marks to indicate subject matter likely to appear on tests, including information the instructor displays or gives as handouts.
- Specific questions that might help you on a test.

Use abbreviations and numerical clues to save space. For example, "? apartheid" can stand for "What is the definition of *apartheid*?" "Effects C. War (5)" could stand for "What were five effects of the Civil War?" Make sure you don't write the answers in the margin under the questions because you'll want to use the material in the margins to test yourself later.

Experiment to learn what works best for you. Use the margin in different ways to accommodate the subject matter of different courses. For example, in a math class you might note key equations in the margin, while in an English class you might write the names of authors and their works.

Boer War (History 201)	Oct. 14, 1993
Boer—Zulu war	Bantus migrating S into same area
	Boers vs. Bantu (Zulu) genocidal struggle
	Boers won - echoes still felt today
	(Rose?)
Cecil Rhodes	1870-1880 Cecil Rhodes carved out his fortune
his dream?	at Cape. His dream was Cape to Egypt RR
1880s gold	Rhodes exploited political—social situation
discovered where?	1880s Gold discovered in Dutch Transvaal/
diamonds disc.	Orange
	Europeans. Americans flooded in
	Boers did not like
Boer reaction?	Diamonds discovered. Boers becoming more
	antagonistic-taxing heavily.
	1880 Rhodes tried coup d'etat
1880 Jameson raid	Jameson raid - allegedly to aid settlers in
	Orange Free state
Effect of	While Gladstone was in, British backed off.
Gladstone?	
1899 Boer War	1899 Boer War
	dirty war:
guerilla	Boers were good fighters - fought guerilla war
concent. camps	British started concentration camps - families
	World opinion against British

SELF-TESTING

When reviewing or studying your notes, don't simply reread them. Test yourself on their content. You can work alone or with a study partner or group, exchanging notes and testing each other. Here is a popular method for self-testing:

1. With a separate sheet of paper, cover your notes in the large column. Look at the words, phrases, and questions you wrote in the margin. Turn the words and phrases into additional questions.

2. Recall as much information as you can to answer each question. Recite the information aloud to yourself or to someone in your study group.

3. Uncover your notes and check to see how you've done. Were your answers accurate and complete? For example, if your marginal note or question called for four causes of World War I, did you recall them all?

4. Circle any questions in the recall column that you missed. Study these missed items on another day. Recite the information aloud, write it in the air, and make **mnemonic** connections (connections that aid the memory) between the answers and familiar items. (See Chapter 19.)

5. Test yourself on only the missed items. The next day, test yourself again on all the items in your marginal notes—those you missed as well as those you got right.

6. If you have time, repeat the process by again studying the items you missed and then retesting yourself on all the items.

7. If you have only a day or two to prepare for a test, leave an hour between Steps 4 and 5 and between Steps 5 and 6.

PERIODIC REVIEW

Reviewing your notes every week or two will help you remember more of what you learned in class. Schedule a weekly review period that is right for you, and stick to it. You'll also find that reviewing material cumulatively reduces the time needed to study for tests.

PORTFOLIO

Assignment 1:
Adding Marginal Notes

Refer to the notes you saved from Activity B on page 235 of Chapter 11. For each set of notes, add study notes to the margin: questions, key words, and phrases that can help you learn and remember the material. Save this assignment in your portfolio.

PORTFOLIO

Assignment 2:
Taking Notes on a Radio or TV Program

With a study partner or group, agree on a radio or television documentary that you will listen to or watch. Take notes, review your notes, and use the margin to write questions. Then with your partner or group review the program content. Recall the main ideas and as many of the details as you can. Note any important ideas or details you may have missed. Save this assignment in your portfolio.

PORTFOLIO

Assignment 3:
Getting Feedback From Your Instructor

Give your instructor an opportunity to help you with your note-taking skills. Complete these steps:

- Select one page of notes from two different classes.
- Include marginal study notes you added after class.
- Attach to each page of notes a "SELF-EVALUATION" cover sheet with your answers to the following questions.

1. Are my class notes accurate and complete? If not, how could they be improved?
2. Are my class notes and marginal study notes useful? If not, how can they be improved?
3. Could I have recorded the same information in less space or less time? If so, how?
4. Do I have good notes for self-testing? If not, how can I improve them for that purpose?

- Make a copy of these pages, and give them to your instructor for comments. Save this assignment in your portfolio.

Assignment 4:
Revising and Applying Your Guidelines

PORTFOLIO

Complete these steps:

- Review the guidelines you and your group prepared for evaluating the quality of lecture notes in Chapter 11 (page 212). Revise the guidelines, based on what you have learned in this chapter.

- Choose a page or more of your notes. Fill in missing words and details, rewrite illegible words, and clarify any confusing phrases and incomplete ideas. Add self-test notes if you need to.

- Exchange papers with another student. Evaluate and then discuss each other's work using the guidelines that your group developed. Make concrete and constructive suggestions and comments. Your goal is to help each other sharpen your note-taking skills.

- Work independently to make changes to your notes.

- Evaluate the checklist of guidelines that your group developed. Work together to improve it. Write the guidelines on a separate piece of paper. Refer to these guidelines periodically to evaluate your notes. Save this assignment in your portfolio.

EVALUATING LECTURE NOTES

Here is an excerpt from a world history lecture. Read the lecture and evaluate the student's notes using the checklist that follows.

> The teachings of Confucius have been eagerly studied and followed by the Chinese people in the past, and the Chinese have founded not only their educational procedure, but, until recently, much of their governmental practice as well, in his words. The Chinese have followed Confucius' teachings with zeal because they have confidence in his character and in the traditions of his life.
>
> Confucius probably was born in 551 B.C., the son of aristocratic refugees. His father died shortly after his birth, and Confucius' early struggles were those of the common man performing menial tasks. Due to his mother's sacrifices, however, Confucius was able to study under a tutor in his village. Soon he developed a consuming interest that would make him a lifelong student of the historical and poetic traditions of

ancient China. In his late twenties, Confucius became a teacher, offering instruction in areas such as poetry, government, music, and propriety. Disciples joined him, some of whom were to follow him all his life. Confucius is known to have held several government offices, but he often fell under the suspicion of government officials and was forced to move from one feudal district to another. Confucius spent his last years in retirement. Upon his death in 497 B.C., Confucius' disciples were more determined than ever to carry on his teachings and aims.

It is largely through his disciples that we learn the teachings of Confucius. Their interpretations and recollections of the words of Confucius are found in the Four Books:

1. The *Analects*—This is a collection of the sayings of Confucius and of some of his disciples.

2. The *Great Learning*—This was initially designed to function as the basis for the education of gentlemen in general, and of princes in particular.

3. The *Doctrine of the Mean*—This deals with certain fundamental aspects of Confucian philosophy, in particular with the relation of human nature to the underlying moral order of the universe.

4. The *Book of Mencius*—This book dates from the 3rd century B.C. and includes a collection of the sayings and writings of early Confucian thinkers.

The ethical thought of Confucius was based upon two beliefs regarding the China of his day: first, the society was disturbingly corrupt; and second, the moral condition of the country was not beyond repair. What Confucius was saying was that, even though man's practices had grown corrupt, man himself was not yet corrupt—it was still as likely that man could lead a good life as that he could lead an evil life. The reason man's actions had grown corrupt, according to Confucius, was because he had failed to live by *li,* as his ancestors had done. One translation of *li* is an ideal social order in which everything is in its place. According to Confucius, man was not living by *li,* and as evidence, Confucius pointed to the feudal order which was then breaking down.

(Pauk, Salamanca, et. al., Ed., from *Listen and Read*)

Where do Chinese use C. teach? (2)	Confucius teaching-Chinese use education governmental practice
C. born?	C. Born 551 BC approx.
Early life?	father died mother sacrificed so he had tutor
Taught? (4)	late 20s became teacher poetry. govt.. music. propriety
Worked?	worked for govt.. retired
Died?	Died 497 BC
Where did we learn teach of C.?	Learned about him from his disciples. their interp his 4 books
Name C. 4 books	Analects collection of sayings
Describe each	Great Learning education of gentlemen. princes
	Doctrine of the Mean rel. of human nat. to moral order
	Book of Mencius 3rd cent. sayings of early C'fucian writers
What did he base his ethical thoughts on (2)	Ethical thought based-2 beliefs @ China 1. Society corrupt 2. Could be fixed Society corrupt but man was not

Checklist

Rate the student's notes for each item on the following checklist. Circle *3* for "excellent," *2* for "good," or *1* for "poor."

1. The notebook paper leaves enough marginal space.   3   2   1

2. All class notes are in the center of the page.   3   2   1

3. The notes are clearly written and easy to read.   3   2   1

4. The notes are organized in outline form.   3   2   1

5. Main chunks of information are separated by blank lines.   3   2   1

6. The notes are written in the student's words.   3   2   1

7. All special terms are defined word-for-word.   3   2   1

8. The notes include all important information from the lecture.   3   2   1

9. Recall questions and key concepts are included in the margin.   3   2   1

10. The recall or self-test column includes abbreviations and numbers that are clues to important information.   3   2   1

11. The recall or self-test column does not include answers to questions.   3   2   1

12. The notes are adequate for preparing for a test.   3   2   1

Scoring

Add your rating of the student's points. A score of 28 to 36 means the student's note-taking skills are in good shape. A score lower than 28 means the student's skills could be improved.

For each item you rated *2* or *1*, describe a problem in the notes and tell how the student might improve them.

_____

_____

_____

_____

_____

_____

_____

_____

_____

_____

_____

_____

_____

_____

_____

_____

_____

_____

_____

_____

_____

_____

_____

_____

WRAPPING IT UP

SUMMARY

- Your lecture and textbook notes can help you prepare for a test.
- Strategies for *using notes after class* include
  1. Rapid review
  2. Making marginal notes
  3. Self-testing
  4. Periodic review
- You should review your notes within 24 hours after writing them.
- Marginal notes include recall questions, key words, and phrases that help you recall important information.

THINKING IT OVER

- Which ideas and strategies from this chapter are most important?

  _____

  _____

  _____

- How will you apply what you learned to using your notes after class? Be specific.

  _____

  _____

IN YOUR JOURNAL

Review the goal you set at the beginning of this chapter. In your journal, evaluate the progress that you have made toward that goal. Revise your goal as appropriate.

Improving Your Reading Skills

As you begin work at the college level, you'll face demanding reading tasks—tasks that require you to sharpen the reading skills you have and to learn new ones. This section will help you take charge of your reading skills and upgrade them. Chapter 13 guides you in improving your word study skills. In this chapter you'll learn ways to expand your vocabulary. Chapter 14 helps you develop techniques for previewing textbook and chapter content. Chapter 15 focuses on main ideas and guides you in recognizing the most important ideas in the material you read. Chapter 16 emphasizes improving your rapid reading techniques. You'll review skimming and scanning, and you'll work on improving your reading rate. Chapter 17 takes you step by step through the process of reading a textbook chapter effectively. Chapter 18 helps you sharpen your critical thinking and critical reading skills. You'll learn techniques that will help you master new material through analyzing, judging, and making decisions about what you read.

13

IMPROVING WORD STUDY SKILLS

OBJECTIVES:

- To infer or draw a conclusion about the benefits of an expanded vocabulary.

- To develop skill in using the dictionary as a resource.

- To use context to determine meanings for unfamiliar words.

- To apply word analysis skills to unfamiliar words.

- To learn high-frequency roots, prefixes, and suffixes as a way to decode unfamiliar words.

How Can I Learn
New Words?

In daily life you are accustomed to identifying objects based on only limited information. What items do you recognize in the picture, based on their shape and location?

The surrounding objects in the setting are a context that you can use to interpret and identify information. You do the same thing when you read and encounter a word you don't know: you use the context—the surrounding words in the sentence and paragraph—to figure out the meaning of the new word. In this chapter you'll learn ways to expand your vocabulary.

GETTING STARTED

Your **vocabulary**—the words you use when you speak, listen, and write—is a good indicator of how much you know. The following statements will help you informally evaluate your vocabulary skills. Read each statement, circling *A* for "always" or "almost always," *F* for "frequently," or *N* for "no" or "never."

1. I find the dictionary helpful for finding words I don't know.   A   F   N

2. I can use the pronunciation symbols in the dictionary.   A   F   N

3. I can find definitions in the dictionary.   A   F   N

4. I can choose the correct dictionary definition for a word.   A   F   N

5. I quickly get the meaning of new words.   A   F   N

6. I can figure out a word in a sentence by using the other words and the meaning of the sentence.   A   F   N

7. I'm not afraid to use new words.   A   F   N

8. I can break a word into parts and determine what the parts mean.   A   F   N

9. I know the meaning of most common prefixes, roots, and suffixes.   A   F   N

IN YOUR JOURNAL

Set a goal for improving your vocabulary. The questions you answered with *N* or *F* indicate skills to work on. You might express your goal in the following way: "I'd like to improve my skills in determining the meanings of new words from the context."

DISCUSSING WORD POWER

GROUP
ACTIVITY

In your group, discuss some of the ways you actively try to improve your vocabulary. Begin by discussing the word-study strategies listed in the Data Bank. Which ones have you tried? Which ones have worked? Which ones have not? What other strategies have you tried for developing your vocabulary?

Identify different situations in which vocabulary problems arise, such as when you read a textbook, when you attend a lecture, when you go for a job interview, and when you read non-textbook material such as newspapers and magazines. Have you encountered vocabulary problems that are specific to one type of reading, listening, or speaking? Develop a set of guidelines for improving vocabulary skills based on the experiences of the group members.

_____

_____

_____

_____

_____

_____

_____

_____

_____

_____

_____

- Keeping a list of new words.
- Making vocabulary cards.
- Using a "Word-a-Day" calendar.
- Taking a vocabulary-building course.

- Reading a vocabulary-improvement book.
- Using the dictionary often.
- Using vocabulary-building tapes.

ENCOUNTERING NEW WORDS

DEVELOPING VOCABULARY POWER THROUGH READING

The most natural and valuable method of building your vocabulary is through reading. When you read, you are actively working to understand the meaning of words. The more words you read and understand—especially words that are unfamiliar to you—the larger your vocabulary grows.

DISCOVERY ACTIVITY

• What are some of your favorite reading materials?

_____

_____

_____

_____

• What are some words that you've learned as a result of reading? List five words and their definitions.

_____

_____

_____

_____

_____

• Do you master a word and its meaning the first time you read it, or do you need to see the word several times in different reading materials before you have mastered it? Explain the way you master new words.

_____

_____

_____

_____

READING AND LISTENING

The advantage of expanding your vocabulary through reading is that you see new words spelled and used correctly in a context. If you can't figure out the meaning of a word using the context, at least you can check the meaning of the word in the dictionary because the correct spelling is there in front of you.

Of course reading is not the only way to expand your vocabulary. You may encounter new words in any communication situation—when you listen to others speak, when you watch movies or television, and so on. In these situations you hear words and use the spoken context to figure out meanings. If you can't understand the meaning from context, you can spell the word as accurately as you can and find the word in the dictionary.

- What are some words that you first encountered through listening? Did you learn the meanings at the same time or later? Explain what happened.

_____

_____

_____

Talking with other students about material you're studying is a good way to use and remember new vocabulary.

Here are some suggestions for expanding your vocabulary through reading and listening.

- Be on the outlook for new words. You hear and read new words everywhere. Notice them. Enjoy them. Write the ones that interest you on notecards, or keep a book in which you record new words in alphabetical order.

- Read different kinds of material each day: newspapers, magazines, science fiction, history, romance, poetry, and so on. Each type of material will provide different words for your vocabulary. Notice words that show up in more than one kind of material. Examine the contexts in which the words are used. Seeing the same word in different contexts helps you learn the word faster.

- After watching a movie that you like, find out if there is a book on which the movie is based. Read the book. You'll gain a greater understanding of the characters and plot—and you'll increase your vocabulary too.

GROUP
ACTIVITY

Activity A: The Book, the Movie

In your group, discuss a recent movie or popular book. Questions to discuss include: How do the book and movie compare? What differences exist in vocabulary between a book and a movie and why? Summarize your discussion.

_____

_____

_____

_____

_____

_____

CLUES IN CONTEXT

The surrounding words in a sentence or paragraph often provide clues to the meaning of a word that is unfamiliar to you. Read the following example. What meaning can you infer for the word *raptors*? What words give you a clue?

Small animals, including rabbits, mice, and fish, are the favorite foods of such raptors as eagles, falcons, and hawks.

The sentence context helps you recognize the meaning of *raptors* by giving you two important clues:

1. A description of something they do—eat small animals

2. Examples of what they are, introduced by the words "such...as."

As a result, you can infer that *raptors* are flying birds that eat small animals.

Kinds of Context Clues

Several kinds of context clues can help you infer the meaning of words that are unfamiliar to you.

Your Own Experience. Sometimes you can infer meaning by using what you already know.

> I could, by placing my nose against the floor, and by being very patient, find the smallest button or lost item that *evaded* my family's search. (Gus Lee, *China Boy*)

• Based on your experience of looking for something, what does the word *evaded* probably mean?

_____

_____

_____

Comparison or Contrast Clue. Sometimes the context provides information that compares one thing or idea to its opposite.

> Except for the kitchen, which had a look of permanence, the rest of the house had a hotel feel about it—a kind of sooner or later leaving appearance: a painting or two hung in an all right place but none was actually stationed or properly lit; the really fine china was still boxed and waiting for a decision nobody was willing to make. It was hard to serve well in the *tentativeness*. (Toni Morrison, *Tar Baby*)

- Based on the description of the house, what does *tentativeness* probably mean?

_____

_____

Synonym Clue. Sometimes the context provides a **synonym** for an unfamiliar word—another word or phrase that means the same thing.

> By living—struggling, losing, meditating, imbibing, aspiring, achieving—he wrote himself into *ineraceable* [sic] evidence— an evidence that can be and often has been ignored, but never totally destroyed. (Luther Standing Bear, *Land of the Spotted Eagle*)

- Based on the synonym clue, what meaning does *inerasable* probably have?

_____

_____

Direct Definition Clue. Sometimes the context provides an exact definition of a word.

> Some time ago, I was traveling in the state of Morelos in Central Mexico, looking for the birthplace of Emiliano Zapata, the village of Anenecuilco.
> I stopped on the way and asked a *campesino*, a laborer of the fields, how far it was to that village. (Carlos Fuentes, "If We Had Left at Daybreak We Would Be There By Now," Commencement address given at Harvard, 1983, printed in the *Harvard Gazette*, June 1983)

- Based on the context clue, what does *campesino* mean?

_____

_____

USING CONTEXT CLUES

When you come across a word that is unfamiliar to you, don't immediately stop reading to look it up in a dictionary. If you stop, you'll lose your train of thought, and your comprehension may suffer as a result. Instead, continue reading. Make a guess as to the possible meaning of the word. Look for context clues that will help you decide if your guess is right. Try your inferred meaning in place of the original word to see if the meaning makes sense. If the passage seems to make sense, keep going. If you start feeling confused, stop reading and look up the word in the dictionary. Reread the passage using the correct meaning.

WHEN CONTEXT DOESN'T HELP

Occasionally you need an exact definition of a word that's unfamiliar to you. The context clues may be vague or may suggest several possible meanings. The context clues may themselves be unfamiliar. When you sense that the unfamiliar word is an important or key word, check the word in a dictionary.

GROUP
ACTIVITY

Activity B: Words in Context

In some of the material you are reading, find passages that contain unusual words. Use context clues to try to infer the meaning of the word. Then exchange passages with someone in the group. Use the context to infer the meaning in the passage you receive. Then discuss the kinds of clues you found and how you inferred the meaning. What conclusions can you draw about using context clues, based on the group's experience? Summarize your ideas in the space provided.

_____

_____

_____

_____

_____

USING THE DICTIONARY

An up-to-date abridged dictionary will meet most of your needs during your time in college. Avoid pocket dictionaries, which are usually satisfactory only as sources for correct spellings. Their compact size forces them to leave out a great deal of information, including multiple definitions of some words.

When you're shopping for a dictionary, look for these features:

• *Finger Tabs Marking the Beginning of Each Alphabetical Section.* This feature helps you look up words faster.

• *Pronunciation Guides Along the Bottom or Top of Each Page.* This feature saves you from having to flip back and forth between the front of the book and the word you're looking up.

• *Word Origins Included in the Entry Definitions for Words.* Once you have your own dictionary, become thoroughly familiar with it. Study all of the special features including the pronunciation key and the order of information within an entry. This feature helps you learn words with similar origins.

• *Special Sections at the Front or Back.* These are features such as the guide to the use of the dictionary; articles on word usage and word origins; lists of abbreviations; a guide to grammar, punctuation, and mechanics; a guide to writing and editing a paper; a table of weights and measures; a list of special signs and symbols; a list of foreign words and phrases; a list of colleges and universities; forms of address; biographical and geographic names.

• *The Pronunciation Key.* Read through the examples, saying the words aloud to yourself.

• *The Order of Information Within an Entry.* Here is an example from *Merriam Webster's Collegiate Dictionary,* Tenth Edition:

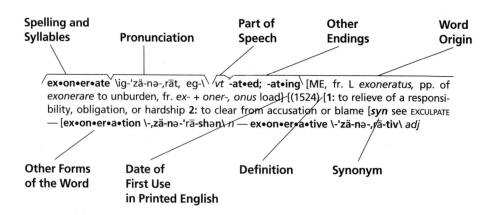

Here is a guide to examining the kinds of information found in a dictionary entry.

• *Spelling and Syllables.* The spelling of the word will be the standard American English spelling. Sometimes a word may have an alternative spelling (often a British spelling) that will appear after the first spelling. The first spelling is always the preferred one. The syllabication helps you pronounce the word and hyphenate it correctly if you need to.

• *Pronunciation.* The pronunciation given is for standard American English. A word may have an alternate pronunciation following the preferred one. Pronunciation symbols can vary from dictionary to dictionary, but they are generally easy to use. Notice the placement of the accent mark or marks. If you need further help in pronouncing a word, refer to the pronunciation key.

• *Part of Speech or Speech Category.* The part of speech is usually abbreviated. The speech category tells you how the word is correctly used in a sentence. Sometimes a word belongs to more than one speech category, usually by a change in pronunciation. For example, a written document may be a *record* (*n*) or someone may *record* (*vt*—verb transitive, a verb that takes an object) a message on your answering machine. Some dictionaries show these as two different entries; others include alternate pronunciations and definitions within the same entry.

• *Other Endings.* Some words undergo a change in spelling, depending on how they are used in a sentence. Some nouns change spelling to show number (*valley, valleys; goose, geese*). Many verbs change spelling to show tense (*resist, resisted, resisting; speak, spoke, spoken*). Some adjectives and adverbs change spelling to show comparison (*calm, calmer, calmest; lovely, lovelier, loveliest*). These grammatical forms of words are called **inflectional forms**.

• *Word Origin or Etymology.* The word origin (or **etymology**) helps you understand the meaning of a word and, sometimes, how the word came to have several meanings. In the case of the word *exonerate*, the word is from a Middle English word, *exoneraten*, which is from a Latin word, *exoneratus*, which is a form of the Latin word *exonerare*, which means "to unburden." The Latin word *exonerare* is itself made up of two roots *ex-*, which means out of, and *oner-* or *onus*, which means load.

- *Date of First Use in Printed English.* Some dictionaries cite the first recorded date that a word was used in print in the English language.

- *Definition.* Many words have more than one definition. An entry gives the definitions in the order that they are most frequently used, beginning with the most frequent. If you're not sure which meaning a word has in a certain context, you'll need to reread the context, substituting meanings until one makes sense.

- *Synonym.* Some dictionaries give synonyms for certain words. The synonym can help you understand the meaning of the entry word. For example, if you looked up the word *exculpate,* you would find this definition: to clear from alleged fault or guilt. This meaning is similar to that of the word *exonerate.*

- *Other Forms of the Word.* By adding different **suffixes** or endings, the word can function in other speech categories. Many dictionaries provide the spelling, syllabication, and speech category for these variations.

GROUP
ACTIVITY

Activity C: Examining Dictionary Entries

With a partner from your group, examine an entry in a dictionary. Identify all the features. Describe what you found most interesting or unusual about the word and its entry.

_____

_____

_____

_____

_____

_____

_____

_____

_____

_____

_____

_____

USING THE DICTIONARY FOR VOCABULARY BUILDING

Your primary source for building your vocabulary should be the reading you do in a variety of printed materials. The dictionary, however, is an important resource and support for building your vocabulary. Try this strategy: When you encounter a new word and look up the word in the dictionary, place a dot by it. While you are on the page, look for another word you don't know and read the definition. Try to use the new word in conversation the same day. When you have made three dots by a word—that is, you have looked up the word three times—take the time to memorize the spelling and meaning of the word.

Special Dictionaries

Your reading may take you into special areas of knowledge where you encounter many new words. For most of those words, the context will provide the meaning; for others any desk-size dictionary will do. From time to time you may want more information than you can find in a general-use dictionary. You may need to know the meaning a word has in a special subject area, such as law, psychology, or sociology.

In your school or community library, you'll find special subject dictionaries, including ones for sociology, criminal justice, chemistry, music, art, geography, and biography. Some of these dictionaries are more like encyclopedias than dictionaries; others include words specific to the subject area and expanded definitions.

The thesaurus is a specialty dictionary. It lists synonyms and near synonyms for various words. Some versions of the thesaurus also include antonyms. Use a thesaurus with care. Most thesauri do not provide definitions. They list words that are related in meaning, but the connotations of the different synonyms can vary.

Before you choose a substitute for a word, make sure the substitute has the meaning you want. You may have to use a dictionary to determine the exact meaning of a synonym.

PORTFOLIO

Assignment:
Using a Special Dictionary

Read a chapter of a book, or a magazine or journal article on a subject of interest to you. Identify a key word—a person, term, place, or event—that you want to learn more about. In the library, find a special dictionary on the subject, and look up the word. Write a summary of the information you find. Save this assignment in your portfolio.

WORD ANALYSIS: DIVIDE AND CONQUER

Another key to building vocabulary power involves recognizing prefixes, roots, and suffixes—the building blocks of word meaning. A **prefix** is a word part added to the beginning of a word that changes the meaning of the word, such as *re-* in *reapply* and *pre-* in *precaution*. A **root word** is a core unit of meaning, such as the Greek root *graph*, which means "to write," and the Latin root *dict*, which means "to speak." These roots form the core of words such as *paragraph*, *holograph*, *contradict*, and *dictator*. A **suffix** is a word part added to the end of a word that changes the meaning of the word, such as, *-able* in *believable*, *-tion* in *constitution*, and *-ology* in *bacteriology*.

English Word	Prefix	Latin Root	Suffix
transpiration	trans- (across)	spirare (to breathe)	-ation (the act of)
toxicology	_____	toxicum (poison)	-ology (study of)
inducement	in- (toward)	ducere (to lead)	-ment (action)

ENGLISH WORDS, FOREIGN SOURCES

The English language belongs to a family of Germanic languages, which also includes Dutch, Yiddish, and Flemish. The Germanic family of languages is itself one of several subgroups of a language known as Indo-European that was spoken in northern Europe 5,000 years ago. The core vocabulary of everyday English tends to come from German. Many words, however, have Greek or Latin origins. These words are found in abundance in science and other fields of special knowledge. By recognizing different parts of a word—prefix, root, suffix—and knowing the meanings of the parts, you can often infer the meaning of a long word. The 18 prefixes, 13 roots, and 18 suffixes presented in the remainder of this chapter are used in more than 14,000 English words. You already know some of these word parts and roots. By learning others, you will increase your ability to unlock the meanings of thousands of words—that's thousands more than you *already* know.

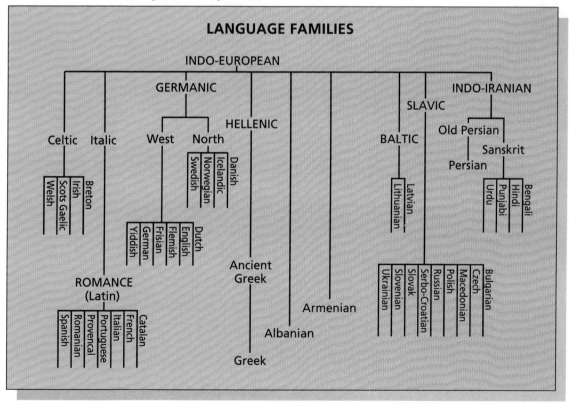

(Victoria A. Fromkin and Robert Rodman, *An Introduction to Language*)

PREFIXES

A prefix can create an opposite meaning, for example, from *cooperative* to *uncooperative*, from *qualify* to *disqualify*, from *profit* to *nonprofit*. Prefixes can also add meanings that indicate categories of meaning such as time, location, degree, number, and judgment. Here are 18 key prefixes. In the space provided, write the category of meaning to which each prefix belongs.

PREFIX	MEANING	EXAMPLE	CATEGORY OF MEANING
1. a-, ad-	to, toward	admission	_____
2. de-	away, down	depression	_____
3. dis-	apart, not	disassemble	_____
4. epi-	upon	epidermis	_____
5. in-	into	inference	_____
6. in-	not	insubstantial	_____
7. inter-	among, between	intercede	_____
8. mis-	wrong	misplace	_____
9. mono-	one, alone	mononucleosis	_____
10. o-, ob-	against	obstinate	_____
11. over-	above	overcome	_____
12. pre-	before	prepayment	_____
13. pro-	for, forward	proponent	_____
14. re-	back, again	reproduction	_____
15. sub-	under	subconscious	_____
16. super-	above, greater	supernatural	_____
17. trans-	across	transmutation	_____
18. un-	not	unclear	_____

ROOTS

English contains many Greek and Latin roots because England, like much of continental Europe, was at one time part of the Roman

Empire, from the first century A.D. to the fifth century A.D. The Romans spoke Latin, a language that had itself borrowed many Greek words, especially in areas of science and academic study. With the explosion of technology in the modern age, Greek roots such as *micro* (small) and *tele* (distant) and Latin roots such as *min* (as in *mini*, meaning "small") figure even more prominently in everyday English.

The following 13 roots are among the most common in English words. Write another example for each root in the space provided.

GREEK ROOTS	MEANING	EXAMPLE	EXAMPLE
1. graph	write	autograph	_____
2. logo	word, study of	logotype	_____

LATIN ROOTS			
3. cap(t)	take, seize	captive	_____
4. duc(t)	lead	production	_____
5. fac(t)	make, do	factory	_____
6. fer	bear, carry	conifer	_____
7. mitt, miss	send	remission	_____
8. plic, plex	fold	complex	_____
9. pon, pos	place, put	proponent	_____
10. scrib, script	write	scribble	_____
11. spect	see	spectacles	_____
12. sta(t)	stand	status	_____
13. ten, tain	hold, have	retain	_____

SUFFIXES

Suffixes or word endings serve two purposes: to indicate a specific meaning and to express a grammatical relationship between one word and other words in a sentence. A word may have two suffixes, indicating changes of meaning and grammatical position. Notice the following example:

Elba gracefully drew the shawl around her shoulders.

The word *gracefully* has two suffixes—*ful* which means "full of" and *-ly* which means "in the manner of." The second suffix is required to make *graceful* fit grammatically in the sentence.

Four groups of words often require suffixes for grammatical purposes: nouns, verbs, adjectives, and adverbs. The following are 18 common suffixes. Write another example in each space.

NOUN SUFFIXES	MEANING	EXAMPLE	EXAMPLE
1. -er, -ar, -or	one who	teacher, doctor	_____
2. -ess	female	heiress	_____
3. -ment	product or thing	document	_____
4. -ness	quality of being	shrewdness	_____
5. -ology	study of	psychology	_____
6. -tion, -sion	act or process	admission	_____

VERB SUFFIXES

7. -ate	to make	captivate	_____
8. -ed	past tense	cautioned	_____
9. -en	to make	strengthen	_____
10. -ing	act or process	pardoning	_____
11. -ize	to make	popularize	_____

ADJECTIVE SUFFIXES

12. -en	made of	earthen	_____
13. -ic	relating to	democratic	_____
14. -ive	inclined to	restive	_____
15. -less	without	thoughtless	_____
16. -ous	full of	nervous	_____

ADVERB SUFFIXES

17. -ily, -ly	in what way	steadily, quickly	_____
18. -ly	to what degree	occasionally	_____

WORD ATTACK

When you encounter a word that is unfamiliar to you, you have three options that can help you infer the meaning of the word.

1. Use context clues.

2. Look up the word in the dictionary.

3. Analyze parts of the word, identifying the meanings of the prefix, root, and suffix.

In addition to these three options, you can build your vocabulary power by using these three strategies.

1. Write new words and their definitions on word cards or in a notebook.

2. Keep a spelling list.

3. Use new vocabulary words often in your writing and in conversation.

GROUP
ACTIVITY

Activity D: Picking Words Apart

Choose a paragraph in a novel, newspaper, textbook, or other source. With members of your group, identify all the words that have prefixes and suffixes, and explain their meanings. Notice words that have Greek or Latin roots. What do these roots mean? List the word parts and their definitions in the space provided.

_____

_____

_____

_____

_____

_____

_____

_____

_____

_____

_____

Wrapping It Up

Summary

- The more words you read and understand—especially words that are unfamiliar to you—the larger your vocabulary grows. A good way to build your vocabulary is to read different kinds of material every day.

- Context clues are important guides to the meaning of a new word.

- A dictionary is an essential tool for vocabulary building.

- A dictionary should have the following features: spellings, syllables, pronunciations, parts of speech or speech categories, word origins or etymologies, definitions, usage examples, and other forms of a given word.

- A key to unlocking the meaning of an unfamiliar word is to identify the parts that make up the word—its prefix, root, and suffix.

Thinking It Over

- What material from this chapter did you find most helpful?

_____

_____

_____

_____

_____

_____

- How will you apply the information and ideas in this chapter to building your vocabulary?

_____

_____

_____

_____

_____

_____

_____

IN YOUR JOURNAL

What progress have you made toward the goal you set at the beginning of this chapter? What new words have you added to your vocabulary? What strategies have you begun to practice to build your vocabulary? What new goals have you set?

OBJECTIVES:

- To identify parts of a textbook and chapter to be previewed.

- To develop previewing skills.

- To describe common patterns of text organization.

- To adjust reading strategies and speed according to patterns of organization, prior knowledge, and chapter content.

What Will I Be Reading?

The woman in the picture is trying to decide which book to buy. What is she doing that will help her make her decision?

The picture shows an everyday situation in which we preview or get an advance look at items or information. In some situations the preview is provided by a producer who hopes you will pay to see an upcoming movie or watch a television show. In other cases you initiate the preview to satisfy your curiosity, such as when you preview a magazine or a paperback novel before buying it. In this chapter you'll learn to preview your textbook as a way to read and study more effectively.

GETTING STARTED

How would you rate your previewing skills? Use the following checklist to indicate your experience with previewing textbooks. Circle *A* for "always" or "almost always," *F* for "frequently," or *N* for "no" or "never."

1. I preview my textbooks at the beginning of the term when I buy them.   A   F   N

2. I preview a book in two stages. First I preview to get an idea of the general organization or structure. Then I preview to recognize special book features.   A   F   N

3. I can identify the special features found in most textbooks.   A   F   N

4. As part of my preview, I notice how information in the chapter is organized.   A   F   N

5. I notice patterns of organization in chapter material, such as information arranged in chronological order.   A   F   N

6. I adjust my reading rate based on what I'm reading, my purpose for reading, and what I already know about the topic.   A   F   N

IN YOUR
JOURNAL

Set a goal for improving your ability to preview textbook material based on statements in the checklist that you responded to by circling *F* or *N*. For example, if you circled *N* or *F* for statement 3, you might express your goal as follows: I'd like to improve my ability to recognize special features found in most textbooks.

Discussing Previewing

GROUP ACTIVITY

In your group, discuss some of your previewing experiences. Choose among the situations listed in the Data Bank. Discuss guidelines for previewing in different situations: what to look for, how much time to take, how to use your past experience, the best time to preview, and questions to ask yourself or others. Write your guidelines in the space provided.

_____

_____

_____

_____

_____

_____

_____

_____

_____

_____

_____

_____

_____

_____

_____

- Reading a textbook or other nonfiction book.
- Reading a newspaper.
- Choosing a magazine to read.
- Watching a preview of a movie.
- Watching a preview of a television show.

DATA BANK

- Trying out a video game or other software.
- Deciding what to order in a restaurant.
- Planning a trip by car.
- Buying a car or other vehicle.
- Buying a CD or tape.

BUILDING A FRAMEWORK

PREVIEWING YOUR TEXTBOOKS

Your textbooks are important tools for the tasks you encounter in college. In learning to use your texts as tools, you first need to understand their special features. These features include the table of contents, preface, introduction, headings and subheadings, and index. These features make the text easier to use and increase the value of the information the book contains.

DISCOVERY ACTIVITY

- Look through the remainder of this textbook. Make a list of the special features of the book.

  _____

  _____

  _____

  _____

  _____

  _____

  _____

  _____

  _____

- Which features seem familiar?

  _____

  _____

  _____

- Which features are unfamiliar to you?

  _____

  _____

_____

_____

_____

- Which features are you sure you know how to use? Describe what they're used for or how they help you.

_____

_____

_____

_____

_____

_____

WHEN TO PREVIEW YOUR TEXTBOOKS

The best time to preview your textbooks is at the beginning of the term, when you buy them. At that time the general plan and contents of each book will give you a good idea of what you'll be studying during the term. By becoming familiar with the features of the book early in the course, you can make better use of the book throughout the term.

HOW TO PREVIEW A TEXTBOOK

To preview a textbook, follow this three-step strategy:

1. Preview for general structure.
2. Preview for special features.
3. Preview each chapter.

Spend no longer than half an hour to preview the general structure and special features of an entire textbook. Spend no longer than ten to fifteen minutes previewing a single chapter. The benefits you gain are well worth the time, for this kind of preview both speeds and strengthens the learning process. When you preview the whole book, you create in your mind a kind of framework upon which you can later hang new concepts and related details.

Previewing for General Structure

A preview of the general structure includes three steps.

1. *Flip through the book.* Note the appearance of the print. Look at the illustrations—photographs, charts, and other visuals. Notice the chapter titles and features (for example, a list of special vocabulary, terms in boldface type, chapter questions, and chapter summary).

2. *Examine the table of contents.* See which topics are covered and in what order.

3. *Read the introduction and the summary of each chapter.* If the chapter does not have an introduction, read the first paragraph in the chapter.

Previewing for Special Features

Special features are at the front of the book, at the end of the book, and in every chapter.

Three features are usually found at the front of the book: table of contents, preface, and foreword.

1. *Table of Contents.* Almost every textbook has a table of contents. This list shows the titles of the chapters and the order of the chapters in the book. Some tables of contents are skeletal; others

list every chapter title, subheading, and sometimes even a brief description of the chapter content.

2. *Preface.* In the preface the writer tells you something about the book. The writer may explain why the book was written, how it is organized, and how it can best be used. The preface may also include acknowledgments. At the very least, skim the preface for any hints that can make your study easier.

3. *Foreword or Introduction.* Occasionally someone other than the writer wants to tell you something about the book. This person may be the editor or an academic colleague of the writer who wants to praise or introduce the book or the writer. Skim the forward or introduction for information that may help you understand and use the book.

Three features at the end of the book are the glossary, index, and appendixes.

1. *Glossary.* This feature is one of the most helpful elements a book can have. A **glossary** is a kind of dictionary that includes words that are specific to the book or to the subject.

2. *Index.* The **index** is an alphabetical listing of the specific items of information in the book. The list includes all key words and the pages on which these words appear. Some books also include a second index of illustrations—diagrams, maps, photographs, and so on. Literature books often include an index of writers and titles of works that appear in the book.

3. *Appendixes.* The writer may include notes, documents, maps, a bibliography, and other information that supports material in the main part of the book. For example, political science texts often include a copy of the United States Constitution in an appendix.

Previewing Each Chapter

Chapter features include an introduction, a summary, and questions. Preview each chapter as your instructor assigns it. By previewing the chapter as it is assigned, you will focus your attention only on the material you'll be studying, which will improve your understanding of the chapter content. Here are the steps for a good chapter preview, which should take only ten to fifteen minutes.

1. *Start by looking quickly through the chapter.* Note the main features—the introduction, summary, and questions. Note the topic,

bold-type heads and subheads, illustrations, special tips, and highlighted material. As you preview, form questions and ideas about the chapter topic. Here's an example of what might occur to you as you preview an illustration in a chapter:

There are photographs of people's faces showing various kinds of emotions. I guess this chapter must be on emotions. Oh, the heading says "Nonverbal Behavior." I know that emotions are nonverbal and that people's facial expressions are clues to their emotions.

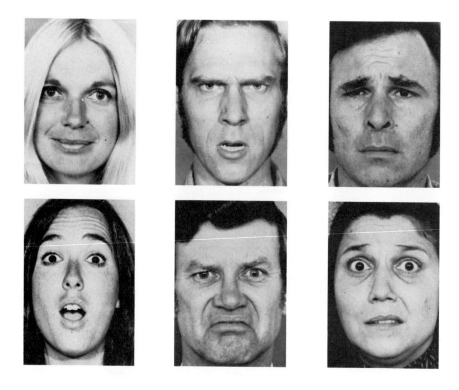

This sort of preliminary dialogue with yourself will assist your memory when you study the chapter, whether or not your half-formed questions and expectations are accurate.

2. *Skim the introduction.* When you **skim**, you glance rapidly over the material, reading only the most important information to get a general idea of the content. This should be your second look at the introduction. (Remember the book preview?)

3. *Skim the chapter summary.* By skimming the chapter summary *before* reading the chapter, you'll recognize the key ideas when you study the chapter.

4. *Skim the chapter questions or exercises.* The questions and exercises are written to draw your attention to the most important information in the chapter. Skimming them will help you recognize the key concepts when you study the chapter.

PORTFOLIO

Assignment 1:

Describing How to Preview a Chapter

In your own words, describe the steps in the chapter preview and explain why previewing is valuable. As a part of this assignment, you may want to develop a preview checklist for use in Acitvity A below and for later use in previewing chapters in this and other texts. Your checklist may include space to make some quick notes as you preview, or it may simply serve as a reminder of the previewing steps until you have them fixed firmly in your mind. Save this assignment in your portfolio.

GROUP
ACTIVITY

Activity A: Preview

With your group, apply the steps of the chapter preview to a chapter of this book that has not yet been assigned. Allow ten to fifteen minutes for the preview, and then use the information you gain to discuss what you expect to learn from the chapter.

RECOGNIZING SEVEN PATTERNS OF ORGANIZATION

Knowing the organization of the material you are reading can make you a more successful reader. You can adjust your reading strategy to the pattern of organization the writer has used. You can predict what is coming next, look for answers to questions, and keep track of information in an orderly way. The seven main patterns of organization writers use are (1) chronological, (2) how-to or process, (3) definition, (4) cause and effect, (5) order of importance, (6) classification, and (7) physical or spatial.

Chronological Pattern

In the **chronological pattern**, writers organize information in time order. Events are described from earliest to most recent, or, in reverse chronological order, from most recent to earliest. When you are reading information written in chronological order, you can make a time line to remember the order of events.

STRATEGY: When you read material organized in the chronological pattern, make a time line or list of the main events in the order in which they occurred. In the following example, note that the dates are B.C.

> In 246 B.C., the man who would unify China succeeded to the Ch'in throne at the age of thirteen. He grew to be vigorous, ambitious, intelligent, and decisive. He is famous as a Legalist autocrat; but he was also well liked by his ministers, whose advice he usually followed. In 232 B.C., at the age of twenty-seven, he began the campaigns that destroyed the six remaining territorial states. On completing his conquests in 221 B.C., he adopted the glorious title we translate as "emperor"—a combination of ideographs hitherto used only for gods or mythic heroes—to raise himself above the kings of the former territorial states. He is known to history as the First Ch'in Emperor. Then, aided by officials of great talent, he set about applying to all of China the reforms that had been tried and found effective in his own realm. His accomplishments in the eleven years before his death in 210 B.C. were stupendous.

- In which of your textbooks are you likely to find the chronological pattern? Why?

  _____

  _____

  _____

- In what other publications are you likely to find the chronological pattern?

  _____

  _____

  _____

How-To or Process Pattern

In the **how-to** or **process pattern**, writers present information as a set of steps or directions to be followed in a certain order. The goal is for readers to be able to do something by following the steps.

STRATEGY: When you read material organized in the how-to or process pattern, separate the steps from the other information the writer presents. As you read the following example, write the steps of the process in your words.

Still Playback

When the VCR is in the playback mode, press the PAUSE/STILL button to view a still picture.

- The Still indicator "PLAY > <" and the Still Remain time (maximum 5 minutes) will appear in the display.
- To continue the normal playback, press the PLAY button or PAUSE/STILL button.
- If the tape is recorded in the SP or LP mode, the picture will not be clear.
- If the VCR is left in the still mode for 5 minutes (after the Still Remain time shows OMOOS), the unit will resume the playback automatically to protect the tape and video heads.

> - **What should be done if the picture rolls when viewing a still picture?**

With certain televisions, when viewing a still picture (stop action), the picture may roll. To correct this problem, insert a driver into the STILL Adjustment under the front compartment, and turn it either left or right.

- In which of your textbooks are you likely to find examples of the how-to or process pattern? Why?

_____

_____

- In what other publications are you likely to find the how-to or process pattern?

_____

_____

Definition Pattern

In the **definition pattern**, writers introduce special terms or vocabulary—often in boldface type—followed by the definition or explanation. The writers of most introductory college texts include many special terms and new terms by using the definition pattern. The writer may first give the specific name or term, then the category it falls into, and then more details. Here's an example:

The margay is a kind of wild cat that lives in Central and South America.

The writer may also give the class or category first, then follow with the specific kind and details. Here's an example:

One unusual kind of wild cat is the margay, native to Central and South America.

Definitions may be short, as in the two examples above, or they may be expanded, running for several pages. Some books are essentially long definitions, as when a writer writes about a subject such as feminism, jazz, literacy, or conservation.

STRATEGY: When you read material organized in the definition pattern, pause frequently and summarize the writer's main ideas in your words.

• What is an example of the definition pattern from one of your textbooks?

_____

_____

_____

• What other publications are likely to use the definition pattern?

_____

_____

_____

Cause and Effect Pattern

In the **cause and effect pattern,** writers describe the impact of one event on another. The event that brings about a change is the cause; the event that results is the effect. Sometimes a single cause can have many effects.

STRATEGY: When you read material organized in the cause and effect pattern, make a chart showing the causes in one column and the effects in another column. In the following example, notice that the writer introduces two main effects of mineral deposits.

Distribution and Importance

Mineral resources are not spread evenly around the continents. This creates the have and the have-not nations. A mine or other mineral deposit is a rare feature, geologically speaking.

The importance of mineral deposits to people cannot be overemphasized. The wealth of nations is dependent on their natural resources. Although not always emphasized, mineral deposits have played a very important role in history. In ancient times, wars were fought and civilizations prospered or failed because of gold and silver deposits. In recent times, metals and energy-producing materials, such as iron, coal, and petroleum, have determined the course of history.

• In which of your textbooks are you likely to find the cause and effect pattern? Why?

_____

_____

_____

_____

• In what other publications are you likely to find the cause and effect pattern?

_____

_____

_____

_____

_____

Order of Importance Pattern

In the **order of importance pattern**, writers present important information first, followed by less important information.

STRATEGY: When you read material organized in the order of importance pattern, make a chart or concept map that shows the most important items followed by the less important items. As you read the following example, notice how the writer has described the gases that make up air in order of their importance.

> Air is a mixture of gases. The most important gases making up this mixture are oxygen and nitrogen. Oxygen is essential to the life processes of nearly every plant and animal cell living on earth. Nitrogen is needed to form protein in all plant and animal tissue. Oxygen and nitrogen make up about 99 percent of air. The remaining 1 percent is made up of gases such as carbon dioxide, which is used by plants as part of their food-making process; water vapor, which condenses and falls to the earth as rain or snow; argon; krypton; helium; hydrogen; xenon; ozone; and neon.

- In what other subject areas are you likely to find the order of importance pattern? Why?

  _____

  _____

- In what other publications are you likely to find the order of importance pattern?

  _____

  _____

Classification Pattern

In the **classification pattern**, writers show the relationship between a topic and its component parts. An American history or government text, for example, presents the branches of the United States federal government—judicial, executive, legislative. Each category may then be broken further into its divisions and agencies.

STRATEGY: When you read material organized in the classification pattern, make a diagram to see the relationship of the parts to the whole. Notice how the following diagram shows the relationship of the parts of the federal government.

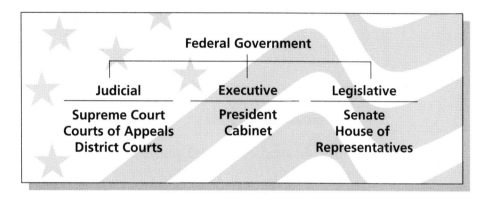

In the following excerpt from a table of contents, notice the classification of the political system of Late Imperial China.

- In what other subject areas are you likely to find the classification pattern? Why?

  _____

  _____

- In what other publications are you likely to find the classification pattern?

  _____

  _____

Physical or Spatial Pattern

In the **physical** or **spatial pattern**, writers describe how an object looks and how it is located in relation to other objects. For example, a writer of a health book may describe parts of the human body by their position in relation to each other. A writer of an astronomy book may describe stars, planets, and galaxies in relation to their distances from each other. A writer of a travel book will describe specific features of a place in relation to one another. Charts, diagrams, photographs, and other visuals help clarify material presented in the physical or spatial pattern.

STRATEGY: When you read material organized in the physical or spatial pattern, create a mental image of the relationships presented. As you read the following selection from a geology textbook, notice how the planets are described in relation to each other. On the chart that accompanies the selection, notice the order in which the planets are listed. Numbering the planets can help you remember some of the information.

> The nine planets all revolve in the same direction around the sun. The orbits are all elliptical, very close to circular, and lie close to a single plane, except Pluto, whose orbit is inclined. Seen from Earth, the sun and the planets follow the same path across the sky. The inner planets, Mercury, Venus, Earth, and Mars, form a group in which the individual members are more or less similar in size. The next four planets, Jupiter, Saturn, Uranus, and Neptune, form a similar grouping of much larger planets. Pluto is much smaller than the other outer planets and has a tilted, eccentric orbit. Between Mars and Jupiter are several thousand small bodies, the asteroids, that are probably the origin of most meteorites.

Planet Data

Body	Distance from Sun (average)		Radius		Specific Gravity	Atmospheric Pressure at Surface (Earth = 1)	Composition of Atmosphere
	Millions of Kilometers	Millions of Miles	Kilometers	Miles			
SUN	—	—	695,088	432,000	1.4	—	—
Mercury	58	36	2,414	1,500	5.4	—	None
Venus	108	67	6,114	3,800	5.2	90	Mainly carbon dioxide
Earth	150	93	6,376	3,963	5.5	1	78% nitrogen 21% oxygen
Mars	227	141	3,379	2,100	4.0	0.007	Mainly carbon dioxide, possibly minor water
Jupiter	777	483	69,992	43,500	1.3	200,000	Mainly hydrogen and helium; some methane and ammonia
Saturn	1,426	886	59,533	37,000	0.7	200,000	Same as Jupiter
Uranus	2,869	1,783	25,342	15,750	1.2	8	Similar to Jupiter, with more methane, no ammonia
Neptune	4,494	2,793	26,549	16,500	1.7	?	Same as Uranus
Pluto	5,899	3,666	1,500 (?)	900 (?)	?	?	?

- In which of your textbooks are you likely to find examples of the physical or spatial pattern? Why?

_____

_____

- In what other publications are you likely to find the physical or spatial pattern?

_____

_____

Questions

What patterns of organization do you see in the following brief selections? For each selection, write the pattern of organization, and circle any clues that helped you recognize that pattern.

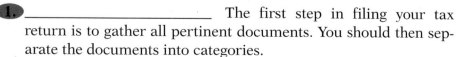

1. _____ The first step in filing your tax return is to gather all pertinent documents. You should then separate the documents into categories.

2. _____ Beginning in the 1830s, opposition to slavery was growing, both in the United States and abroad. About this time John Brown began to raise supporters; later he turned to violence.

3. _____ New Mexico is located in the southwestern United States, bordered on the north by Colorado, on the east by Texas, and on the west by Arizona.

4. _____ Criminal behavior may be divided into crimes against property and crimes against people.

5. _____ A very strong relationship exists between cigarette smoking and the development of lung cancer.

6. _____ In a counseling situation the establishment of rapport takes first precedence. Only after rapport and trust are established can the therapist proceed to the next steps.

7. _____ The third important kind of white cells are the macrophages. They are the largest of the white cells and are produced in the bone marrow along with the B and T cells.

Patterns In Other Sources

Not only textbooks but also lectures and other class presentations are usually organized using one or more of the patterns. Once you recognize patterns, you'll be able to anticipate how the information is likely to flow, and you can record more of the lecture information in your notes.

ADJUSTING YOUR READING RATE

You are not likely to read everything at the same rate. You read some materials faster than you read others. Your reading rate depends on several factors, including the kinds of material you are reading, your purpose for reading, and the knowledge you already have.

During the course of a day you read many different kinds of materials, from traffic signs to textbooks.

• What are some of the different kinds of materials you read?

_____

_____

_____

• Which materials do you read slowly and carefully? Which ones do you read quickly? Explain why you read different materials at different speeds.

_____

_____

_____

_____

WHAT ARE YOU READING?

You can recognize different types of material and different patterns of organization. Among the kinds of reading material you listed in the discovery activity, you might have included textbooks, newspapers, magazines, roadside advertisements, junk mail, letters from friends and relatives, and novels. Your experience tells you that, page for page, you can read a novel faster than you can read a textbook. Your reading speed is influenced by three factors:

1. The level of writing—the degree of difficulty—in the publication.

2. The level of interest in the task—how motivated you are to read the material.

3. Your knowledge of the subject.

When the writing is at a more difficult level, your reading rate is likely to be slower. If you are not eager to read the material, you may read slowly. If the subject is unfamiliar to you, you will also read slowly.

• What makes a piece of writing difficult to read?

_____

_____

_____

_____

WHY ARE YOU READING?

You're usually aware of why you're reading something. Your reasons for reading might include studying for a test, learning directions, being entertained, and learning how to do something. When you read for entertainment, you use a different reading rate than when you read to prepare for a test. When you're glancing at book titles in a bookstore, you read faster than when you read a story in a news magazine. In general, when your purpose is to remember main ideas and details or to understand new concepts, you tend to read more slowly. Also, if you read something more than once, you probably use a faster rate on the second, third, or fourth reading.

- Name three different kinds of materials you've read recently. Then describe your purpose for reading each one.

_____

_____

_____

_____

_____

WHAT DO YOU ALREADY KNOW?

How fast you read may depend on how familiar you are with the subject. When you already have some knowledge about a subject, you read faster. If you have a strong background in the treatment of Native Americans in nineteenth-century America, for example, you can cover information about that period at a faster rate than if you knew very little about the subject.

- Name an area in which you have good background knowledge. Describe how your background knowledge has recently helped you read and understand something.

_____

_____

_____

WHEN DO YOU SLOW DOWN OR SPEED UP?

You may find as you read that you hit a tough spot and have to slow down. You may come to an easier part and find that you can read more rapidly. As you read, remember to adjust your reading rate to match the difficulty of the material, your purpose for reading, and your knowledge of the subject.

GROUP
ACTIVITY

Activity B: Setting the Speed

With your group, choose a selection from a newspaper, magazine, novel, nonfiction book, or textbook. Describe the subject and the organization of the selection. Brainstorm ideas about possible purposes for reading the selection. Identify the different purposes for reading the selection, and estimate how long it might take to read the selection for different purposes.

_____

_____

_____

_____

_____

_____

_____

_____

_____

_____

_____

_____

PORTFOLIO

Assignment 2:
Finding Patterns of Organization

Over the next few days, find examples of the different kinds of organization in your textbooks and in other reading material. On a separate sheet of paper, describe the examples you found and any adjustments you made in your reading strategy to better understand the information. Save this assignment in your portfolio.

WRAPPING IT UP

SUMMARY

- Special features of textbooks include a table of contents, preface, introduction, headings and subheadings, and index.
- The best time to preview your textbooks is when you buy them at the beginning of the term.
- Previewing a textbook is a two-step strategy:
  1. Preview for general structure
  2. Preview for special features
- Writers use seven main patterns of organization:
  1. Chronological
  2. How-to or process
  3. Definition
  4. Cause and effect
  5. Order of importance
  6. Classification
  7. Physical or spatial
- These strategies can help you successfully read material organized in different patterns:
  1. Making and using time lines and diagrams
  2. Summarizing ideas
  3. Restating steps in your own words
- Your reading rate depends on several factors, including the level of difficulty of the material you are reading, your purpose for reading, and the knowledge you already have.

THINKING IT OVER

- What material from this chapter did you find most helpful?

  _____

  _____

  _____

  _____

  _____

  _____

  _____

  _____

- How will you apply the information and ideas in this chapter to previewing your textbooks, recognizing patterns of organization, and adjusting your reading rate?

  _____

  _____

  _____

  _____

  _____

  _____

  _____

  _____

  _____

IN YOUR
JOURNAL

Describe the progress you've made toward the goal you set at the beginning of this chapter. What new goals have you set, based on reading this chapter?

15

IDENTIFYING
MAIN IDEAS

OBJECTIVES:

- To define **main idea**.
- To identify main ideas in different contexts.

How Do I Recognize Main Ideas?

A picture usually conveys one big idea that is easy to understand. What is the big idea of the picture on this page?

In written and spoken material the big idea, often called the main idea, is not always so easy to recognize. The main idea is the most important thought expressed by an author or a speaker about a topic. Recognizing the main idea is perhaps the most important skill in comprehending written or spoken material. This chapter will help you strengthen your ability to recognize main ideas in different contexts.

GETTING STARTED

How confident are you of your ability to identify main ideas when you read and when you listen to others speak? Use the following checklist to analyze your ability in this area. Circle A for "always" or "almost always," F for "frequently," or N for "no" or "never."

1. I know what a main idea is.   A   F   N

2. I can tell the difference between a main idea and a topic.   A   F   N

3. I can tell the difference between a main idea and a detail.   A   F   N

4. I know where in a paragraph the main idea is likely to appear.   A   F   N

5. I know how to draw a conclusion about or infer the main idea when it is not directly stated.   A   F   N

6. I am an active or strategic reader: I form questions and carry on a silent dialogue with the author as I read.   A   F   N

IN YOUR JOURNAL

Use your answers on the checklist to set a goal for improving your ability to recognize main ideas. The questions you answered with N or F indicate skills to work on. You might express your goal in the following way: "I'd like to improve my ability to infer the main idea when the main idea is not directly stated."

DISCUSSING MAIN IDEAS

GROUP
ACTIVITY

In your group, discuss your methods of recognizing the main idea in written and spoken material. Begin by discussing the items in the Data Bank. See if you can identify which item in each group is a main idea and which items are details. Then discuss how you made your decision. Did you ask yourself questions? What were the questions? Did you look for clues? What were the clues? Describe your procedure in the space provided.

_____

_____

_____

_____

_____

_____

_____

_____

_____

_____

_____

_____

Group 1

   A. Ruth Bader Ginsburg was appointed by President Clinton in 1993.

   B. Sandra Day O'Connor, the first female justice, was appointed by President Reagan in 1981.

   C. The appointment of women as Supreme Court justices is a recent event in the long history of the Court.

Group 2

   A. Sequoyah, a Cherokee Indian, developed a system of writing for the Cherokee language.

   B. Sequoyah was born in 1760 in eastern Tennessee.

   C. By 1821, Sequoyah perfected 86 symbols, which represented all the syllables in the Cherokee language.

IDENTIFYING MAIN IDEAS

BECOMING AN ACTIVE OR STRATEGIC READER

As you read any piece of writing or listen to someone speak, you frequently ask yourself "What's the point?" or "What is the author/speaker telling me?" These questions are part of being an active or strategic reader or listener. You set a purpose for reading or listening—to find the main idea, for example—then you use a strategy to achieve that purpose.

DISCOVERY
ACTIVITY

• Describe something you've read recently and your purpose for reading it.

_____

_____

_____

_____

• How did your purpose for reading help you understand the information?

_____

_____

_____

_____

ACTIVATING PRIOR KNOWLEDGE

As you've read in Chapter 14 about adjusting your reading rate, whatever you read is filtered through what you already know. You can gain a greater benefit from this interaction of the new and the old by taking time to do the following before you read:

- Identify the subject.
- Think about what you already know about the subject.
- Skim the selection to get an idea of the contents.
- Form questions based on what you already know and on what you'd like to know.

You may not have a great deal of prior knowledge, but you can apply your knowledge in way that will help you get the most out of what you read and hear. Follow the example of Edward Gibbon, a noted British historian of the eighteenth century. Gibbon reported that he spent most of a day recalling every piece of information in his mind on a subject before he began to read a new book on the subject. His goal was to apply all of the information he already knew to the task of reading the new book. In this way, Gibbon began reading on a more equal footing with the author than if he had made no preparation.

A DIALOGUE WITH THE AUTHOR

Many readers and listeners find that having a silent dialogue with the text or speaker helps focus on what's important. As you read or listen, respond to ideas by asking questions of and making statements to yourself. Your comments come from the knowledge you already have and from your ability to analyze what you read and hear. When you ask questions and make comments, you are an active participant in understanding what you read and hear. When you're active, you learn more. Here's an example of the type of dialogue you might have with written material.

> **TEXT:** Social definitions of "problem drugs" change frequently over time. Within American society different groups commonly disagree over such definitions.

> **YOU:** *What are "problem drugs"? What do different groups say about them?*

> **TEXT:** This has been the case with such addictive drugs as morphine and heroin.

> **YOU:** *I knew heroin was addictive, but morphine? They gave that to my brother when he was in the hospital!*

Activity A:
Writing Your Silent Dialogue

Choose a passage in a textbook or fiction book. Read the passage aloud, pausing after each sentence. Share your questions and comments with the group.

- In the space provided, record any questions and comments that group members have. Continue in this way through the passage.

_____

_____

_____

_____

_____

_____

_____

_____

_____

_____

- Notice the variety of questions and comments your group had. Which questions were answered by the passage?

_____

_____

_____

_____

_____

_____

_____

_____

- Evaluate this way of reading or listening. Do you learn more as an active reader/listener? Why?

_____

_____

_____

_____

FINDING A DIRECTLY STATED MAIN IDEA

From an author's point of view, the best way for readers to understand the main idea is to state the idea clearly in a position where readers can easily recognize it. As a reader you should be aware that not all authors follow this strategy. Finding the main idea of a paragraph or selection may involve some detective work. Your work is easier, however, if you know where and how authors are likely to present main ideas.

Beginning a Paragraph

Textbook authors often begin paragraphs with a sentence that states the main idea. They then support the main idea with facts, examples, and other details. When you're looking for the main idea, begin at the first sentence of a paragraph. Use your questioning strategy, asking, for example, "Is this the author's main point?" As you read the remaining sentences, ask whether they support the main idea.

Activity B: Identifying the Main Idea

Read the following paragraph, and underline the main idea.

The Achaemenid State
   Perhaps the greatest achievement of the Achaemenids was the relative stability of their rule. They justified their title of *Shahanshah*, "king of kings," as a universal sovereignty entrusted to them by Ahura Mazda. Their inscriptions reflect their sense that their justice and uprightness earned them this trust; their elaborate court ceremony and impressive architectural

monuments underscored it. They acted as priests and sacrificers in the court rituals and symbolized their role as cosmic ruler by burning a special royal fire throughout each reign. The talents and evident charisma of their early leaders strengthened the force of their claim to special, divinely sanctioned royal status among their subject peoples. Yet alongside this, they were tolerant of diversity in ways earlier empires had not been. In part, the sheer size of their realms demanded this. Even Darius' conversion to Zoroastrianism did not bring forced conformity or conversion, as his lenient treatment of the Jews vividly shows.

- What pattern did you notice in the placement of the main ideas?

  _____

  _____

  _____

  _____

Ending a Paragraph

Sometimes an author chooses to begin a paragraph with details, building up to the main idea, which is then expressed in the last sentence. Your questioning strategy can help you identify this pattern. When you ask "Is this the author's main point?" and the sentence is a detail sentence, your own judgment will tell you the sentence does not contain the main idea. Your next question, then, might be, "What main idea does this detail support?" Here's an example of a paragraph with the main idea expressed in the last sentence.

A man recalls the name of his first grade teacher but forgets the name of the person he has just been introduced to. Millions of people remember just where they were when the space shuttle Challenger exploded but have vague memories of where they were at a specific hour a week ago. This phenomenon has attracted the attention of psychologists who study the thinking process. *The psychologists use the* term primacy of memory *to describe the fact that a person's early important memories are often stronger than later, less important memories.*

Questions

1. What clues helped you recognize the main idea?

_____

_____

2. Was the main idea clearer or easier to identify and understand at the end of the paragraph? Explain.

_____

_____

_____

In the Middle of the Paragraph 〰〰〰

The main idea sometimes—but rarely—appears in a position other than the first or last sentence in a paragraph. Here is an example:

> They grew maize, the staple of the Maya, and beans, on which the Maya also had lived. In the highlands, they grew wheat, in the lowlands sugar. Everywhere they grew fruit—apples and quinces in the interior of Guatemala, oranges and limes along the coasts. They raised cattle, horses and mules. Almost everything they produced, whether food or tobacco, cotton or wool, was intended not for export but for their own needs. The only major exceptions were hides, cocoa, and indigo, source of the blue dye then vastly popular in Europe. These were produced on the great estates, and they made the estate owners wealthy.

(Harold Lavine and The Editors of LIFE, from _Central America._)

Questions

1. What is the main idea of the paragraph?

_____

_____

2. What important detail comes _after_ the main idea is expressed?

_____

_____

Activity C: Finding Main Ideas

With your group, read the following paragraph, and discuss the main idea. Underline the main idea, and explain how you reached your decision about it.

Not all social groupings involve social interaction; caterpillars from a hatch, for example, all feeding on a single leaf, act entirely as individuals. But where there is true collective activity, the social behavior is adaptive; cooperation within a group tends to promote the survival of individuals, and with survival, the likelihood that they will reproduce successfully. A small fish is less likely to be eaten if it swims in a large school; a prairie dog in a colony can warn or be warned of approaching predators; a lion in a pride can hunt more effectively; and a person in a society can trade one specialized type of labor for food, clothing, shelter, and other necessities of survival.

(From *Essentials of Biology* by Janet L. Hopson and Norman K. Wessells. Copyright © 1990 by McGraw-Hill, Inc. Reprinted by permission of McGraw-Hill.)

_____

_____

_____

_____

_____

_____

_____

_____

_____

_____

Identifying an Implied Main Idea

In a conversation with a friend, suppose you heard the following: "I hadn't seen Ben for several years when I saw him at the theater this weekend. Wow, what a change! I would hardly have known him if he hadn't spoken to me. I'm telling you, he could hardly fit into the seat."

Questions

1. What did your friend imply about Ben's appearance?

_____

_____

_____

_____

2. What exactly did your friend say that led you to your conclusion about Ben?

_____

_____

_____

_____

An author can express a main idea directly by using exact words, as you've seen. An author can also suggest or imply a main idea by providing clues that help readers infer an important point. When an author implies a main idea, you need to use a strategy of "reading between the lines." As you read, look for clues and ask yourself, "What important point do these clues lead to?" This process helps you infer the main idea.

GROUP
ACTIVITY

Activity D: Reading Between the Lines

In your group, read the following selection, and discuss the main idea. Then answer the questions.

Many adolescents experience skin eruptions between the ages of 13 and 18. These skin problems are often serious enough to demand medical attention. Weight problems also become evident at this time and may make teenagers feel embarrassed and isolated. Other developments associated with puberty—the voice change and beard growth for boys, onset of menses and breast growth for girls—add to the concerns that take great prominence at this time.

Questions

1. What is the implied main idea about this period of adolescence? Write the main idea in a single sentence.

_____

_____

_____

2. What clues helped you infer the main idea?

_____

_____

_____

Read and discuss the paragraph below; then answer the questions.

> During the 1960s, the Peace Corps was founded, and many idealistic young people went to serve in foreign lands. Some who remained at home joined the fledgling civil rights movement, traveling to the South to participate in voter registration drives. On college campuses thousands protested the Vietnam War and held demonstrations calling for its end.

Questions

1. What implied main idea comes across to you in this passage? Write the main idea in a single sentence.

_____

_____

_____

2. What clues helped you infer this main idea?

_____

_____

_____

_____

_____

_____

_____

Read and discuss the following paragraph; then answer the questions about the selection.

> Thomas soon tired of watching the daytime TV shows. He did not read well, so that avenue of escape was not appealing to him. Looking for jobs soon became unbearably discouraging. Nobody seemed to want to hire a high school dropout even to pump gas. Worst of all was the fact that he no longer got to see his friends. They were attending school, doing homework, or attending football games and other events where Thomas no longer felt welcome.

Questions

1. What main idea does the author imply about this period in Thomas's life? Write the main idea as one sentence.

_____

_____

2. What clues helped you infer this main idea?

_____

_____

PORTFOLIO

Assignment:
Finding an Implied Main Idea

In one of your textbooks or in other reading material, find a passage in which the main idea is implied rather than directly stated. Copy the passage on a separate sheet of paper, and write a sentence that states the main idea. Underline clues in the passage that helped you infer the main idea. Save this assignment in your portfolio.

WRAPPING IT UP

SUMMARY

- Becoming a strategic reader involves setting a purpose for reading and asking yourself questions as you read.
- To activate your prior knowledge as an aid to strategic reading, follow these steps:

    1. Identify the subject.

    2. Think about what you already know about the subject.

    3. Skim the selection to get an idea of what it contains.

    4. Form questions based on what you already know and on what you'd like to know.

- Entering into a silent dialogue with the text or speaker helps you focus on what's important in a selection.
- A main idea may be directly stated or implied.
- A stated main idea may appear at the beginning, at the end, or in the middle of a paragraph.
- To infer an unstated main idea, look for clues as you read, and ask "What important point do these clues lead to?"

THINKING IT OVER

- What material from this chapter did you find most helpful?

_____

_____

_____

• How will you apply the information and ideas in this chapter to improving your reading skills?

_____

_____

_____

_____

_____

_____

_____

_____

_____

_____

IN YOUR JOURNAL

Describe progress you've made toward the goal you set at the beginning of this chapter. Analyze your ability to identify the main ideas in written and spoken information. Do you know what to look for and where to look? Do you know what questions to ask yourself? What problems do you have in identifying the main idea, if any? Describe any problems you have, and set goals for solving those problems.

16

EFFICIENT READING TECHNIQUES

OBJECTIVES:

- To develop efficient reading techniques.
- To apply efficient reading techniques.

How Can I Read Faster?

L ike the student in the picture, you have much reading to do in college. What thoughts might be going through the mind of the people in the picture?

Most college students want to read faster. Some people do indeed read faster than other people; however, the desire to read faster often leads to unrealistic expectations about how much you can improve your reading rate. A faster reading rate does not necessarily mean that you comprehend more than you do when you read at your normal rate. A more realistic expectation is the ability to use different strategies for different reading purposes. In this chapter you will learn techniques for more efficient reading.

How well do you know your own method of reading? Are you aware of the techniques you use as you read? The following checklist will help you analyze some of your reading strategies. Answer each question by circling *A* for "always" or "almost always," *F* for "frequently," or *N* for "no" or "never."

1. I use skip reading or skimming for some kinds of reading, skipping words and reading rapidly to get a general idea of what the material is about.　　　　　　　A　F　N

2. I use scanning to pick out specific pieces of information from a larger context, such as an encyclopedia article, a phone directory, or an index.　　　　　　　A　F　N

3. I activate my prior knowledge when I'm scanning material written on a subject I know something about.　　　　　　　A　F　N

4. When I read, I focus on groups of words rather than on one word at a time.　　　　　　　A　F　N

5. I regularly practice reading faster.　　　　　　　A　F　N

IN YOUR JOURNAL

Use your answers on the checklist to set a goal for improving your ability to read more efficiently. The questions you answered with *N* or *F* indicate strategies to work on. You might express your goal in the following way: "I'd like to improve my ability to use skimming or skip reading to get an idea of the general content of a piece of writing."

ANALYZING YOUR READING RATE

GROUP
ACTIVITY

Read the selection in the Data Bank at your normal reading rate. Keep track of how many minutes and seconds you need to read the selection. After you finish reading the selection, answer the questions that follow.

I began writing around the time I was twenty-two years old. I am now thirty-four and feel that after all this time I am just beginning to learn to write. I am only now beginning to comprehend what poetry is, and what it can mean. Each time I write I am in a different and wild place, and travel toward something I do not know the name of. Each poem is a jumping-off edge and I am not safe, but I take more risks and understand better now how to take them. They do not always work, but when they do it is worth it. I could not live without writing and/or thinking about it. In fact, I don't have to think about it; it's there, some word, concept always being born or, just as easily, dying.

I walk in and out of many worlds. I used to see being born of this mixed-blood/mixed-vision a curse, and hated myself for it. It was too confusing and destructive when I saw the world through that focus. The only message I got was not belonging anywhere, not to any side. I have since decided that being familiar with more than one world, more than one vision, is a blessing, and know that I make my own choices. I also know that it is only an illusion that any of the worlds are separate.

It is around midnight. I often write at this time in my workroom near the front of an old Victorian-style house near downtown Denver. Tonight a thick snow has muffled the sounds of traffic. The world is quiet except for the sound of this typewriter humming, the sometimes dash of metallic keys, and the deep breathing of my dog who is asleep nearby. And then, in the middle of working, the world gives way and I see the old, old Creek one who comes in here and watches over me. He tries to make sense of this world in which his granddaughter has come to live. And often teases me about my occupation of putting words on paper.
(Joy Harjo, from "Ordinary Spirit")

- What is the author's attitude toward writing?

  _____

  _____

  _____

  _____

  _____

  _____

- How does the author's attitude change toward her heritage?

  _____

  _____

  _____

  _____

  _____

  _____

- What happens after the writer settles down to work?

  _____

  _____

  _____

  _____

  _____

  _____

  _____

Calculate your reading speed by dividing the number of words in the selection (345) by the number of minutes it took you to read the selection. Write your group's average reading rate in the space provided (average rate = sum of everyone's rate divided by the number of people in the group). Discuss any problems you had.

Personal Reading Rate _____

Group's Average Rate _____

RAPID-READING TECHNIQUES

SPEED READING?

One skill that captures the imagination of many students is speed reading. Workshops claiming to double or even triple a student's reading rate draw crowds wherever they are presented.

DISCOVERY
ACTIVITY

- What ideas do you have about improving your reading rate?

  _____

  _____

  _____

  _____

- Have you taken a speed reading course? What effect did it have on your reading rate?

  _____

  _____

  _____

- What are your biggest problems in reading?

  _____

  _____

  _____

  _____

Speed reading workshops are often expensive; and there is a catch: the human eye-brain structures have a natural limit that is much the same for everyone. They can take in so many letters or words at a time, and no amount of training can change that.

However, you can improve your ability to read more efficiently—by choosing different reading techniques to accomplish different reading tasks. Three such techniques are skip reading (also called skimming), scanning, and phrase reading.

SKIP READING OR SKIMMING

When you **skip read** (or skim) a selection, you glance rapidly over a selection, reading only the most important information to get a general idea of the content. You're probably already familiar with skip reading or skimming in your daily life. Think of the way you handle junk mail. Do you read every word of it? No, you look quickly to see who it's from, what it's about; then you decide if you'll read further or throw it away.

These are the steps in skip reading or skimming:

1. Read the title and subtitle if there is one.
2. Read each boldface or italic heading.
3. Read the first paragraph.
4. Quickly read the first sentence in each remaining paragraph.
5. Read the last paragraph.
6. Quickly read visuals, including charts, diagrams, captions, and boxed features.

Skip reading is easy, but this technique also has a narrow purpose. You skim only to see if a closer or more careful reading is warranted. If it is not, you have lost very little time. If you decide to do a closer reading, you already have the first step out of the way. The preview provides pegs for you to hang the more detailed information on during your closer reading.

Skim the following selection, just to get a general idea of what the selection is about. Don't spend more than one minute to do this. Then answer the questions without looking back at the selection.

Checking on Your Coverage
What to do to make sure your insurance company is on the up and up
Americans spends billions each year to safeguard their homes, lives and livelihoods. Yet "most people put more time and effort into buying a car or refrigerator than they do into buying insurance," laments Massachusetts Insurance Commissioner Kay Doughty. But a little spade-work can help consumers avoid the lemons. Some rules of thumb:

- **Know your insurer.** Before checking on an insurer, you must determine who actually covers you. For instance, roughly two thirds of all workers—some 100 million people—are in health plans where the employer pays medical claims directly, retaining the insurer or other administrator just to process the paperwork. Such self-insured pools are not regulated by state insurance departments, however, and thus do not qualify for bailouts if claims go unpaid. The same holds true for reinsurers. To see who ultimately backs your policy, ask an employee benefits officer or check with your agent for any "cut through" letter identifying reinsurers.
- **Check the registration.** "If you do nothing else," advises Michael Donio, of the People's Medical Society, a consumer group in Allentown, Pa., "make sure the insurer is licensed in your state." That at least guarantees that a company has met solvency and financial-reporting standards. Most state insurance departments offer toll-free numbers for consumer inquiries. And though none will divulge an insurer's financial status, several—notably California, Florida, New York and Texas—now rank underwriters according to the number of complaints per premium volume. For extra security, "make sure the company is licensed in New York," suggests Robert Hunter, president of the National Insurance Consumer Organization in Alexandria, Va. The Empire State boasts some of the country's toughest regulations and requires insurers to meet them wherever they do business.
- **Ask about safety nets.** All states maintain "guaranty funds" to pay claims in case of default. But the rules governing contributions vary greatly, and consumers can get burned if their insurer is exempt. Fewer than half the states, for instance, guarantee Blue Cross and Blue Shield plans. Self-insured companies and some group-health plans also do not qualify for state bailouts.
- **Ferret out finances.** Few policyholders have the expertise to fathom the elaborate financial statements insurers must file with state insurance commissions. However, several rating agencies, including Standard & Poor's, A.M. Best Co. and Moody's Investors Service, grade the creditworthiness of insurance companies. Public libraries usually have copies of such tomes as *Best's Insurance Reports.* Most insurance departments also will cite a rating. Since a few spectacular flops have received high marks in the past, experts advise reading more than one evaluation.

Unlike the big rating services, Weiss Research Inc. (2200 N. Florida Mango Road, West Palm Beach, FL 33409; 407-684-8100) writes for consumers. It also provides the only ranking of the nation's 72 Blue Cross and Blue Shield plans. Consumers may obtain a letter grade of their health insurers by phone for $15 or a one-page "Personal Safety Brief" for $25. For $2, Weiss will mail its 24-page layman guide, including a fill-in-the-blank postcard questionnaire on how to determine an insurer's financial sturdiness.

- **Don't decide in the dark**. The industry-sponsored National Insurance Consumer Helpline, (800-942-4242) fields questions on a wide variety of topics weekdays from 8 A.M. until 8 P.M. Eastern time and can refer consumers to appropriate sources for complaints. For tips on what types of policies to avoid, National Insurance Consumer Organization (121 N. Payne Street, Alexandria, VA 22314; 703-549-8050) offers a $3 "Buyers Guide to Insurance."
- **Sound off**. Above all, says Mary Griffin, an insurance counsel at Consumers Union in Washington, D.C., register any complaint. That's often the only way regulators know there is a problem. Most insurance departments have consumer advocacy offices and toll-free numbers to handle gripes—New York alone fielded over 30,000 last year, while California has more than 65 caseworkers and 40 hot-line specialists to handle the load. Texas recently went a step further, establishing a separate Office of Public Insurance Council to give consumers a voice in the regulatory process.

Unfortunately, even the most diligent research won't enable you to spot all swindles. But as failed Florida insurance broker Skip Searle notes, "it's better than flipping coins." Searle should know: He signed up with the fraudulent health plan he helped market—and wound up losing his own insurance.

(Copyright May 24, 1993, *U.S. News & World Report*)

Questions

1 What is the general topic of the selection?

_____

2 What advice does the selection give?

_____

_____

_____

- What method did you use as you skimmed the selection? Identify the parts you read and those you did not read.

_____

_____

_____

Activity A: Skimming Academic Material

Practice skimming the two pages from an anthropology textbook on pages 327–328. Spend no more than 30 seconds per page.

CULTURAL CHANGE AND ADAPTATION

Domesticated Animals

Many agriculturalists use animals as means of production—for transport, as cultivating machines, and for their manure. For example, the Betsileo of central Madagascar incorporate cattle into their agricultural economy based on rice production (Kottak 1980). First the Betsileo sow rice in nursery beds. Then, once the seedlings are big enough, women transplant them into flooded rice fields. Before transplanting, the men till and flood the fields. They bring cattle to trample the prepared fields just before transplanting. Young men yell at and beat the cattle, striving to drive them into a frenzy so that they will trample the fields properly. Trampling breaks up clumps of earth and mixes irrigation water with soil to form a smooth mud into which women transplant seedlings. Like many other agriculturalists, the Betsileo collect manure from their animals, using it to fertilize their plots, thus increasing the yield.

Irrigation

While horticulturalists must await the rainy season, agriculturalists can schedule their planting in advance, because they control

water. The Betsileo irrigate their fields with canals from rivers, streams, springs, and ponds. Irrigation makes it possible to cultivate a plot year after year. Irrigation enriches the soil because the irrigated field is a unique ecosystem with several species of plants and animals, many of them minute organisms, whose wastes fertilize the land.

An irrigated field is a capital investment that usually increases in value. It takes time for a field to start yielding; it reaches full productivity only after several years of cultivation. The Betsileo, like other irrigators, have farmed the same fields for generations. In some agricultural areas, including the Middle East, however, salts carried in the irrigation water can make fields unusable after fifty or sixty years.

Terracing

Terracing is another agricultural technique the Betsileo have mastered. Central Madagascar has small valleys separated by steep hillsides. Because the population is dense, people need to farm the hills. However, if they simply planted on the steep hillsides, fertile soil and crops would be washed away during the rainy season. To prevent this, the Betsileo, like the rice-farming Ifugao of the Philippines, cut into the hillside and build stage after stage of terraced fields rising above the valley floor. Springs located above the terraces supply their irrigation water. The labor necessary to build and maintain a system of terraces is great. Ter-

Agriculturalists use domesticated animals as means of production, for transport, as cultivating machines, and for their manure. Here a woman and water buffalo plow a rice field in Yangshuo, China.

(From Kottak, C., *Cultural Anthropology*, 6th Edition. Copyright © 1994, 1991, 1987, 1982, 1979, 1978, 1975, 1974 by McGraw-Hill, Inc. Reprinted with permission of McGraw-Hill, Inc.)

CHAPTER 16: EFFICIENT READING TECHNIQUES **327**

CULTIVATION

In some areas of Irian Jaya, Indonesia (which is on the island of New Guinea), labor-intensive cultivation in valleys involves the construction of long drainage ditches. Here, members of the Dani tribe use their bare hands and feet to maintain such a canal.

race walls crumble each year and must be partially rebuilt. The canals that bring water down through the terraces also demand attention.

Costs and Benefits of Agriculture

Agriculture requires human labor to build and maintain irrigation systems and terraces. People must feed, water, and care for their animals. Given sufficient labor input and management, agricultural land can yield one or two crops annually for years or even generations. An agricultural field does not necessarily produce a higher single-year yield than does a horticultural plot. The first crop grown by horticulturalists on long-idle land may be larger than that from an agricultural plot of the same size. Furthermore, because agriculturalists work harder than horticulturalists do, agriculture's yield relative to labor is also lower. Agriculture's main advantage is that the long-term yield per area is far greater and more dependable. Because a single field sustains its owners year after year, there is no need to maintain a reserve of uncultivated land as horticulturalists do. This is why agricultural societies are more densely populated than are horticultural ones.

The Cultivation Continuum

Because nonindustrial economies can have features of both horticulture and agriculture, it is useful to discuss cultivators as being arranged along a **cultivation continuum**. Horticultural systems stand at one end—the "low-labor, shifting-plot" end. Agriculturalists are at the other—the "labor-intensive, permanent-plot"—end.

We speak of a continuum because there are today intermediate economies, combining horticultural and agricultural features—more intensive than annually shifting horticulture but less intensive than agriculture. These recall the intermediate economies revealed by archeological sequences leading from horticulture to agriculture in the Middle East, Mexico, and other areas of early food production. Unlike nonintensive horticulturalists, who farm a plot just once before fallowing it, the South American Kuikuru grow two or three crops of **manioc**, or casava—an edible tuber—before abandoning their plots. Cultivation is even more intense in certain densely populated areas of Papua-New Guinea, where plots are planted for two or three years, allowed to rest for three to five, and then recultivated.

Questions

1. What is the general topic of the textbook excerpt?

_____

2. What are three methods of agricultural production?

_____

_____

_____

3. The illustrations show people from which two nations?

_____

Skimming: A Survival Strategy in Today's Print Explosion

New technology has resulted in an information explosion, and the fallout is a print explosion. Homes, libraries, offices, and classrooms are terminals for the flow of enormous amounts of printed information. As an educated person, you must decide quickly what information is worth taking time to read thoroughly. Skimming can help you survive the print explosion. One of the most useful applications for skimming will be when you go to the library to do research for a paper. As you look at the indexes, books, journals, and magazines, skimming will help you quickly decide which ones meet your needs.

SCANNING: A RAPID-READING TECHNIQUE

DISCOVERY ACTIVITY

Scanning is another technique that you probably use every day. When you scan, you look for one specific piece of information in written material, such as a name in a phone directory.

• What other kinds of material have you scanned?

_____

_____

• In what ways has scanning helped you?

_____

_____

To scan effectively, you need to recognize how the written material is organized. Once you discover the organization, you can figure out how to glance quickly through the material to find exactly what you want. Probably the easiest writings to scan are those which are in alphabetical order, such as the phone book or a dictionary. Your task is easier if the term or section of a text you're scanning is italicized or boldfaced.

Activity B: Scanning

Suppose you are doing a research paper on Dizzy Gillespie, the musician. You've looked up his name in the index of a book on American music and have found a page reference. The following excerpt reproduces that page. Time yourself as you scan to find Gillespie's name.

FROM SLAVERY TO FREEDOM

Vocalists have fared much better. Although Leontyne Price retired from the Metropolitan Opera to devote herself to the concert stage, Shirley Verrett, Grace Bumbry, and Jessye Norman became the mainstays and, in addition, captivated audiences on both sides of the Atlantic. There were several bright stars at the Met and elsewhere. Kathleen Battle joined the select few as a leading coloratura soprano, Leona Mitchell inherited much of the Price repertoire, Barbara Hendricks added important new roles, including *Der Rosenkavalier*, and Simon Estes, fresh from European triumphs, became a leading bass at the Metropolitan. The Met's production of George Gershwin's *Porgy and Bess* in its 1985-1986 season provided several new opportunites for Negro singers since Gershwin stipulated that only blacks should sing in the opera. Thus, men such as Gregory Hubbard, Bruce Everett, Gregory Baker, and Vinson Cole secured opportunities not only to perform in that opera but to take on numerous other roles as well.

The vibrancy and creativity that had characterized black musical expression during the Depression and war years continues down to the present. The growth in the influence of black popular music as an expression of aesthetic, political, and religious values widely held in

(From Franklin, J. and Moss, A., *From Slavery To Freedom: A History Of Negro Americans*, 6th Edition. Copyright © 1988, 1980, 1974, 1956, 1947 by McGraw-Hill, Inc. Reprinted with permission of McGraw-Hill, Inc.)

the Afro-American community was directly related to the increased earning power of many blacks during the postwar years. Those able to secure jobs with decent or better wages in industry, the service sector, the civil service, or through work in the professions, now had the means to patronize those theaters, night clubs, and cabarets in which their favorite artists performed and, more important, to purchase their records. Recordings enhanced and established the reputations of artists by giving them access to larger audiences; and, in some cases, they provided black artists with their most stable source of income, thus encouraging them to continue to refine and develop their skills in the face of many other discouragements.

Jazz, both instrumental and vocal, continued to show great dynamism. Instrumentalists such as Charlie Parker, Dizzy Gillespie, Thelonious Monk, and Max Roach, all of whom had begun their careers as innovative developers of the jazz idiom on the eve of World War II, were joined during the postwar period by equally talented and inventive younger figures such as Miles Davis, John Coltrane, Cannonball Adderly, and the composer Quincy Jones. In the 1970s, the ascendancy of Wynton Marsalis, who received acclaim for his performances on both the jazz and classical trumpet, provided another expression of the versatility and musical sensitivity of black artists. Jazz vocalists played an important role in the popularization of jazz; Sarah Vaughan, Dinah Washington, Al Jarreau, and Lou Rawls were among the most popular.

- How long did you take to find the name?

_____

_____

- What other words besides *Dizzy Gillespie* helped you find the name?

_____

_____

Scanning becomes even easier when you have prior knowledge to help narrow your search. Looking among the names of opera singers at the top of the page would only have prolonged your scanning. However, if you were aware that Dizzy Gillespie was a famous jazz musician, you might have been guided by the word *jazz* as well as by his name. If you had never heard of Dizzy Gillespie, you could not have used that strategy.

WHAT HAPPENS WHEN YOU READ?

Some time ago, researchers developed a device—a specialized kind of camera—that records eye movements during reading. Data provided by the device contradicted what we would have expected to happen when we read.

EXPECTATION: The eyes move smoothly over the lines of print from left to right.

FACT: The eyes make very jerky back-and-forth movements called **saccades**. To check this phenomenon, watch a reader's eyes closely.

EXPECTATION: The eyes keep moving forward except when you consciously go backward in the text.

FACT: The eyes very often move backward or regress over text that the eyes have already seen. These regressions seem to be necessary to the physical and mental process of reading. Approximately 15 percent of an average reader's saccades are regressions. Regressions are not a bad thing unless a person goes back consciously and repeatedly in addition to the unconscious and necessary regressions.

EXPECTATION: Reading takes place when the eyes move over the text, during the saccades.

FACT: When the eye is moving, no information is relayed to the brain, no "reading" is taking place. Reading takes place only when the eye stops between saccades. At that time the images the eye has seen are interpreted by the brain and given meaning. The eye stops are called **fixations**. They are so common that you make many fixations during the reading of a single page of text. A fixation lasts about a quarter of a second.

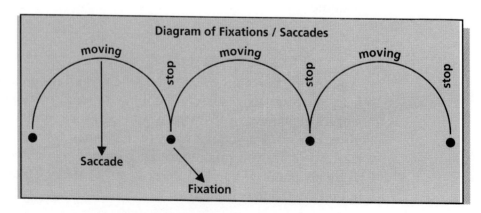

Diagram of Fixations / Saccades

- Which of these facts was most surprising to you? Why?

  _____

  _____

  _____

- What do these facts suggest about ways to improve your reading speed?

  _____

  _____

  _____

  _____

PHRASE READING

The facts from reading research indicate two ways to improve your reading speed:

1. Learn to make fewer fixations per second.

2. Learn to take in more words per fixation.

You can do both at once by reading words in groups or phrases rather than one at a time.

Activity C: Follow the Dots

Read the short passage below. But instead of looking directly at the word groups, look at or fixate on the dots below the words, taking in the phrases above the dot in your peripheral vision.

As you read	try to push	your eyes ahead.
•	•	•
Your eyes	stop-and-go,	stop-and-go
•	•	•
across the line.	Each "go" movement	is very fast;
•	•	•
it is merely	a quick dart.	Your eyes read
•	•	•
one group of words	at each stop.	Make each stop
•	•	•
as short as possible.	Do not linger	on any word.
•	•	•

- What was easy—or difficult—about this activity?

  _____

  _____

- Would practicing the activity help to increase the number of words you take in during each fixation? Explain.

  _____

  _____

  _____

Activity D: An Exercise to Help You Read Groups of Words

In the following passage, two or more words are separated by a string of dots. As you look at each group of words and dots, focus your eyes on the dots. You should notice that you are able to see the words on either side of the dots, even though you are looking *only* at the dots. Keep your eyes moving from group to group, but don't push hard enough to frustrate yourself or cause eye strain. As you continue through the passage, you should notice that your eyes are able to take in more words in a single fixation than you might have thought possible.

As........Gregor Samsa   awoke......one   morning.......from
    uneasy.....dreams   he......found   himself....transformed
        in......his   bed......into   a........gigantic
insect......He was   lying on his.........hard,
    as it were......armor-plated,   back and when......he lifted
his head a......little he could   see his dome-like.......brown
    belly divided......into stiff segments
on top of which....the bed quilt   could hardly........keep in
    position and was.......about to slide   off.......completely.
His numerous.......legs, which were   pitifully thin......compared
    to the rest.......of his bulk, waved
        helplessly before......his eyes.

(Franz Kafka, from *The Metamorphosis*)

- What difficulties, if any, did you have?

  _____

  _____

- How might activities such as this one help to improve your reading speed?

_____

_____

Improving Your Reading Speed

As a gifted young college player, Michael Jordan developed his extraordinary abilities by studying and practicing the game. He achieved Superstar status as a player for the Chicago Bulls.

Phrase reading is a skill that you need to practice. Be aware, however, that speed alone is not the goal. Comprehension is far more important. For this reason, your textbooks are not very good for practicing your phrase reading, at least not until you have some experience. Start with magazines, newspapers, and other light reading material. Over time, you'll develop your skill so that you can read more demanding material without sacrificing accuracy in your comprehension.

Time yourself as you read the selection. Practice reading in groups of words instead of word by word. After you've read the selection, answer the questions. Check your answers. Then determine your reading rate by dividing the number of words in the selection by the minutes and seconds you took to read the selection. (Round the seconds to the nearest quarter—0.25—of a minute.)

Like many young men, Jordan felt most comfortable when playing, thinking or talking about sports. He had been a gifted Little League pitcher, throwing two no-hitters before moving on to greater truimphs in Wilmington's Babe Ruth League. "My favorite childhood memory, my greatest accomplishment was when I got the Most Valuable Player award when my team won the state baseball championship," he told Sam Smith of the Chicago Tribune. "That was the first big thing I accomplished in my life, and you always remember the first. I remember I batted over .500, hit five home runs in seven games and pitched a one-hitter to get us into the championship game."

Michael's greatest friend and toughest opponent in those years was his brother Larry. Larry worked harder at athletics than Michael did, and he possessed a startling leaping ability.

His younger brother revered him. On the Laney High School basketball team Michael requested number 23, because it was roughly half the 45 that Larry wore.

This fraternal regard, however, was not immediately evident to James and Deloris as they watched the two boys trying to pound each other into the dirt of their backyard basketball court. In these initial showdowns, Larry doled out defeats that often sent his brother into a fury. The games became increasingly heated during the younger Jordan's sophomore year, when Michael sprouted to 5-foot-11 while Larry remained a shade under 5-foot-8.

In those contests, many of which ended in fights, Michael developed perhaps the essential element in his personality: a passion for competition. Jordan hates to play on the losing side in a Bulls scrimmage. He once stormed out of a practice because he felt former coach Doug Collins was not keeping score fairly. However casual a game might seem, Jordan pursues victory relentlessly and accepts almost any challenge. This can seem a bit obsessive, a bit juvenile at times, but Michael regards competition as an unmixed blessing. For him, it has been the key to self-discovery.

(Jim Naughton, from *Taking to the Air: The Rise of Michael Jordan*)

Number of Words in the Selection: 315

Your Reading Time: _____ minutes _____ seconds

Comprehension Questions

Circle the letter of the correct answer.

1. As a child, Michael Jordan won the state's Most Valuable Player award for

    a. baseball **b.** basketball
    c. football **d.** hockey

2. As a child, Michael's brother, Larry, was known for

    a. pitching no-hitters
    b. shooting baskets from center court
    c. a startling leaping ability
    d. batting .500

3. The author calls Michael Jordan's competitiveness

    a. "his toughest opponent"
    b. "destructive"
    c. "the essential element of his personality"
    d. "embarrassing"

4. In his sophomore year, Michael was shorter than his brother Larry.

    a. true   **b.** false

5. Doug Collins was

    a. Michael's junior varsity coach
    b. a former Bulls coach
    c. Michael's best friend
    d. a reporter for the *Chicago Tribune*

Number correct: ————

Multiply the number correct by 20   ———— × 20

Your score: ————

Your reading rate (Divide 315 words by your reading time stated in minutes.): ————

Try reading this second selection a little faster than you read the first selection. Remember to read groups of words instead of one word at a time.

Jordan was a late bloomer by athletic standards. Many top basketball prospects are contacted by college recruiters before their voices change, but Michael was all but ignored outside North Carolina. He didn't even make a list of the nation's top 300 college prospects published before his senior year in high school.

The lack of attention, though painful at the time, had beneficial side effects. Jordan was spared the pressure that accompanies youthful athletic acclaim. He had no reason to imagine himself a star, and felt little temptation to presume his athleticism would excuse poor grades or bad conduct. His late athletic development afforded Michael the luxury of a normal adolescence.

In the summer before his senior year, Jordan attended a camp conducted by Bobby Cremins at Appalachian State University. Cremins, now the head coach at Georgia Tech, is normally an astute judge of talent, yet he never even realized Jordan was in his program. When Michael broke the news to him a few years later, the coach was incredulous.

After Cremins' clinic Jordan moved on to Chapel Hill, where Dean Smith, a Carolina institution, offered the most prestigious high school basketball camp in the area. Michael's suitemate there was Buzz Peterson. The two boys played the same position and played it as well as anyone in the state. Over the next two years, they would compete—first for statewide high school honors and then for a starting spot on the Carolina varsity. In the process these opponents became extremely close friends.

The local experts thought Peterson was a better college prospect. He was headed for Howie Garfinkel's Five Star Camp in Pittsburgh, where the nation's best high school players were drilled by a top-notch coaching staff and evaluated by scouts from almost every major college program in the country. Playing well there was the surest way to win a scholarship.

(Jim Naughton, from *Taking to the Air: The Rise of Michael Jordan*)

Number of Words in the Selection: 315

Your Reading Time _____ minutes _____ seconds

Comprehension Questions

Circle the letter of the correct answer.

1. Jordan was listed among the top 300 basketball players before his senior year in high school.

   a. true   **b.** false

2. Being a "late bloomer" helped Michael Jordan

   a. have a normal adolescence outside of North Carolina
   b. become recognized
   c. focus entirely on developing his athletic skills
   d. all of the above

3. Bobby Cremins

    a. was conductor of the camp at Appalachian Sate University
    b. became head coach at Georgia Tech
    c. never realized Jordan was in the program at Appalachian State
    d. all of the above

4. Michael's roommate at Chapel Hill was

    a. Dean Smith   **b.** Brendan Malone
    c. Buzz Peterson   **d.** Roy Williams

5. America's best high school basketball players were sent to

    a. Appalachian State University
    b. Five Star Camp in Pittsburgh
    c. Kansas University
    d. Georgia Tech

Number correct: _____

Multiply the number correct by 20   _____ $\times\, 20$

Your score: _____

Your reading rate (Divide 315 words by your reading time stated in minutes.): _____

- How does your rate on this selection compare to your rate on the first selection?

  _____

- How does your comprehension on this selection compare to your comprehension on the first selection?

  _____

Try reading the last selection a little faster than you read the first and second selections. Remember to read groups of words instead of one word at a time.

Basketball's counterculture grew up outdoors on the nation's playgrounds. Young black athletes didn't have access to college coaching gurus, who plied their trade at segregated schools. Instead, they learned their craft in neighborhoods where the game was looked on, in Bill Russell's words, as a combination of art and war. Sinking a jump shot was fine, but if it had the arc of a rainbow, so much the better. Protecting the ball was useful, but dribbling through the other team was thrilling. Rebounds were essential, but snatching coins from atop the backboard is what made your name.

The Harlem Globetrotters played this quicker, more free-flowing brand of basketball, and in 1948 they took two of three games from George Mikan and the Minneapolis Lakers, champions of the National Basketball League. Many white strategists looked down their noses at the Globies, and considered them nothing more than a minstrel show, but "scientific" basketball was about to be overwhelmed by the talented black athletes who began flooding into the NBA in the late 1950s. Elgin Baylor, the Lakers' marvelous forward, was the harbinger of this new style. He could jump over defenses and around opponents who had boxed him off the boards. What really popularized this acrobatic style, however, was white fans' discovery of the black playground.

It happened in the late 1960s when Pete Axthelm wrote *The City Game*. A student of the Harlem summer leagues, Axthelm captured the great gifts and grim lives of men like Earl Manigualt and Herman "The Helicopter" Knowings for a mainstream audience. David Wolf, who wrote *Foul: The Connie Hawkins Story*, took the tale one step deeper, showing how black playground stars were denied the educations they needed to attend college and, hence, the experience they needed to earn a shot at the NBA. The ghetto heroes who emerge from these books are something more than basketball players. Like the great blues singers, they turned their rage into art and became symbols of flickering transcendence.

(Jim Naughton, from *Taking to the Air: The Rise of Michael Jordan*)

Number of Words in the Selection: 310

Your Reading Time: _____ minutes _____ seconds

Comprehension Questions

Circle the letter of the correct answer.

1 According to Bill Russell, basketball in some black neighborhoods was

    a. an alternative to playing at segregated schools
    b. preparation for college-level playing
    c. a combination of art and war
    d. a form of "scientific" basketball

2 In 1948 the Harlem Globetrotters won two of three games against the

    a. Minneapolis Lakers   **b.** Chicago Bulls
    c. Detroit Pistons   **d.** Philadelphia 76ers

3 The new style of playing exhibited by black basketball players was quicker, more free-flowing, and acrobatic than the playing of white players.

    a. true   **b.** false

4 *The City Game*, a book by Pete Axthelm, describes

    a. the life of Elgin Baylor
    b. Michael Jordan's early career
    c. the author's collaboration with David Wolf on another book
    d. basketball playing among the Harlem summer leagues

5 The author compares early black basketball heroes to

    a. opera singers   **b.** painters
    c. blues singers   **d.** acrobats

Number correct: _____

Multiply the number correct by 20 $\times\,20$ _____

Your score: _____

Your reading rate (Divide 315 words by your reading time stated in minutes.): _____

- How does your rate on the third selection compare to your rate on the first and second selections?

  _____

- How does your comprehension on the third selection compare to your comprehension on the first and second selections?

  _____

- Describe your reactions to the activity. What conclusions did you draw about your ability to read faster?

  _____

  _____

  _____

Reading Faster with Practice

The material on which you practiced improving your reading is from a nonfiction book, a biography. It is the kind of book you are likely to read for entertainment or pleasure, not for a difficult college course. However, by practicing with material such as this—including newspapers, fiction, and other nonfiction books—you may be able to improve your ability to read more difficult material faster without losing comprehension. In fact, you may improve your comprehension.

Assignment 1:
Reading New Material

Follow these steps to practice improving your reading rate and comprehension:

1. Work with a partner. Each of you should bring a book you are reading for entertainment.

2. Have your partner choose a section of the book you have not read, read the section, and write some questions about it.

3. Read the section yourself, time your reading, and answer your partner's questions.

4. Change roles, choosing a section of your partner's book and asking questions about it after your partner has read the selection.

5. Repeat Steps 2 through 4 with two more sections from your books.

Save your questions in your portfolio.

Assignment 2:
Practicing

The three techniques you've studied—skimming, scanning, and phrase reading—can help you read more efficiently. To achieve this goal, however, you must practice. For the next five days, keep a record of situations in which you use each of the three techniques. On a separate sheet of paper, describe the kinds of printed materials you skimmed, scanned, and phrase read. Explain your purpose for using each technique. Save this assignment in your portfolio.

WRAPPING IT UP

 SUMMARY

- The human eye-brain structures have a natural limit that is much the same for everyone. However, you can become a more efficient reader by practicing three techniques:
  1. Skip reading or skimming
  2. Scanning
  3. Phrase reading

- In skip reading or skimming, you rapidly glance over a selection, reading only the most important information to get a general idea of the content.

- In scanning, you look for one specific piece of information in written material, such as a name in a phone directory. The key to effective scanning is to recognize how the written material is organized.

- Researchers have found that, contrary to what you might expect, your eyes make jerky back-and-forth movements or saccades when you read. Your eyes also make regressions, moving back over text you've already seen. In the reading process, information is relayed to the brain only during the eye stops between saccades, called fixations.

- You can increase your reading speed by practicing phrase reading, which involves learning to make fewer fixations per second and learning to take in more words per fixation.

- What material from this chapter did you find most helpful?

  _____

  _____

  _____

  _____

  _____

- How will you apply the information and ideas in this chapter to becoming a more efficient reader?

  _____

  _____

  _____

  _____

  _____

IN YOUR
JOURNAL

Describe the progress you've made toward the goal you set at the beginning of this chapter. What techniques from this chapter have you practiced on your own? What were the results? What new goals have you set?

17

USING TEXTBOOK-READING STRATEGIES

OBJECTIVES:

- To review previewing technique for textbooks.

- To apply strategies for learning new vocabulary.

- To use outlining as an aid to textbook reading.

- To write marginal questions as an aid to textbook reading.

- To create study maps as an aid to textbook reading.

- To apply the SQ4R method in textbook reading.

What
Textbook-Reading
Methods Will Help Me?

Reading a textbook is not like reading a novel or magazine. The task requires preparation and strategies that enable you to understand and remember as much as possible. Notice the materials being used by the student in the picture. How will the student use these materials in the process of reading the textbook? Textbook reading demands more of you as a reader and a thinker. This chapter will help you learn some of the strategies that can help you read your textbooks more efficiently.

You have been reading textbooks for many years. You probably have learned some techniques for mastering difficult subject matter.

Evaluate your own textbook-study methods by circling *A* for "always" or "almost always," *F* for "frequently," or *N* for "no" or "never."

1. I preview parts of the book and chapter before I read.   A   F   N

2. I turn headings into questions.   A   F   N

3. I highlight important information.   A   F   N

4. I write questions in the margin.   A   F   N

5. I test myself using my notes or questions.   A   F   N

6. I copy new vocabulary words and write definitions in my own words.   A   F   N

IN YOUR JOURNAL

Select one or more of the items for which you circled F or N. Rewrite each statement into a goal for improving your textbook reading skills. For example, if you circled N for "I test myself using my notes or questions," you might write a goal like this:

"As I study a chapter, I'll take notes in a way that will allow me to self-test later." As you study this chapter, remember your goal and take steps to achieve it.

EVALUATING YOUR TEXTBOOKS

GROUP ACTIVITY

By now you should be familiar with many textbook features, such as the table of contents, index, and glossary. You should also be familiar with other aspects of your textbooks, such as the pattern of organization, level of difficulty, and style of writing. In your group, discuss the features that you find helpful and those that create problems for you. Use the list in the Data Bank. For the problem areas, brainstorm possible solutions. Write your recommendations in the space provided.

_____

_____

_____

_____

_____

_____

_____

_____

_____

Pre- and Post-Chapter Features
Table of Contents
Preface
Foreword
Introduction
Appendices
Glossary
Subject Index
Author Index
References

Within-Chapter Features
Chapter Objectives
Overview

Beginning Questions
Bold Headings and Subheadings
Visuals: Charts, Graphs
Visuals: Pictures, Photos, Cartoons
Sidebars
Summary
Ending Questions
Assignments, Exercises

Other Features
Pattern of Organization
Style of Writing
Level of Difficulty

STRATEGIES TO READ TEXTBOOKS

IDENTIFYING USEFUL STRATEGIES

No matter how efficiently you read, you're likely to face special challenges when you read textbooks. You've studied strategies for improving your word study skills (Chapter 13); for previewing, recognizing patterns of organization, and adjusting your reading rate (Chapter 14); for identifying main ideas (Chapter 15); and for improving your reading efficiency (Chapter 16).

In this chapter you'll learn additional strategies that will help you meet the challenges of reading textbooks.

DISCOVERY ACTIVITY

- Besides the strategies you've already studied, what other strategies might you need to make efficient use of your textbooks?

_____

_____

_____

_____

_____

PREVIEWING A CHAPTER: A REVIEW

As you learned in Chapter 14, the first step in approaching a textbook chapter is always to preview it. What key points do you recall about previewing a chapter?

_____

_____

_____

_____

_____

_____

_____

Check your answers against the information on pages 283–287.

> Remember these two important guidelines for previewing:
> 1. Recall your previous knowledge about the subject.
> 2. Form questions and ideas about the chapter content based on your reading of the introduction and summary and your preview of headings and illustrations.

LEARNING NEW TERMINOLOGY

Your subject areas and textbooks have their own special terminology. Four strategies can help you with what may sometimes seem like an overwhelming number of new terms.

STRATEGY 1: USE YOUR GLOSSARY

When you preview the book, notice whether the text provides a master glossary. If not, your chapter preview might reveal glossaries for individual chapters. Checking new terms in the glossary is a convenient way to learn the definitions. The only drawback is that you must interrupt your reading to turn to the glossary to check a word. If you don't find the word in the glossary, check the word in a dictionary. Write the definition of the word in the margin near the text where you first saw the word.

STRATEGY 2: WAIT TO LOOK IT UP

Instead of automatically checking the glossary for an unfamiliar term you encounter, keep reading. Perhaps in the next sentence or two you'll find an exact definition for the word or be able to infer the meaning from the context in which the word is used. Of course, if you do not understand what you're reading, you should take the time to check the word in the glossary or in a dictionary.

STRATEGY 3: MAKE CONCEPT CARDS

Those 3- by 5-inch cards are great vocabulary aids. Write the vocabulary word on one side and the definition on the other. An alternative is to use a sheet of paper: write the word on the left side, the definition on the right side, and fold down the middle to test yourself. The cards have three advantages:

Photosynthesis

Ch. 6
p. 121

1. Manufacture of food within plant
2. Chlorophyll present
3. Sunlight activities

1. Cards are portable. They fit in a pocket, backpack, or purse. You can study them when you're standing in those aggravating lines at the financial aid office, registration office, or supermarket.

2. Cards are sortable. You can sort them into piles such as Pile 1—"I know"; Pile 2—"I don't know." Then you can carry around the troublesome ones for extra practice. Just remember to practice the known ones occasionally so you won't forget them.

3. Cards allow you to change the order of the words. Sometimes when you learn words or concepts in a certain order, you know them only in that order. By writing vocabulary words on cards, you can shuffle the cards and check your knowledge of the words in any order.

If you're making cards for several classes, you may want to use color coding. Here are some examples:

- Green for biology
- Yellow for history
- Blue for math
- Pink for English

Hold the cards for one course in a pack, and color the edges all around with a marker. Use a rubber band to keep them together.

STRATEGY 4: SPELL PHONETICALLY WHEN YOU TAKE NOTES

In a lecture, if you hear a term that you don't recognize, approximate the spelling as closely as you can in your notes. Then you have several choices:

- Ask someone else in the class if he or she recognizes the word when you say it.
- Check the text, glossary, and index to see if you can find the word.
- If you're afraid of being embarrassed by your spelling, ask the teaching assistant or instructor.

Vocabulary is one of the big challenges during the freshman year. Just remember that you probably will never again face so many new words all at once. You came to college to become educated, and learning new words is a big part of this process. Use new words as often as you can in your writing.

Strategies for Careful Reading

After you have previewed the material and chosen a way to handle terminology, your next task is to select a strategy for a careful reading of the textbook. Your close-reading strategy should be one that is active. If you just read, you won't remember very much, regardless of your reading rate. Your reading strategy, therefore, must involve writing.

This chapter presents five textbook-reading methods:

1. Outlining
2. Writing marginal questions
3. Highlighting
4. Mapping
5. SQ4R (Survey, Question, Read, Recite, (W)rite, Review)

IN YOUR JOURNAL

How will you use what you've learned about vocabulary building this term? Evaluate the suggestions you've just read. Set specific goals for yourself in a class that has a heavy vocabulary load.

Textbook-Reading Principles

Even before you study various text-reading methods, consider these eight basic principles of text reading.

1. *A textbook is not a novel and cannot be read like one.* Rather than being a story, a textbook is usually a description of theories, concepts, processes, and facts. Your job is to interact in a deep enough way with the information so that you really understand it. You must also put the facts into perspective rather than just memorizing them. Facts are usually presented to prove or support a concept. You must be able to fit the facts into their proper places as supporting data.

2. *Short periods of text reading are more effective than long stretches of study.* Break up your available time into half-hour chunks of intense concentration with ten-minute breaks between the reading periods. Research shows that you will learn more using the spaced readings. In fact, your mind continues processing and learning during the break periods.

3. *Previewing is always the first step of any text-reading method.* The preview is an easy but essential way to set up a mental structure or framework for information you are about to learn. A chapter preview should take you only ten to fifteen minutes and is time well spent. See pages 283–287 if you want to review the steps in previewing.

4. *Each text is different and may require different techniques and levels of effort.* You will generally have less trouble with a text that is:

   - Well written with many special features to help you.

   - Written about a subject you understand and in which you have a good background.

   - Written on a subject that interests you.

   Of course not all textbooks you'll read will be so "friendly." You're likely to have at least one book that will present you with considerable difficulties. Once you have determined the level of "friendliness" of a text, you can better judge the time and effort that reading will require. Allocate your time accordingly. Choose the technique most appropriate for each text, but be willing to try a different technique if the one you initially choose doesn't work.

5. *When reading a textbook, don't just sit there—do something!* Activity stimulates attention, interest, and learning. If you write, talk, or move while you are reading, your mind will stay alert longer, and you'll learn more. Consider some of your learning style preferences (Chapter 5) when you begin to read a textbook. If you have a strong tactile preference, for example, you might pick up your book and walk around. Change positions, stand, kneel in the chair, do simple exercises. If your tactile preference is low, you might study more effectively by sitting quietly and taking notes as you read.

Stay away, however, from that soft, comfortable chair or bed. Don't try to tell yourself that you will learn more if you're comfortable. You may fall asleep instead. The same is true for being too warm and cozy. We learn better when we are a little uncomfortable and a little cooler than is our preference.

6. *Get in the habit of asking questions.* Whether you ask questions aloud or just say them to yourself silently, when you form questions and read to answer them, you remember more. You've already learned to use information from your preview to form questions.

7. *For all but the easiest of your textbooks, select a text-reading method that provides for self-testing.* You are reading your textbook to gain knowledge. You also want to do well on tests to show what you have learned. A textbook study method that enables you to self-test will help ensure that your test performance shows what you really know.

When you are testing yourself, remember that you must not be able to see the answers. This is the reason for the split-page (Cornell) formats you learned in Chapter 11. You'll apply the same principle when you study the marginal questions, modified outlining, and SQ4R methods in the next part of this chapter. The only alternative to using split-page formats to self-test is having someone quiz you when you are not looking at your notes.

8. *When you are no longer productive, quit reading.* If you find yourself reading the same page repeatedly because you remember nothing, stop reading. When you are really tired, go to sleep and set the alarm early. You will accomplish far more in less time when you are refreshed.

- Which of the eight principles have you already applied in your textbook reading?

_____

_____

_____

_____

_____

_____

- Describe your experience with one or more of these principles. What have you found easy? What was difficult?

_____

_____

_____

_____

_____

_____

_____

_____

TEXTBOOK-READING TECHNIQUES

The eight principles you just studied provide the background that will help you improve your approach to reading textbooks. Now you'll study five specific techniques that will sharpen your textbook-reading skills even further. The five techniques are outlining, writing marginal questions, highlighting or underlining, mapping, and SQ4R.

DISCOVERY
ACTIVITY

- You may already have used one of these five techniques. Which of them is familiar to you?

_____

_____

_____

_____

_____

_____

_____

_____

_____

- Describe when and how you used the technique.

_____

_____

_____

_____

OUTLINING A TEXTBOOK CHAPTER

In Chapter 11 you learned how to take notes during a lecture. Taking outline notes from a textbook is much easier. In a lecture you have to write fast enough to keep up with the speaker. Sometimes the information comes so fast that you can't use the outline form.

When you outline a textbook chapter, however, you can work at your speed. Outlining has several advantages as a textbook-reading method:

- Outlining forces you to condense and frame information in your words.

- You have to decide which ideas are main ideas and which are supporting or secondary to enter them in the outline.

- When you're preparing for a test, studying your outline is easier than rereading your textbook.

- What kinds of material have you outlined in the past?

_____

_____

_____

- How did making an outline help you?

_____

_____

_____

- What has been your biggest problem with outlining?

_____

_____

_____

Formal and Informal Outlines

A formal outline has this structure:

I. First main idea

    A. Point supporting first main idea

    B. Second point supporting first main idea

       1. Support for B

          a. Support for 1

          b. Support for 1

       2. Support for B

          a. Support for 2

          b. Support for 2

II. Second main idea

    And so on.

An informal outline is just a simpler version of a formal outline, without the numerals and letters. An informal outline has this structure:

First main idea

    Supporting point for main idea indented

    Supporting point for main idea indented

       Support for point above indented further

          Indent even further if supporting point indented above

Second main idea

    And so on.

Activity A: Making a Formal Outline of This Chapter

With your group, develop a formal outline of this chapter. Record the main ideas and supporting details.

_____

_____

_____

_____

_____

GROUP
ACTIVITY

Activity B: Creating an Informal Outline

In your group, change the formal outline of this chapter to an informal outline.

_____

_____

_____

_____

_____

_____

_____

_____

_____

In your group's opinion, what is lost or gained by using the informal instead of the formal structure?

_____

_____

_____

_____

GROUP
ACTIVITY

Activity C: Choosing Outlining Methods

In your group, discuss the information covered by a chapter in one of your textbooks. Using your judgment and your preview of each chapter, decide which outline method—formal or informal—would be best. Describe your reasons for your choices.

_____

_____

_____

_____

_____

_____

_____

A Horizontal Outline

Most of us have learned to outline in a vertical fashion as shown on page 359. A *horizontal outline* can also be helpful when you want to test yourself on chapter content. You can cover the right side of the paper and try to recall the supporting details for each main idea. You can cover the left side and recall the main ideas supported by the specific details. Here is an example of a horizontal outline.

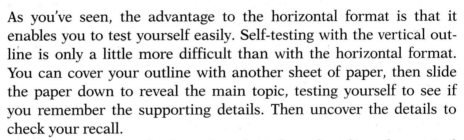

Horizontal/Vertical Self-Testing

As you've seen, the advantage to the horizontal format is that it enables you to test yourself easily. Self-testing with the vertical outline is only a little more difficult than with the horizontal format. You can cover your outline with another sheet of paper, then slide the paper down to reveal the main topic, testing yourself to see if you remember the supporting details. Then uncover the details to check your recall.

Whether you use the formal or the informal outline, the vertical or the horizontal method, you must self-test without being able to see the points you are trying to recall. This feature of self-testing is crucial, as you will see Chapter 19, which includes a description of knowledge illusions.

MARGINAL QUESTIONS

The second textbook-reading method involves writing questions in the margins of your textbooks. Writing in your textbook is a way to make the book work for you. When you review and self-test, your comments are right there on the page to help you. If you're studying a new chapter in a book and you need to review material from a previous chapter, you can quickly look back to your written comments for the important points. The following example shows marginal questions written for a textbook page.

<table>
<tr><td>What are assets and asset returns?</td><td>

ASSETS AND ASSET RETURNS

Assets fall into two broad categories, <u>financial assets and tangible assets.</u> A further subdivision identifies four main asset categories in the economy: <u>money; other interest-bearing assets (credit market instruments or bonds for short); equities, or stocks; and tangible, or real, assets.</u> Table 1 shows the main categories of assets held by U.S. households in 1991. These asset holdings are reported by the Federal Reserve in its publication *Balance Sheets for the US Economy.* We now comment briefly on each category.

</td><td>- 2 categories of assets

- 4 assets categories in the economy</td></tr>

<tr><td>What kinds of assets are money and other deposits?</td><td>

MONEY AND OTHER DEPOSITS

The money stock proper consists of <u>assets that can be immediately used for making payments. Money includes currency (notes and coins) and also deposits on which checks can be written.</u> At the end of 1991, currency and checkable deposits (a measure of money called <u>M</u>1) amounted to $898 billion. A broader measure of money (called <u>M</u>2) includes in addition to checkable deposits at banks also <u>money market mutual funds and other deposits such as savings accounts.</u> This measure of money was $3,440 billion at the end of 1991.

From the 1930s until the mid-1970s, no interest was paid on checkable deposits. During that period, people held checkable deposits purely for the convenience. Now interest is paid on checkable deposits. Thus they are now held partly because <u>they pay interest</u> but also because <u>they offer a convenient way of making payments.</u>

</td><td>- meaning of "money"

- other kinds of money

- advantages of checkable deposits</td></tr>
</table>

(From Dornbusch, Rudiger, and Fisher, Stanley, *Macroeconomics*, 6th Edition. Copyright © 1994, 1990, 1987, 1984, 1981, 1978, by McGraw-Hill, Inc. Reprinted with permission of McGraw-Hill, Inc.)

Before you write marginal questions for any chapter, you should have already previewed the chapter. Then follow these five steps:

1. Read or reread the introduction to the chapter—the part between the chapter title and the first boldfaced heading.

2. Read the first boldfaced heading. Convert it into a question. For example, "ASSETS AND ASSET RETURNS" becomes "WHAT ARE ASSETS AND ASSET RETURNS?" Write this question in the margin as close to the heading as you can.

3. Read the section between this heading and the next, remembering the question and looking for the answer. Do not highlight or underline while you read.

4. After you complete the section, ask yourself the question in the margin. Then highlight or underline the answer. Insert numbers if you need to (for example, four stages of psychological development). If there are terms and definitions in the section, write the terms in the margin, and highlight the definitions.

5. Repeat the procedure with the remaining headings and sections until you've completed the chapter.

GROUP
ACTIVITY

Activity D: Writing Marginal Questions for This Chapter

Reread part of this chapter, writing marginal questions and underlining or highlighting answers. In your group, discuss the marginal questions members wrote. Then discuss the marginal questions method, comparing it with the outlining method.

• What problems did you have with each method?

_____

_____

_____

_____

_____

_____

_____

_____

_____

_____

- What did you like about each method?

  _____
  _____
  _____
  _____
  _____
  _____
  _____
  _____
  _____
  _____
  _____

- Which method was your preference?

  _____
  _____
  _____

- Which method works best for the chapter part you chose? Explain your choice.

  _____
  _____
  _____
  _____
  _____
  _____
  _____
  _____
  _____
  _____
  _____

Studying Marginal Questions

You can easily adapt marginal questions to help you self-test. Simply cover the textbook page with a piece of paper, leaving the questions exposed. Answer each question as completely as you can, then uncover the page and see if you are correct. Continue through the chapter, covering one section at a time.

HIGHLIGHTING/UNDERLINING

Highlighting or underlining is a very popular method of textbook study. By itself, however, highlighting brings only mediocre results. To benefit from highlighting, combine it with writing questions in the margins. The three steps in highlighting are:

1. Don't highlight during your first reading. Read part of a chapter between headings. Then reread the part, and highlight the important points during your rereading. Highlight main ideas, key words and terminology, and important details.

2. When in doubt, highlight less. Don't make your text look like a child's coloring book. If that much material looks important, your background in the subject is probably weak, and you need a more effective strategy than highlighting.

3. Write a question for self-testing in the margin opposite each important section you have highlighted. In other words, the highlighted portion is the answer to the question you write.

What caused the deterioration of England's relations with Spain?

DETERIORATION OF RELATIONS WITH SPAIN

A series of events led inexorably to war between England and Spain, despite the sincerest desires on the part of both Philip II and Elizabeth to avoid a direct confrontation. Following Don John's demonstration of Spain's seapower at the famous naval battle of Lepanto in 1571, <u>England signed a mutual defense pact with France</u>. Also in the 1570s, <u>Elizabeth's famous seamen,</u> John Hawkins (1532-1595) and Sir Francis Drake (1545?-1596), <u>began to prey regularly on Spanish shipping in the Americas</u>. Drake's circumnavigation of the globe between 1577 and 1580 was one in a series of dramatic

5 main causes

①

②

③

demonstrations of English ascendancy on the high seas. In 1585, <u>Elizabeth signed a treaty that committed English soldiers to the Netherlands</u>. These events made a tinderbox of English-Spanish relations. The spark that finally touched it off was <u>Elizabeth's reluctant execution of Mary, Queen of Scots</u> (1542-1587) on February 18, 1587, for complicity in a plot to assassinate Elizabeth. Philip II ordered his Armada to make ready.

④

⑤

(Paul Weinberger, from *The Heritage of World Civilization*)

MAPPING: A VISUAL ALTERNATIVE

When you used the learning styles checklists in Chapter 5, you may have found that you are primarily a visual learner. **Mapping** is a method for recording information from textbooks that often appeals to visual learners. A map shows visually the relationship between main ideas and supporting facts or details.

Maps can take many regular geometric arrangements, including a wheel and spokes (see Figure 1 below) and a set of boxes (see Figure 2 on page 367). On page 368 you will find a variety of other geometric arrangements that you can use to create concept maps.

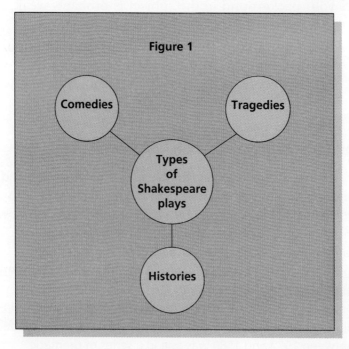

Figure 1

Comedies

Tragedies

Types of Shakespeare plays

Histories

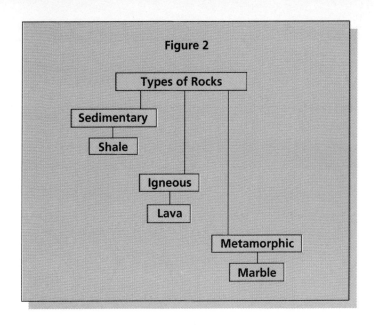

Figure 2

Types of Rocks

Sedimentary

Shale

Igneous

Lava

Metamorphic

Marble

An animal husbandry student once mapped a chapter onto the shape of a steer (see Figure 3), placing some concepts on ribs and legs. He said that when he closed his eyes during a test, he could see the steer in his mind and read the facts written there.

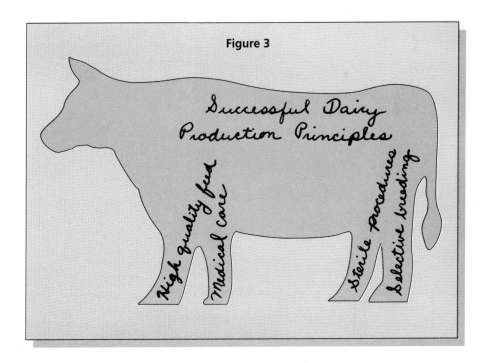

Figure 3

Successful Dairy Production Principles

High quality feed

Medical care

Sterile procedures

Selective breeding

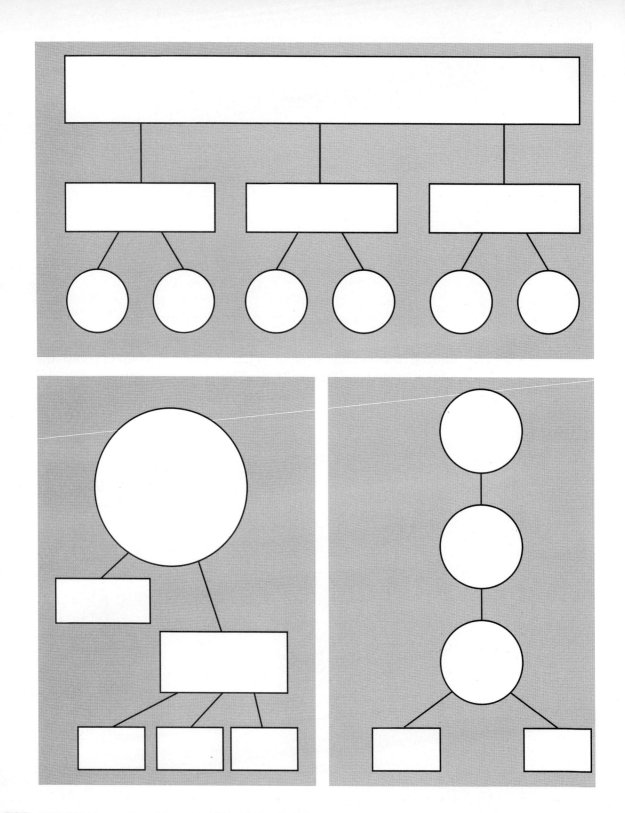

Perhaps you don't relate so strongly to steers, but another shape for a concept map might be helpful for you to memorize. You can adapt that form as a base when you make a map. Here are some tips for mapping:

- Keep your maps simple; avoid crowding your map with too many words.
- Make several maps for a chapter.
- Use your maps to self-test by closing your eyes and visualizing the image, recalling the words you've written on the map.

PORTFOLIO

Assignment 1:
Making a Visual Map

Create a visual map of the main ideas and supporting information presented on pages 365–366 of this chapter. Use one of the shapes shown in Figures 1 through 4, or design your own. Save this assignment in your portfolio.

SQ4R

The SQ4R method is a six-step method of textbook study.

Use SQ4R for difficult textbooks. This method takes more effort than other methods, but the results are worthwhile. SQ4R requires more effort early in the term, allowing you to use your notes to self-test later in the term. The first time, SQ4R may take several hours

for a long and technical chapter. Each time you use this method, however it will take less time. Once you have taken SQ4R notes from a chapter, you will not need to open that chapter again. Most students read a chapter once when it's assigned, again before a test, and maybe a third time before a final examination. Those separate reading times add up to more time than you would spend doing SQ4R once.

How to Use the SQ4R Method

Some of the six SQ4R methods may already be familiar to you.

1. *Survey (preview).* Preview the chapter content just as you learned to do in Chapter 14 of this book. Read the headings, introductory paragraphs, and the summary. Notice illustrations and read the captions. Form questions in your mind as you preview. This preview should take ten to fifteen minutes.

2. *Question.* As you did with the marginal questions method, turn each heading into a question, but don't write your questions in the book. Fold a piece of paper in half lengthwise, and write the question on the left side of the fold. Use only one side of the paper. When you fold your notes for self-testing, the paper will wear out if you fold it both ways. Also, some students like to overlap their SQ4R notes for a whole chapter, leaving only the question side showing. Then, they review by quickly going down the sheets to see if they can answer the questions.

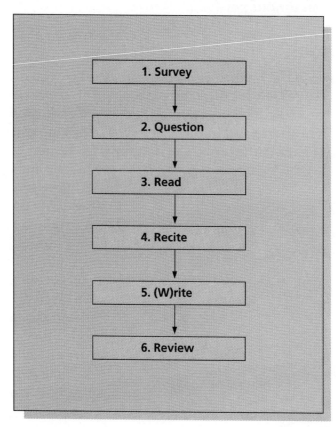

1. Survey

2. Question

3. Read

4. Recite

5. (W)rite

6. Review

If the section between headings is really long and seems to have information other than that answering the heading question, you may need to write extra questions. Some textbook authors are better than others about sticking only to the subject of the heading. Write the extra questions under the main question for the section.

3. *Read.* Read to answer your question, but read only from one question heading to the next heading. Don't go any further.

4. *Recite.* Say your question to yourself, aloud if possible. If not, say it in your mind. Then briefly, answer the question from what you just read in that section. Recite the answer *in your words*.

5. *Write.* Briefly write the answer you just recited on the right side of the paper, opposite the question. The answer must be in your words. Sample questions and answers are shown in the example below.

Q	A
Why is the fourteenth century of interest today?	Similar to events today: chaos, disintegrat. of standards, plague (AIDS)
What were the feudal classes?	Peasants, nobles, clergy, merchants (few)
What duty did the peasant owe his lord (noble)?	Provide food. Take care of animals, farming.
What duty did the noble owe the peasants?	Protect from raids of other lords or foreign forces.
Did the compact work well?	Not really. Lords didn't always defend.
What were sumptuory laws?	How fancy your dress could be: colors, ornaments, styles.
Were the sump. laws enforced?	Rarely

Now repeat Steps 2 through 5 until you have finished the chapter or half of the chapter. Since SQ4R requires intense effort, you should divide a chapter into halves or thirds, depending on the length. Spread your note taking over several days.

6. *Review.* Fold the paper in half along the vertical fold line. Ask yourself the questions, and try to answer them. When the time comes to prepare for a test, repeat this review step. When you miss a question during your self-testing, circle the question on the left, so that you can review those problem points intensely.

Handling Vocabulary Terms With SQ4R

Write the vocabulary word on the left side of your paper. If the word has a very precise, technical meaning, you'll need to memorize that meaning word for word. Copy the meaning on the right side of your paper. If the word has a less precise meaning, put that meaning in your words, and write your definition on the right side of your paper, as shown in the example below. When you're ready to self-test, you can test for vocabulary as well as for main ideas.

Phonology	Study of the sounds of words
Phoneme	Single unit of sound (p)
Morphology	Study of physical form or shape of words
Morpheme	Smallest meaning-bearing unit of language (con)
Grapheme	Single written symbol of language, often a letter (s)
Syntax	The way words are ordered and structured to create meaning
Semantics	The meanings of words

Here is another example of self-test questions. Notice that the student has not yet completed Step 5 of the SQ4R method, writing answers to the questions.

Is spelling ability
related to:
    intelligence?
    reading ability?
    reading method?
2 spelling routes or
methods:
    lexicon (def)
    VOI (def)
What types of words are
spelled phonologically?

Are there good spellers
who read poorly?

Are there good readers
who spell poorly?

What is the correlation
between reading ability
and spelling
ability?

How are VOI images
formed?

When are VOI images
formed?

What reading style
may effect spelling?
    logographic (def)

How is spelling
disability related to
learning disability?

What three things can
improve the spelling of
good readers—poor
spellers?

PORTFOLIO

Assignment 2:
Using SQ4R

Use SQ4R to study the sample chapter in the appendix of this book, or use SQ4R to study a chapter in another textbook. Before you start, fold four or five pages in half vertically, and label them at the top with the subject and chapter number. When you've completed the method, use the "Reviewing Your SQ4R Notes" checklist on page 375 to see how you did. Save the completed checklist in your portfolio.

GROUP
ACTIVITY

Activity E : Comparing Methods

With your group, make a chart comparing and contrasting the five textbook-reading methods you studied in this chapter: outlining, writing marginal questions, highlighting, mapping, and SQ4R. On your chart, indicate the materials each method requires and how each method helps you identify main ideas and supporting details.

- Name the steps you took:

S _____ Q _____ R _____

R _____ R _____ R _____

- Is your paper folded in half vertically?
- Is your paper labeled with subject and chapter number?
- Is there a question for each heading?
- Are the answers expressed in your words?
- Did you need to write extra questions?
- Did you define all vocabulary terms?
- What did you do during the Recite step?

_____

_____

_____

_____

_____

- Describe what you did during the Review step.

_____

_____

_____

_____

_____

Wrapping It Up

Summary

- Four strategies for learning new terminology are:
    1. Use the glossary.
    2. Wait to look up a word, checking context for clues to the meaning of the word.
    3. Make concept cards.
    4. Spell phonetically when you take notes.

- Five methods of textbook study are:
    1. Outlining
    2. Writing marginal questions
    3. Highlighting
    4. Mapping
    5. Using SQ4R

- Eight textbook-reading principles are:
    1. Recognize that textbooks require special reading strategies.
    2. Study in short periods with a break in between.
    3. Preview.
    4. Recognize that textbooks are different from each other and require different reading techniques.
    5. Become an active reader.
    6. Ask questions.
    7. Select a textbook-reading method that provides for self-testing.
    8. Stop when your studying is no longer productive.

THINKING IT OVER

- What material from this chapter did you find most helpful?

  _____

  _____

  _____

  _____

  _____

- How will you apply the information and ideas in this chapter to studying your textbooks?

  _____

  _____

  _____

  _____

  _____

  _____

  _____

IN YOUR
JOURNAL

What steps have you made toward achieving the goal you set at the beginning of this chapter? Describe the steps. Describe your most recent experience with one or more of the textbook-study methods. Which ones seem to work best with your learning style and the amount of effort you are willing to spend? What problems do you foresee? What advantages do you foresee?

18

CRITICAL THINKING AND READING

OBJECTIVES:

- To identify instances of critical thinking in daily life.

- To identify steps in the critical thinking process.

- To apply steps in the critical thinking process.

- To investigate and apply the critical reading process.

How Do I Analyze
Something?

What is the person in the picture doing that suggests he might be thinking carefully and using judgment? What thoughts might be going through his head?

One of the meanings of the word *critical* is "characterized by careful analysis and judgment." Critical thinking and critical reading are skills that you apply often in daily life. These skills involve analyzing and making judgments—not necessarily to find fault, but to understand fully so that you can describe what you think and what you've read. Critical thinking and critical reading are especially important to success in college. This chapter will help you recognize the importance of these skills and how to improve your use of critical thinking and critical reading.

Critical thinking involves taking something apart, seeing how it is put together, and making a judgment about it. Your judgment may take one of the following forms:

- Evaluation
- Inference
- Interpretation

In **evaluating**, you decide whether something is good, bad, worth buying, worth seeing, and so on. For example, the person in the picture on pages 378-379 was evaluating the quality of two packages of meat.

In **inferring**, you obtain a meaning that is not specifically stated in the information or objects you analyzed. You have studied the process of inferring an unstated main idea in Chapter 15.

In **interpreting** something, you express—in your own way—the meaning you've gained from your analysis. You might interpret a poem, for example, by describing in your words the meaning you find in the poem.

- Describe a situation in your life or work in which you have analyzed something and made a judgment based on your analysis. In your description tell whether you made an evaluation, an inference, or an interpretation.

_____

_____

_____

_____

_____

_____

_____

_____

• Suppose you are about to make an important decision. List sources from which you might obtain information to analyze before you make your decision.

_____

_____

_____

_____

_____

_____

_____

_____

_____

_____

_____

_____

_____

_____

_____

_____

_____

_____

_____

IN YOUR
JOURNAL

Based on what you know about critical thinking and critical reading at this point, describe how you would like to improve your skills in one or both of these areas. For example, you might want to improve your ability to analyze new information. Set a goal, and describe steps you will take to achieve it.

WHAT MAKES THINKING "CRITICAL"?

GROUP ACTIVITY

What do people actually do when they think critically? Discuss ideas within your group. Use the two scenarios in the Data Bank as a source for discussion. Both shoppers are new to the supermarket in which they're shopping. Which shopper uses critical thinking? Explain your choice.

_____

_____

_____

_____

_____

Catherine, in a rush as usual, burst into the supermarket and grabbed a cart. Beginning at the center of aisle 6, she raced down the aisle looking for detergent, but all she saw were cookies and other baked goods. At aisle 7 she grabbed two boxes of cereal and a loaf of bread off the shelves. In aisle 8, still looking for detergent, she spotted a new kind of frozen food dinner she'd advertised on television and bought six of them. In aisle 9 she couldn't resist stopping to look at the latest magazines. Soon she was engrossed in reading an article about a famous movie star who was involved in a messy divorce. Suddenly Catherine realized she was late and dashed to the checkout counter. As she carried the groceries out to her car, she had the nagging feeling she'd forgotten something.

Entering the supermarket, Paula pulled her shopping list out of her wallet and grabbed a cart. The first item on her list was toilet paper. She was pressed for time, but she decided to take a minute to go past each aisle and read the aisle directories to find out how the store arranged its products. She made a quick mental note of the arrangement and then headed for aisle 2, which contained household cleaning supplies and paper products. Checking her list, she saw that she also needed bathroom cleanser so she picked up a bottle after locating the toilet paper. The other items on her list were in aisles 7, 8, and 9 so she skipped the aisles in between. At aisle 7 she picked out a new cereal her daughter wanted. At the checkout counter she gave the cashier coupons that saved her 10 percent on some of her purchases.

CRITICAL THINKING AND READING

CRITICAL THINKING

Critical thinking is a logical process that involves the following steps:

Analyzing	Judging	Making Decisions
looking at something closely, examining it in detail, to understand as much as possible	forming an idea or opinion about something; making an evaluation, inference, or interpretation	making a choice or taking action based on your understanding

DISCOVERY
ACTIVITY

- Think about something you did recently in which you used critical thinking. Describe what you analyzed, what judgment you made, and what decision you made.

_____

_____

_____

_____

_____

ANALYZING

Analyzing is the first step of critical thinking. If you kept a record of your thoughts, you'd probably find yourself analyzing situations and printed material all the time. When you analyze, you ask questions such as these:

- What am I seeing (reading, hearing, touching, smelling)?

- What's going on?

- What's the problem?
- What do I already know?
- What else do I want to know?
- What do I need to know to make a decision?

The questions help you analyze information as you think and read. Together, your questions and answers lead you to a thorough understanding of what you're analyzing.

Suppose the community where your school is located is divided over the issue of gun control. Some people feel that licenses for guns should be harder to get; others feel that the right to bear arms should not be restricted. You're interested in the issue and want to know more about it. You analyze the situation. You might talk to other students and to people in the community. You read the local papers to find the arguments on both sides of the issue. All of this information becomes part of your analysis and helps you understand the issue of gun control.

JUDGING

In the next step of critical thinking, you form a judgment based on your analysis. Your judgment is the way you interpret the information you acquire during your analysis. You might decide, for example, that some of the violence committed in the community is due to the prevalence of guns. On the other hand, you might decide that ownership of guns has kept crimes such as theft from increasing. You might decide that the mayor, who loves hunting, has helped popularize the idea of owning a gun.

When you're ready to express your judgment in speaking or in writing, you can support your judgment by citing evidence you gathered during your analysis. Suppose, for example, your judgment is that handgun sales should be restricted. You might cite police reports of gun sales and statistics that show a rise in injuries caused by guns.

MAKING DECISIONS

In the third step of critical thinking, you make a decision. Based on your analysis and judgment, you may decide to act or you may decide not to act. If your judgment leads you to agree with those opposed to limiting gun sales, you might decide to join a rally to protest legislation that would curb handgun sales. On the other hand, if your judgment leads you to agree with those who want stricter gun controls, you might decide to sign a petition, donate money, or do volunteer work to help this group.

Your decisions can take you in any direction. If you're really using critical thinking, however, you don't make a decision until after you've analyzed and formed a judgment.

Critical thinking and problem solving go hand in hand. In *Problem Solving and Comprehension* (1982), Whimbey and Lochhead studied how good problem solvers work—especially how their *thinking* works—by having problem solvers think aloud while working problems. These studies were done mainly with academic problem solving, such as predicting the next number in a series or identifying differences among a set of items.

Whimbey and Lochhead's findings can also certainly apply to the process of solving nonacademic problems. The researchers identified ineffective and effective problem solving attitudes and strategies, shown below.

Ineffective Attitudes and Strategies
- Thinking that you are either able to solve a problem right away or you aren't.
- Thinking that if you don't see the solution immediately, you should give up.
- Going through a problem too quickly, which results in misunderstanding the problem.
- Making premature conclusions.

Effective Attitudes and Strategies
- Believing that problems can be solved.
- Having patience when problems seem confusing.
- Compulsively checking and rechecking for accuracy.
- Reading a problem several times.
- Breaking problems into steps and taking one step at a time.
- Avoiding guessing.
- Approaching problems actively, including thinking aloud, creating mental pictures, writing ideas, making diagrams, counting on fingers.
- Using other strategies when one approach isn't working.

Whimbey and Lochhead's study suggests that successful critical thinkers develop skills that improve their thinking. The aim of critical readers is to make their thinking clear and accurate. To achieve this aim, critical thinkers practice the steps of critical thinking and use self-discipline to apply and improve their skills.

GROUP
ACTIVITY

Assignment 1:
Using the Critical Thinking Process

Identify a current problem or issue at your college or in your community. Apply the critical thinking process to this problem or issue. Brainstorm what you and other group members already know. Investigate additional information that you want or need to know. Express your judgments in writing, supporting your judgments with evidence from your analysis. Finally, make decisions about what you can do regarding the problem or issue. Describe your decision in writing. For example, you might develop a possible solution to the problem. Save this assignment in your portfolio.

PORTFOLIO

CRITICAL READING

Much of the reading you've done has been critical reading. Critical reading is a process that shares the analyzing and evaluating (or judging) steps with critical thinking. Some experts consider critical reading—along with listening, writing, and speaking critically—to be part of the general critical thinking process. In critical reading, you actively enter into a silent dialogue with the writer of the material you're reading. The writer's words form one part of the dialogue; your questions and ideas form the other part.

• Describe a recent situation in which you believe you used critical reading. Tell what you read, what steps you took as you read, and how you used what you learned.

DISCOVERY
ACTIVITY

_____

_____

_____

ANALYZING AND EVALUATING

In critical reading, the analyzing step includes two parts: literal and interpretive. The word *literal* comes from the Latin word *littera*, meaning "letter," as in letters of the alphabet. You understand the literal meaning of a selection when you make sense of the words the writer has used. The interpretive part of critical reading involves reading the selection from the point of view of the writer and recognizing such elements as the writer's purpose and tone. Using these two critical reading steps—analyzing and evaluating—you get a thorough understanding of written material. The following checklist will help you achieve this understanding.

Checklist for Analyzing and Evaluating in Critical Reading

Analyzing. This step has two parts:

Literal—In this part, you ask these questions:
- What is the subject of the selection?
- Is the selection fiction or nonfiction?
- What are the main ideas?
- What facts does the writer present?
- What opinions does the writer express?
- What important details support the main ideas?

Interpretive—In this part, you ask these questions:
- What is the writer's purpose?
- What is the writer's tone—the way in which the writer expresses feelings toward the audience and the writer's attitude toward a subject?
- What denotative meanings does the writer use—meanings that are direct and specific?
- What connotative meanings does the writer use—meanings that are suggested or implied but not directly stated?

Evaluating. In this step, you ask these questions:
- What are the writer's credentials?
- What bias—an unbalanced way of looking at something—does the writer express?
- How well does the writer support the main ideas?
- How accurate is the information in the selection?
- What overall impression does the selection make on me?

Here is a model for applying critical reading as you read a selection. The questions are the same as those on the critical reading checklist on page 387. Only a few questions appear in the model, as

LITERAL

What is the subject of the selection? The selection is about poetry. The writer tells how Francis Scott Key wrote a poem that became the words to the national anthem of the United States.

Is the selection fiction or nonfiction? The selection looks like nonfiction. I know from my high school history that Francis Scott Key was a real person. He wrote the words that became lyrics for the national anthem.

What are the main ideas? Key wrote a poem, but other people just thought of the poem as words to a song. Americans, in general, don't understand or accept poetry.

OK. Let's start by admitting I'm a poet, and the purity of poetry is close to my heart. When Francis Scott Key wrote it, it was probably on the back of one of the envelopes Americans are famed for writing on. Key is out on a British ship watching the Stars and Stripes withstand one hell of a shelling. As dawn breaks he notices Old Glory is, tried but true, still standing. Hey, Key says to himself, this ought to be noted. Out whips the envelope, feather, penpoint, inkwell. "Oh, say, can you see...," starting one of the best-known poems in history. He finally is brought to shore and probably shows it to a friend, who immediately says, "You oughta take this thing to the Government. We need a good motto." I'm sure Key tried to explain it's not a motto, it's a poem. "We're Americans," his friend says, "we don't get into poetry. But hey! I know a good old English drinking song that if you change a line here and there it'll go to." Poor Key. There was probably some reluctance about changing his lines, but if it was good for the country...well, who is one poet to stand in the way? I mean, does anybody

INTERPRETIVE

What is the writer's purpose? The writer's purpose is to tell the story of a historical event in an amusing way. She is describing the event as if the event happened today.

a way to get you started. You'll find another model with more questions on pages 412–413, after you've studied additional aspects of critical reading.

remember Robert Frost's poem for Jack Kennedy? And that happened in our lifetime! So Key's poem and the British drinking song were combined to make our national anthem. One reason it's so poorly sung, by the way, is you need to hoist a few before trying for those high notes, but that's definitely another discussion.

(Nikki Giovanni, from *Sacred Cows—and Other Edibles*)

EVALUATING

What are the writer's credentials? In the first sentence the writer says she is a poet. I've heard of her before, but I haven't read any of her poems.

What overall impression does the selection make on me? I enjoyed the selection; the writing was interesting. I especially liked the way the writer used today's language to make something historical come alive.

What is the writer's tone? The writer has a humorous attitude toward the subject. She writes in a kind of "street-wise" or "hip" style.

As you can see from the critical reading model on pages 388-389, you do not get a full understanding of a selection until you have used the literal and interpretive parts of critical reading and applied the evaluative step.

Your college courses often require you to analyze and evaluate written selections. You might be asked, for example, to compare the theories or ideas of two or more writers. This task requires more than just reading the words the writers have written. To make a successful comparison, you need to apply critical reading steps—to dig beneath the surface and explore the hidden meanings as well as the apparent meanings. You apply your prior knowledge in the process, and you may even do additional research to enrich your understanding. As with textbook reading, you enter into a dialogue with the writer, asking questions and forming opinions about what you are reading.

- What assignments have you received recently that required you to do critical reading?

_____

_____

_____

- What critical reading steps are you most confident about?

_____

_____

_____

- What critical reading steps are you least confident about?

_____

_____

_____

Literal Meaning

Knowing the literal meaning means identifying the subject, whether the selection is fiction or nonfiction, the main ideas, the writer's use of fact or opinion, and the details that support the main ideas.

To understand the literal meaning of a selection, ask yourself several questions.

• *What is the subject of the selection?* You will find the answer to this question as you preview the selection. Remember that your preview includes reading the first and last paragraphs, reading the headings and turning them into questions, reading the first sentence of each paragraph, looking at the illustrations, and reading the summary (if there is one). As you preview, you will draw conclusions about the subject of the selection. Depending on the length of the selection, you may have the answer to "What is this piece of writing about?" in a matter of seconds.

Note Taking for Critical Reading

Taking notes is an important aid to critical reading. Use the outlining method described on page 358. If you are comparing two or more selections, make separate outlines for each selection.

• *Is the selection fiction or nonfiction?* You'll be able to answer this question fairly quickly, too. Use what you already know about the differences between fiction and nonfiction. Knowing whether the selection is fiction or nonfiction will help you know what to expect as you continue reading the selection. For example, if you know the selection is fiction, look for descriptions of a setting, plot, characters, and so on. If you know the selection is nonfiction, look for main ideas and supporting details.

• What are some differences you would expect to see between a textbook chapter and a short story?

_____

_____

_____

_____

_____

_____

_____

In this scene from *Death of a Salesman,* the main character, Willy Loman, is confronted by his two sons.

• *What are the main ideas?* You have already learned how to determine stated and unstated main ideas in Chapter 15. The main ideas are the important statements the writer makes about the subject. They are the key to understanding what the selection is about. Main ideas are the cornerstones of nonfiction writing. But occasionally you will find that a fiction selection also has unstated main ideas. When you read a fiction selection and you ask yourself, "What is the writer really saying about the subject?," the answer is usually a main idea. For example, Arthur Miller's classic play *Death of a Salesman* makes a statement about the difficulty of growing old in a modern, competitive society in which a person's identity is viewed as synonymous with his or her occupation.

• Think about a fiction selection you've read recently. What ideas was the writer expressing?

_____

_____

• *What facts does the writer present? What opinions does the writer express?* To answer these questions, you must understand the differences between fact and opinion. A **fact** is a statement that can be proved true. The proof may take the form of a demonstration, as when someone drops two objects to the floor to prove the statement that "In the absence of friction, all bodies, large or small, heavy or light, fall to the earth with the same acceleration." The proof may be that a great many people agree that a statement is true. For example, most people would agree that 3 P.M. is 60 minutes later than 2 P.M. and that rain feels wet.

An **opinion** is a statement of belief or judgment that cannot be shown to be true in the same way as a fact. An opinion expresses the belief or judgment of one person, such as when someone says "I think that's a silly idea." Many people may share the opinion, but that does not make the statement a fact. The reason, in this case, is that the word *silly* has no meaning on which everyone would agree. Unlike *wet*, which can be demonstrated and which people can agree on, *silly* means different things to different people.

When you're trying to determine whether a statement is fact or opinion, ask yourself questions such as:

- How can this statement be proved or verified?
- What does this word or phrase mean?
- Would most people agree with this statement?
- Does my own experience support this statement?
- Are there experts who agree or disagree?

One type of opinion is a theory.

Theories: Special Types of Opinions

Sometimes an expert in a certain field, such as a scientist, will make a statement that describes how something happens. Here are two examples:

1. People who are hypnotized behave in a way that they think hypnotized people should behave. They are really playing a role and are not in a different state of consciousness at all.

2. $KE = hf - hf_0$

   (This equation expresses Einstein's theory of photoelectric effect.)

Statements such as these are called **hypotheses** and are often based on experiments and observations. When a hypothesis has been tested and seems to hold true for many cases, the statement is called a **theory**. A theory, however, is still essentially an opinion. A theory is rarely proved 100 percent true. Other theories can explain the same thing a different way. For example, some psychologists believe that when a person is hypnotized, the person goes into a deep state of altered consciousness. This is a different theory than the one stated above. Some theories are eventually disproved and are either replaced by other theories or simply abandoned.

Activity A: Telling Fact From Opinion

With your group, discuss whether each of the following statements is a fact or an opinion, then circle *F* or *O*. If you decide the statement is a fact, describe how it might be proved true. If you decide the statement is an opinion, describe why it could not be proved true.

1. Inflation is bad for the economy.   F   O

_____

_____

_____

2. Cheese is a high-fat food.   F   O

_____

_____

_____

3. Vegetarians think eating meat is immoral.   F   O

_____

_____

_____

4. The eggs of reptiles are inedible.   F   O

_____

_____

_____

5. There are more Cambodians than Thais
in the United States today.   F   O

_____

_____

_____

6. Carbon is an element.   F   O

_____

_____

_____

7. Men cannot give birth.   F   O

_____

_____

8. Women live longer than men, on average.   F   O

_____

_____

9. Women are superior to men.   F   O

_____

_____

_____

10. A red sky in the morning predicts storms.   F   O

_____

_____

_____

GROUP
ACTIVITY

Activity B: Difficulties With Facts and Opinions

One student expressed the problem she had with telling fact from opinion this way: "If I like coffee and dislike tea, that is a fact. If I say that coffee is better-tasting than tea, that's an opinion. It seems to me that they're the same thing." Do you have similar kinds of problems telling fact from opinion? Describe the problems you have. Provide examples from your reading and from your notes. As a group, identify ways to solve some of these problems. List the group's solutions.

_____

_____

_____

_____

_____

• *What important details support the main ideas?* This is another question you'll ask to understand the literal meaning of a selection. Most nonfiction works consist of main ideas and supporting details; however, not every supporting detail is of the same importance. To decide whether a detail is important, compare the detail to the main idea. As you read, keep the main idea in mind, and ask yourself "How does this detail add to the main idea?" You may find that one detail simply supports another detail and is not that important to the main idea. Making an outline can help you interpret levels of importance. Here's an example of a paragraph with a main idea and several supporting details.

There were many Negro officials on the Underground Railroad. Jane Lewis of New Lebanon, Ohio, rowed fugitives regularly across the Ohio River. John Parker, who purchased himself for two thousand dollars, was in league with John Rankin and other white workers on the Railroad. Josiah Henson, born a slave, escaped with his wife and two children to Canada, learned to read and write, and returned south often to assist slaves in their escape. Once he went to Kentucky by a circuitous route through New York, Pennsylvania, and Ohio in order to avoid suspicion. He took 30 refugees out of Kentucky and led them to Toledo within a period of two weeks. Elijah Anderson has been called the general superintendent of the Underground Railroad in northwestern Ohio. From 1850 until his death seven years later in the Kentucky state prison, he worked arduously in behalf of fugitive slaves. By 1855 he had led more than 1,000 to freedom. John Mason, himself a fugitive slave from Kentucky, was one of the most astute conductors. According to William Mitchell, a Negro missionary in Canada, Mason brought 265 slaves to his home in the course of nineteen months. On one occasion he was captured and sold back into slavery, but again he made good his escape. In all he delivered about 1,300 slaves into free territory.

(From Franklin, J. and Moss, A. FROM SLAVERY TO FREEDOM: A HISTORY OF NEGRO AMERICANS, 6th Edition. Copyright © 1988, 1980, 1974, 1956, 1947 by McGraw-Hill, Inc. Reprinted with permission of McGraw-Hill, Inc.)

GROUP
ACTIVITY

Activity C: Identifying Important Supporting Details

In your group, discuss the selection about the Underground Railroad. Identify the main idea. Then discuss each supporting detail. Decide which details are important to the main idea and which support other details. Outline the paragraph.

_____

_____

_____

_____

_____

_____

_____

_____

_____

_____

_____

Interpretive Meaning

When you interpret a selection, you use your experience and knowledge to "read between the lines" to understand hidden information. This hidden—or suggested—information includes the writer's purpose, tone, and use of denotative and connotative meanings.

• *What is the writer's purpose?* A writer writes to tell a story, to describe a person, place or event, to persuade, or to inform. Some pieces of writing serve more than one purpose. A magazine article, for example, may be persuasive as well as informative. Your knowledge and experience will help you identify the writer's purpose. As you read, ask yourself "Why did the writer write this?" and "What am I getting out of this as I read it?" You'll pick up clues from the subject and from the words and phrases the writer uses. To identify the writer's purpose, you may need to read a selection more than once.

GROUP
ACTIVITY

Activity D: Identify the Writer's Purpose

Discuss with your group each selection that follows. Circle the subject and underline the main idea. Then discuss the writer's purpose. What evidence in the selections do you find for your conclusions about the writer's purpose?

Language is the highest and most amazing achievement of the symbolistic human mind. The power it bestows is almost inestimable, for without it anything properly called "thought" is impossible. The birth of language is the dawn of humanity. The line between man and beast—between the highest ape and the lowest savage— is the language line. Whether the primitive Neanderthal man was anthropoid or human depends less on his cranial capacity, his upright posture, or even his use of tools and fire, than on one issue we shall probably never be able to settle— whether or not he spoke.

(Susanne K. Langer, from "The Lord of Creation")

Questions

1. What is the subject of the selection?

_____

2. What is the main idea of the selection?

_____

_____

_____

3. What is the writer's purpose? What evidence supports your interpretation?

_____

_____

. . . I worked as hard on my dancing as I did on my driving to the hoop because I didn't want my dancing to *look* like my driving to the hoop. My teacher was an older boy named Johnny Berg, who didn't know the capital of the United States but knew the two major fast dances. Anyone, even Weird Harold, could do a slow dance: you just leaned on the girl and moved as if you were leaving a crowded bus; but you needed either Astaire or Johnny to teach you the Bop and the Strand.

In the Bop, you circled your stationary partner, trying to stay in orbit and not float off into space like a loose comet; and in the Strand, you strolled across the floor with your partner in your arms and then suddenly flung her away from you, took a few steps, and met her again, as if she were a well-thrown yo-yo. If properly done, the Strand was charming. If improperly done, it looked as if you had disposed of the girl as if she were a frilly banana peel.

My study of these dances took a new direction on the day that my father came home and found Johnny Berg embracing me in our living room.

"Bill," he solemnly said, "can you *explain* this?"

"Oh, sure," I replied. "First you walk a few steps and then you fling him away."

The following day, I changed teachers and began taking lessons with my mother. She was a natural for the Strand. She often felt inclined to throw me away.

(Bill Cosby, from *Love and Marriage*)

Questions

1. What is the subject of the selection?

_____

2. What is the main idea of the selection?

_____

_____

3. What is the writer's purpose? What evidence supports your interpretation?

_____

_____

One of our serious problems in this country is that the public has been conditioned to think when the government does something for them for no charge, it is free. It is not free. We are never going to solve the deficit and debt problem unless everybody in the government from President Clinton on down stops perpetuating the fiction that anything the government does for us is free.

Nothing is free. If you write your suggestions to the U.S. government, Vice President Gore says mark the envelope "reinventing government." And Cabinet members are being asked to dedicate five to ten of their best employees to opening, reading and dealing with this mail. So it's not just the cost of the postage stamp, is it? It's also the cost of the five or ten employees in each department.

Let's say you call the Pentagon's toll-free number. They've had this so-called hot line there since 1979. Last year it received about 15,000 calls at a cost of $1.2 million. That works out to a $80 a call.

(From Charles Osgood, "No Free Lunch," *Reader's Digest*)

Questions

1. What is the subject of the selection?

_____

_____

_____

2. What is the main idea of the selection?

_____

_____

_____

3. What is the writer's purpose? What evidence supports your interpretation?

_____

_____

_____

_____

• *What is the writer's tone?* As a listener, you get meaning from both the speaker's tone and the speaker's words. You can tell when a person is speaking playfully, with serious concern or sadness, with anger, with sarcasm, with indifference, or with a neutral attitude toward the subject. Within your group, try saying the following sentences aloud in as many tones of voice as you can.

> To be, or not to be: that is the question. . . .
>
> (William Shakespeare, from *Hamlet*)

Just as you get meaning from a speaker's tone of voice, you can also get meaning from a writer's tone—the attitude the writer takes toward a subject. A skillful writer can indicate feelings such as playfulness, sympathy, anger, authority, sarcasm, or neutrality toward a subject.

GROUP
ACTIVITY

Activity E: Identifying an Author's Tone

In your group, discuss the writer's tone in each of the following selections. Identify the words and phrases that helped you identify the author's tone.

1. "[marriage awareness training] . . . is an opportunity for the marine to get counsel on one of the single most important decisions of his/her life and benefit from the advice of seasoned marines who have experienced military family life." (Editorial, *The New York Times*, August 13, 1993)

   _____

   _____

   _____

2. "I am standing in my mother's kitchen, waiting for the business of baking cookies to resume. Our Saturday morning ritual had been rudely interrupted by my older sister, who has chosen this cozy family moment to renew her threat to become a nun." (Melissa Anderson Lowry, "Doubting the Reality of God," from Amber Coverdale Sumrall and Patrice Vecchione, *Catholic Girls*)

   _____

   _____

   _____

   _____

3. "There is definitely too much anger in the world today. Pick up almost any newspaper, and the odds are you'll get ink smeared all over your hands. We use a special kind of easy-smear ink, because we know how much it irritates you." (Dave Barry, from "It's A Mad, Mad, Mad, Mad World" from *Dave Barry Talks Back*)

_____

_____

4. "Growing numbers of children are the victims of kidnappers, molesters, and murderers. How are we to protect our children—and our children's children—from this onslaught of violence? We must have renewed moral leadership from the President, and most of all from parents everywhere. Stop the violence." (Carole Christophsen, Letter to the Editor, *U.S. Review*, September 14, 1993)

_____

_____

_____

5. "In addition to preserving life-giving species and protecting millions of living creatures, rain forests regulate the flow of water on earth. Like a gigantic sponge, they soak up water from heavy tropical rainfalls, then release it slowly and steadily, providing a constant supply for people and farmers living hundreds, even thousands of miles away." (Diane MacEachern, *Save Our Planet*)

_____

_____

_____

6. "The man's dead words fell like bricks around the auditorium and too many settled in my belly. Constrained by hard-learned manners I couldn't look behind me, but to my left and right the proud graduating class of 1940 had dropped their heads. Every girl in my row had found something new to do with her handkerchief. Some folded the tiny squares into loveknots, some into triangles, but most were wadding them, pressing them flat on their yellow laps." (Maya Angelou, *I Know Why the Caged Bird Sings*)

_____

_____

_____

- *What denotative and connotative meanings does the writer use?* Would you rather have an instructor *analyze* your term paper or *criticize* it? Would you rather face a *problem* or a *mess?*

The choices show how words have different levels and shades of meaning. Each word has a specific meaning—its **denotative** meaning. Many words also have a **connotative** meaning which consists of ideas and images that have become associated with a word. Some connotations are positive, or favorable; some are negative, or unfavorable.

- What connotations—favorable or unfavorable—do the words *analyze, criticize, problem,* and *mess* have?

_____

_____

_____

_____

Writers choose their words according to their purpose and audience. By choosing words carefully, a writer can describe a person, situation, or event in a way that gives readers a favorable or an unfavorable impression. Here are two examples.

A. The senators haggled endlessly over the proposed budget. They hurled insults and threats at each other like hand grenades.

B. The senators debated the proposed budget for several hours. Their exchanges on the subject were often heated.

Questions

1. Which description creates a favorable view of the senators?

_____

_____

2. Which words help to create the favorable impression?

_____

_____

3. Which description creates an unfavorable view of the senators?

_____

_____

4 Which words help to create the unfavorable impression?

_____

_____

Evaluating 〰〰〰〰〰〰〰〰〰〰〰〰〰〰〰

In the second step of the critical-reading process, you evaluate or judge what you are reading. Several questions guide your evaluation:

- What are the writer's credentials?
- What bias does the writer express?
- How well does the writer support the main ideas?
- How accurate is the information in the selection?
- What overall impression does the selection make on me?

Evaluating what you've read completes your understanding of the material. In the first step of critical reading, analyzing, you identify the main ideas and details, the writer's purpose, and so on. In the evaluating step, you form your own opinion about the material and presentation.

- *What are the writer's credentials?* **Credentials** are the titles, labels, and accomplishments indicating that someone knows what he or she is talking or writing about. Credentials you are likely to see with writers' names in your textbooks are *Ph.D.* or *Dr.* to indicate advanced academic degrees. You may also see words such as *Professor* or *Associate Professor* to indicate the person's position at a college or university.

Knowing the writer's credentials helps you evaluate how reliable or accurate the material probably is. Your textbooks are written by authorities in different subject areas and generally have a high degree of accuracy and reliability. Textbooks are often reviewed before publication by other authorities in the same field.

Textbook reading, however, is only part of the reading you'll do in college. You will often read other nonfiction books on specific subjects as well as articles from magazines, journals, and newspapers. For your nontextbook reading, ask yourself "Who wrote this?" and then make a judgment about the writer's credentials.

Notice whether the writer has any of the following:

- An advanced degree in the subject on which the book is written.
- A position at a respected organization (college, university, hospital, laboratory, newspaper, and so on).
- An identity as a writer of other books on the same or similar subjects.
- An endorsement or recommendation by someone well known in the subject area.

Information about a writer's credentials is often included in the foreword, introduction, or preface to the book. The information may also appear on the back cover of a paperback book or on the paper jacket of a hardcover book.

Writers' credentials can be important when you are comparing the ideas of two or more writers on the same subject. Your judgment about the value of a writer's work may be supported by the kind of credentials the person has. Here are three examples of writer's credentials.

Leonard W. Levy is Andrew W. Mellon All-Claremont Professor of Humanities and Chairman of the Graduate Faculty of History at the Claremont Graduate School. He is the author of the Pulitzer Prize-winning *Origins of the Fifth Amendment* (reissued by Macmillan) and of *The Establishment Clause* (Macmillan). Levy is also Editor in Chief of the four-volume *Encyclopedia of the American Constitution* (Macmillan).

Dennis J. Mahoney received his Ph.D. in constitutional history and government from the Claremont Graduate School, and teaches political science at California State University, San Bernardino. He is Assistant Editor of the *Encyclopedia of the American Constitution.*

Ellen Goodman writes a column for the *Boston Globe* that is syndicated by the Washington Post Writers Group and appears in nearly 300 newspapers across the country. She was awarded a Pulitzer Prize for her columns in 1980. A frequent commentator on both television and radio, Goodman is the author of *Turning Points* and *Close to Home.*

Evaluating a Publication

Just as some writers have biases, some publications also have a point of view that is strongly advocated in the materials they publish. When you are evaluating a selection, consider the source—not only who wrote the material but also who published it. For example, *The National Review* and *The New Republic* have the same initials, but the resemblance ends there. *The New Republic* is a strongly liberal publication while *The National Review* is strongly conservative. Political ideology, however, is only one of many possible biases a publication may have.

PORTFOLIO

Assignment 2:
Comparing Two Sources

Choose a current events topic and read articles by two different writers on the same topic. Identify the writers' credentials and the publications for which they are writing. Describe the major differences you find between the authors' views. Save this assignment in your portfolio.

• *What bias does the writer express?* The ability to recognize bias and slanted writing is an important part of your evaluation of a writer's work. **Bias** is a one-sided, unbalanced way of looking at something. You have probably encountered biased writing in television and newspaper advertisements, in political campaign speeches, and in essays and editorials.

• Describe a specific example of bias you've read or heard.

DISCOVERY
ACTIVITY

_____

_____

_____

_____

_____

Slanted writing is very similar to biased writing, and the two terms are often used interchangeably. In **slanted writing**, the writer presents information that supports a specific point of view but omits information that supports an alternate or opposing point of view. Here's an example.

> We are providing programs that entertain and educate children—programs that also attract sponsors. Our surveys indicate that children enjoy action-packed programs, and that's what we give them. We see no connection at all between so-called violence in television programs and an increase in violence among the general population. On the contrary, when people are watching television, they are passive, peaceful, and nonviolent.

Questions

1. What slant does the argument have?

_____

_____

_____

_____

2. What opposing viewpoint does the argument ignore?

_____

_____

_____

_____

_____

_____

_____

_____

_____

Biased and slanted writing often include **loaded words and phrases**, words that carry a highly charged emotional meaning. Loaded words usually have strong negative or positive connotations. In the following selection, the loaded words have been underscored.

In the coming mayoral election, the voter is given a real choice for the first time in the 10 years that the Democratic <u>machine</u> has <u>dictated</u> the choice of mayor. Cranshaw, the Republican nominee, was a <u>decorated Marine</u> during the Vietnam War. He has a <u>distinguished</u> military record and <u>strong</u> business background. His <u>steadfast</u> adherence to the <u>principles of free enterprise</u> as well as his <u>strong support of family values</u> place him head and shoulders above the other candidates in this race. His opponent, a <u>conscientious objector</u>, espouses all the tenets of the <u>pop-psych</u> and <u>New Age drivel</u> that we have come to expect from the <u>bankrupt</u> ranks of the <u>special-interest party</u>.

Among some of the mud-slinging political campaigns of recent years, the example would not be considered exaggerated. You'll find similar examples in advertisements for various products—from toothpaste to automobiles to breakfast cereal. Recognize the power that such words can have to sway your opinion. When you see or hear such words, you can be sure the writer is presenting information to you with the intent of getting you to agree with his or her bias.

Be Aware of Your Bias

In evaluating a writer's bias, take into account that as a reader, you, too, have biases. Your biases can affect how you evaluate a piece of writing. When you agree with a writer, you have a harder time detecting the shared bias. Detecting bias is easier when you disagree with it.

Bias is hard to avoid. If you detect bias in a selection, don't dismiss the writer or publication. Consider the bias as part of your overall evaluation of the material. Be sure you have a good literal and interpretive understanding of what the author has written. In your evaluation, point out both the strengths and the weaknesses you see. Here's a brief example of an evaluation:

> The writer P. J. O'Rourke has written on the topic of television-watching. His main idea is that there is nothing worthwhile to watch on television, and, therefore, people should spend time doing other things. O'Rourke's humorous treatment of the subject, however, indicates that he is not altogether serious about giving up television-watching.
>
> O'Rourke was formerly the editor of the National Lampoon, a magazine devoted to humor. He correctly identifies some of the problems with television programs—too much violence and sex, for example. However, his light-hearted approach to the subject seems biased in favor of an anything-goes attitude about television. The essay did not take into consideration the possibly serious effects of television on viewers.

• *How well does the writer support the main ideas?* Look for evidence that the writer has made a logical, convincing argument. An argument is logical and convincing if its main ideas are well supported by examples, facts, descriptive details, or anecdotes. A writer has done a good job if he or she has convinced you to agree with the main ideas of the selection.

GROUP
ACTIVITY

Activity G: Evaluating Supporting Information

Read and discuss the following selection. Evaluate how well the writer supports the two main ideas.

> Throughout time, women narrators have written for many reasons: Emily Bronte wrote to prove the revolutionary nature of passion; Virginia Woolf wrote to exorcise her terror of madness and death; Joan Didion writes to discover what and how she thinks; Clarice Lispector discovered in her writing a reason to love and be loved. In my case, writing is simultaneously a constructive and a destructive urge, a possibility for growth and change. I write to build myself word by word, to banish my terror of silence; I write as a speaking, human mask. With respect to words, I have much for which to be grateful. Words have allowed me to forge for myself a unique identity, one that owes its existence only to my efforts. For this reason, I place more trust in the words I use than perhaps I ever did in my natural mother. When all else fails, when life becomes an absurd theater, I know words are there, ready to return my confidence to me. This need to reconstruct which moves me to write is closely tied to my need for love: I write so as to reinvent myself, to convince myself that what I love will endure.

(Rosario Ferre, from "Out of the Frying Pan," from *Lives on the Line: The Testimony of Contemporary Latin American Authors*)

_____

_____

_____

_____

_____

_____

_____

_____

_____

_____

- *How accurate is the information in the selection?* How do you, the reader, know when something is not accurate? The best test is to consult another source. Read material from another expert on the same subject or look up specific details in a reference book such as an encyclopedia or almanac. Don't forget your knowledge. You may already know something about a subject you're reading about. Trust your judgment. If you read something you think is not true, recall your experience and observations. Compare what you've read against what you recall. If your recollection is not strong, look up the information in another source.

PORTFOLIO

Assignment 3:
Eyewitness

Attend a political rally, sports event, concert, or other public event in your community that is likely to be covered in the local newspaper. Carefully observe the event and the people. Then notice how the event is written about in the local paper. Compare your recollection of the details of the event to the published report.

- *What overall impression does the selection make on me?* This is your judgment call. Did you like or dislike the selection? Did the writer do a good job or a poor job? In answering these questions, you sum up what you have learned after reading and rereading a selection (perhaps three or more times). The best way to express your judgment is to cite the evidence you found in the selection. Here are some questions your evaluation should answer.
- Did you find bias? What are some examples?
- Did the writer know what he or she was writing about? What evidence can you cite?
- Did the writer successfully support the main points? What are some examples?
- Is the information accurate? Cite examples.

The model on pages 388-389 showed the two steps of the critical reading process. That model had only a few of the questions you might ask if you were doing a thorough analysis and evaluation of a selection. The model that follows on pages 412-413 shows more questions that you can ask now that you've explored additional aspects of the critical reading process. (The additional questions are preceded by a star.) Compare the two models. Notice how each level of critical reading adds to your understanding of the selection.

LITERAL

What is the subject of the selection? (Same answer as on page 388.)

Is the selection fiction or nonfiction? (Same answer as on page 388.)

What are the main ideas? (Same answer as on page 388.)

★ *What important details support the main idea?* To support the main ideas, the writer describes how Key wrote the poem. She quotes a "friend" of Key's who misunderstands the purpose of the poem, and she describes an event from the inauguration of John F. Kennedy—an event from recent history.

★ *What facts does the writer present? What opinions does the writer express?* I see facts such as the events that led Key to write the poem; I see the names of other people I know were real—Robert Frost and Jack Kennedy. (She means John F. Kennedy.) I see an opinion about why the national anthem is poorly sung.

OK Let's start by admitting I'm a poet, and the purity of poetry is close to my heart. When Francis Scott Key wrote it, it was probably on the back of one of the envelopes Americans are famed for writing on. Key is out on a British ship watching the Stars and Stripes withstand one hell of a shelling. As dawn breaks he notices Old Glory is, tried but true, still standing. Hey, Key says to himself, this ought to be noted. Out whips the envelope, feather, penpoint, inkwell. "Oh, say, can you see...," starting one of the best-known poems in history. He finally is brought to shore and probably shows it to a friend, who immediately says, "You oughta take this thing to the Government. We need a good motto." I'm sure Key tried to explain it's not a motto, it's a poem. "We're Americans," his friend says, "we don't get into poetry. But hey! I know a good old English drinking song that if you change a line here and there it'll go to." Poor Key. There was probably some reluctance about changing his lines, but if it was good for the country . . . well, who is one poet to stand in the way? I mean, does anybody

INTERPRETIVE

What is the writer's purpose? (Same answer as on page 388.)

What is the writer's tone? (Same answer as on page 388.)

★ *What denotative and connotative meanings does the writer use?* The way the writer uses clichés gives a modern twist to an old story. For example, she talks about Key's writing "on the back of one of the envelopes Americans are famed for writing on" and the phrase "tried but true." These examples add humor to the selection.

The writer implies that Key was like a modern poet who is not taken seriously by people who "don't get into poetry."

remember Robert Frost's poem for Jack Kennedy? And that happened in our lifetime! So Key's poem and the British drinking song were combined to make our national anthem. One reason it's so poorly sung, by the way, is you need to hoist a few before trying for those high notes, but that's definitely another discussion.

(Nikki Giovanni, from *Sacred Cows—and Other Edibles*)

★ *How accurate is the information in the selection?* Some of the information about Key is accurate. He wrote a poem about a battle in the American Revolution. Robert Frost wrote a poem for John F. Kennedy when Kennedy became president. The writer also makes up some things, such as the conversation between Key and his friend.

What overall impression does the selection make on me? (Same answer as on page 389.)

EVALUATING

What are the writer's credentials? (Same answer as on page 389.)

★ *What bias does the writer express?* The writer admits that she's a poet and that "poetry is close to my heart," so I believe she is biased toward poetry. I think her bias accounts for a kind of bitter tone when she implies that Americans "don't get into poetry" and when she asks if anybody remembers Robert Frost's poem for Kennedy.

★ *How well does the writer support the main ideas?* The writer supports her points very well by using examples and logical arguments.

WRAPPING IT UP

SUMMARY

- The critical thinking process involves analyzing, judging, and making decisions.
- When you analyze, you ask questions such as "What am I seeing (reading, hearing, touching, smelling)?," "What's the problem?," "What do I already know?," and "What else do I want to know?"
- The critical reading process involves analyzing and evaluating a selection. When you analyze a selection, you recognize the literal and interpretive meanings of the selection. When you evaluate a selection, you decide how well the writer has done his or her job.

THINKING IT OVER

- What material from this chapter did you find most valuable?

  _____

  _____

- How will you apply the information and ideas in this chapter to your thinking and reading?

  _____

  _____

IN YOUR JOURNAL

Do you feel more confident in your abilities to read and think critically after completing this chapter? Evaluate your progress toward the goal you set for yourself early in this chapter.

Improving Your Memory and Test-Taking Skills

Your mind is one of your most valuable assets. Knowing how your mind works can benefit you as you take charge of your life. Your mind is continuously engaged in **cognitive processes**—activities that shape what you know, what you remember, and how well you remember. Remembering specific information is important in many areas of your life. In your college work, remembering specific information is the key to taking tests successfully. The two chapters in this section will help you understand the basic processes your mind uses and how to develop successful test-taking strategies. Chapter 19 describes how your mind stores and retrieves information. This chapter also presents strategies for strengthening your knowledge as you study. Finally, Chapter 19 describes several strategies for improving your memory. Chapter 20 identifies the three basic types of tests and provides strategies for doing well on these tests.

19

IMPROVING YOUR MEMORY

OBJECTIVES:

- To describe a model of how the human brain processes information.

- To identify ways to improve memory.

What Strategies Help My Memory?

We rely on computers to accomplish many tasks, from answering telephones to controlling space vehicles. Like the human brain, a computer can take in information, store it, and produce it on demand. In the picture, how does the computer help the employee perform the job?

Like the people in the picture, your senses are continually bombarded by all kinds of information including sights, voices, random noises, smells, and tastes. Your brain codes and stores most of this information as memory. Storage is the process by which new information becomes a part of human or computer memory. Retrieval is the process by which stored information is recalled for use. In this chapter you will learn how these two processes can help improve your memory.

GETTING STARTED

Like many people, you may take your memory for granted—at least until you forget something. As a student, however, you should appreciate your ability to take in new information and remember it.

- What experience have you had recently that helped you value your ability to process and remember new information?

  _____

  _____

  _____

  _____

- When have you been surprised by your ability to remember—or to forget—information? Describe the circumstances and the result of your remembering or forgetting.

  _____

  _____

  _____

  _____

- What techniques have you learned to help you understand and remember new information?

  _____

  _____

  _____

  _____

IN YOUR
JOURNAL

In your journal, set a personal goal related to taking in, storing, or retrieving information. For example, you might want to improve your ability to remember dates in history or the names of new people you meet.

MEMORY WISH LIST

GROUP ACTIVITY

Many people express dissatisfaction with their memory. Discuss reasons for this in your group. Are group members dissatisfied with their ability to remember? Discuss and list the kinds of information that group members most want to remember. In your discussion, consider the kinds of information listed in the Data Bank. Describe techniques group members have used effectively in learning each kind of information.

_____

_____

_____

_____

_____

_____

_____

_____

_____

_____

_____

- Math formulas.
- Names of new acquaintances.
- Governmental systems.
- Statistics.
- Phone numbers and ZIP Codes.
- Vocabulary.
- Chemical elements in the periodic table.
- How to perform cardiopulmonary resuscitation (CPR).

DATA BANK

- Errands or tasks you need to do on a regular basis.
- Procedures on your job.
- Geological time periods.
- Commands for a word processing program.
- Dates, names, and facts from history.
- Birthdays, anniversaries, or other special occasions.

FROM INFORMATION TO MEMORY

STORAGE AND RETRIEVAL PRINCIPLES

You may not think of your mind as operating like a computer, but in many ways it does. After all, your brain—the human brain—is the model for the way a computer operates. One of the main functions of your brain is a process called **cognition**, which means the mental faculty or process by which knowledge is acquired.

DISCOVERY ACTIVITY

- Describe some similarities and differences between the human brain and a computer.

_____

_____

_____

_____

_____

In the past thirty years psychologists who study cognition have discovered much about how and why individuals remember and forget information. Cognitive psychologists and other researchers have developed a theory about the way the human brain handles information. This **information processing theory** includes concepts that are sometimes used to explain the basic operation of computers. The information processing theory has three main components: encoding, storage, and retrieval.

ENCODING INFORMATION

When you learn information, the information is **encoded**—translated into a code for storage in your brain. The code allows your brain to store the information in a specific place. For example, when you received your social security number, you probably said to yourself that it was an important number. Unconsciously you encoded the number in a way that grouped it with other important numbers such as your telephone number, your address, and so on, for frequent use.

Activity A: Remembering Numbers

In learning your social security number, you consciously thought of a way to make the series of numbers easy to remember. Describe the strategy you used. Describe strategies you've used for remembering other numbers.

_____

_____

_____

_____

_____

_____

_____

_____

STORING INFORMATION

No one really knows how information is stored in the brain. Scientists have several theories that attempt to explain the process, but none of the theories has been proven. Scientists do agree, however, that your brain stores certain kinds of information for a very long time even if you can't recall the information.

Your brain stores information that you've learned very well. Such information includes names of important people and places in your life, skills such as swimming and riding a bicycle, and items you've repeated often, such as song lyrics. Your brain also stores information that has a deep effect on you, such as pleasant and unpleasant experiences.

Even though you don't know how your brain stores information, you can create a visual image of your brain that will help you recall information. Some people visualize their brain as a house with several rooms; some see their brain as a forest with many paths through it; some see their brain as a big filing cabinet with many drawers.

Activity B: Visualizing Your Brain

What visual representation of your brain seems most useful to you? Describe at least six specific kinds of information that are well stored in your brain. Why do you remember these particular items so clearly?

_____

_____

_____

_____

_____

RETRIEVING INFORMATION

When you remember something, you retrieve information from storage in your memory. If the information has been well encoded, you'll remember it more easily than information that has not been well-encoded. Information becomes well-encoded in the following ways:

- You identify the information as important.
- You attach a strong emotional meaning to the information.
- You study the information thoroughly.
- You use the information often.

Activity C: On the Tip of Your Tongue

What information is well-encoded in your brain? Name several examples of information that you retrieve without any effort. How did this information become so well-encoded?

_____

_____

_____

_____

_____

_____

PORTFOLIO

Assignment 1:
Comparing Memories

Time also plays an important role in your ability to remember information. You may not remember some of the things you learned or experienced long ago as well as things you learned or experienced more recently. Discuss an early experience from your life with a family member or longtime friend who was part of the experience. Compare your recollections of the event. Describe details that you each recall. Save this assignment in your portfolio.

IMPROVING YOUR MEMORY

Improving your memory is one of the easiest and most valuable things you can do. All you need is the desire to improve your memory and a willingness to devote time and attention to it. The following four steps can help you improve your memory:

1. Pay attention and intend to remember.

2. Organize and sort information.

3. Involve your senses.

4. Use specific memory-enhancing techniques.

STEP 1. PAY ATTENTION AND INTEND TO REMEMBER

You remember what you intend to remember. The trick is that sometimes you think you want to remember something when in fact you don't want to remember. For example, have you ever forgotten the name of someone you were just introduced to? Even though you smiled and said hello, you may have said or thought to yourself

subconsciously, "I'm probably never going to see this person again in my life" *or* "I hope I never see this person again in my life." You therefore had no intention of remembering the person's name, and that name vanished from your memory.

To remember something, you need to pay attention to it and say to yourself, "I'm going to learn this." For example, if you were just starting a new job and your boss introduced you to someone you'd be working with closely, you'd be likely to remember the person's name.

- What reason would you have for paying attention to this person's name?

  _____

  _____

  _____

  _____

- What might you do to remember the name?

  _____

  _____

  _____

  _____

Activity D: Remembering Names

By this time in the term, you probably know the names of most of your classmates. In your group, have members take a **pseudonym**— a false name. Introduce yourselves, giving your pseudonyms. Then take turns trying to remember each false name. Discuss the methods you used to remember the names. Describe some of the methods.

_____

_____

_____

_____

_____

_____

_____

Forgetting Occurs Quickly

Even with the best of intentions, you will forget new information quickly unless you do something to prevent the loss. You forget most of what you will ever forget about a piece of information within twenty-four hours after you've encoded the information.

Within a day after learning new information, therefore, you need to use a technique to remember as much as you can of the new information. The techniques described in this chapter will help you.

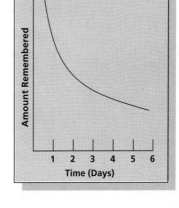

STEP 2. ORGANIZE AND SORT

Psychological studies show that the human brain can immediately retain only seven clumps of random information such as letters and numbers. Each clump can be one or several items, but you cannot retain more than seven of these at a time.

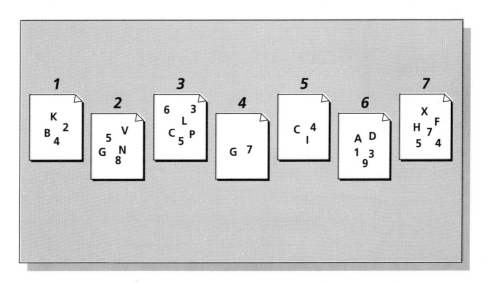

This research suggests that to remember new information, you need to organize or sort the information in a way that makes remembering easy. Suppose, for example, that you had to memorize the following list of animals:

gorilla	gibbon	whale	orangutan	baboon	trout
dolphin	mandrill	shark	chimpanzee	manatee	grouper

You might organize or sort the information into categories:

APES	MONKEYS	FISH	AQUATIC MAMMALS
gorilla	mandrill	grouper	manatee
gibbon	baboon	shark	whale
chimpanzee		trout	dolphin
orangutan			

You now have four clumps of information. Each clump has fewer than seven items in it, so this organization makes the information easy to memorize.

GROUP
ACTIVITY

Activity E: Organizing and Sorting

In your group, brainstorm other ways to organize information you want to remember. For example, how would you memorize the names of the states or capital cities of the United States? Describe the methods you decide on.

_____

_____

_____

_____

_____

_____

_____

_____

_____

_____

_____

_____

Activity F: Organizing and Memorizing Words

Organize the following words and memorize them. In your group, test yourselves on your memorization of the words. Describe the methods you used to memorize the words.

millimeter	metric ton	centimeter	pound
meter	liter	kilogram	Fahrenheit
gallon	kilometer	Celsius	milligram

_____

_____

_____

_____

STEP 3. INVOLVE YOUR SENSES

Each of your five senses is like a powerful antenna picking up information from your environment. You can improve your ability to memorize information by using multiple senses to help you encode the information. To memorize a new word, for example, write, spell, and pronounce the word. In doing so you've used three senses: sight, sound, and touch. The other two senses, smell and taste, might be hard to engage, but you might try to link the word to a familiar smell or taste. Suppose, for example, you are learning the word *gerrymander*. You might link this word to another word that engages your sense of smell or taste, such as *garlic* or *ginger*.

Activity G: Multisensory Memorizing

Use your multiple senses to memorize the following words:

emulate   castigate   avarice   lucid   garrulous   taut

In your group, test each other on your memory of the words. Describe the senses you used and how you used them.

_____

_____

_____

_____

STEP 4. USE SPECIFIC MEMORY-ENHANCING TECHNIQUES

You can improve your ability to memorize information by following the steps you've learned so far: paying attention and intending to memorize the material you want to memorize; ordering and sorting the information; and involving your senses in the process of memorizing information. In addition, several specific techniques can help you easily and reliably memorize new information. These memory-enhancing techniques are:

- Using mnemonics
- Using association
- Using loci
- Rehearsing
- Putting information in your own words
- Using advance organizers

Using Mnemonics

The word **mnemonics** means aiding the memory. Mnemonics refers to tricks people use to help themselves remember new material. Mnemonics usually involves words. For example, to remember the colors of the spectrum of the rainbow in sequence (red, orange, yellow, green, blue, indigo, and violet), take the first letter of each word and form a name: ROY G. BIV. The name can be complete nonsense, as long as it's easy to remember. Another well-known mnemonic is one for remembering the names of the Great Lakes: HOMES (Huron, Ontario, Michigan, Erie, and Superior).

A mnemonic can also be a string of words, such as this one for remembering the names of the cranial nerves of the skull: On Old Olympus' Towering Top, a French and German Vault, Skip, and Hop. The sentence does not make sense; it doesn't have to. The first letter of each capitalized word is a signal for remembering the olfactory, optic, oculomotor, trochlear, trigeminal, abducens, facial, auditory, glossopharyngeal, vagus, spinal accessory, and hypoglossal nerves.

GROUP
ACTIVITY

Activity H: Inventing Mnemonics

In your group, brainstorm mnemonics for lists of names that you need to memorize for your courses. Use either single-word mnemonics or a string of words. Write the mnemonics and what they stand for.

_____

_____

_____

_____

_____

Association

Association is a technique you can use to remember people's names or new vocabulary words. In this technique, you associate or link the new information to something familiar or easily remembered. Suppose you meet a woman named Vera Albright, for example, and you want to remember her name. You might begin by recognizing that her first name means "truth." Or you might think of a vehicle veering or leaning in one direction. For the last name, you might associate her with being very bright (as in "all bright"), or you might associate her last name with sunshine or another bright light.

A similar technique is called the keyword technique. In this technique, you pair a new, unfamiliar word with a familiar word. The familiar word should be similar in sound to the new word, perhaps even rhyming with the new word. The **keyword** technique is helpful when you're learning vocabulary in a foreign language or difficult vocabulary words in a college course. For example, if you were learning the names of certain rocks in a geology course, you might pair the names with familiar words such as the following:

Sedimentary Rock	Possible Keywords
dolomite	termite, dull, dole
chert	church, cherry, shirt, hurt
gypsum	gypsy, gyp
diatomite	diameter, die, dynamite

GROUP
ACTIVITY

Activity I: Association

Identify several new vocabulary words that you need to memorize for a course. With your group, choose key words for the items, and memorize the pairs of words. Test each other on your memory of the terms. Write the word pairs.

_____

_____

_____

_____

_____

_____

_____

_____

Using Loci

The Latin word *loci* means "places." This memory technique involves associating items to be memorized with specific places. A common association is with the rooms of a house. To memorize a speech, for example, you might associate the introduction of the speech with the front door or other entry way of a house. You might associate the main part of the speech with the living room and the end of the speech with the kitchen or back door. By imagining yourself walking through the house, you can recall the key ideas of the speech that you've associated with each part of the house.

You can also use this technique to remember specific items, such as a list of names of people, grocery items, and towns or cities. You can associate each item with a specific place in the house, including furniture, pictures on the wall, carpets, and so on. For example, suppose you wanted to remember this list of grocery items: milk, soap, cereal, potatoes, lettuce, pickles. You might imagine a carton of milk sitting on a table in the hallway, a bar of soap hanging by a string from the doorway to the living room, a box of cereal on the living room TV, a bag of potatoes in your favorite chair, and so on. The strangest associations are the often the easiest to remember.

Activity J: Using Loci

Use the memory technique of loci to memorize the following events in United States history. Try to memorize them in correct chronological sequence.

1607	Jamestown founded
1754-1763	French and Indian War
1804-1806	Lewis and Clark Expedition
1831	Nat Turner's Rebellion
1832	Black Hawk's War
1859	John Brown's Raid
1862	Emancipation Proclamation issued

In your group, test each other on your memorization of these items.

• Describe some of the associations you used.

_____

_____

_____

_____

Rehearsing

When you review your textbook or lecture notes, you are **rehearsing** the information. When you talk to a friend about what you have learned, you are also rehearsing the information. In fact, whenever you bring the new information into your consciousness—including moments when you just casually think about part of the information—you are rehearsing. You can make your rehearsal active—and more productive—by reciting new information and writing comments and questions concerning the new material.

Your brain needs only a few seconds or minutes to encode new information. To remember the information for a long period of time, however, you need to rehearse often, giving the brain opportunities to consolidate and regroup the information. When you rehearse, therefore, do so in brief periods of time—15- to 25-minute segments, for example, with a 5-minute break in between. This strategy is called **spaced rehearsal.** Spaced rehearsal is much more effective than **massed rehearsal**—long stretches of study without a break.

PORTFOLIO

Assignment 2:
How Have You Learned Something?

Describe new information you have recently learned. Describe the strategy you used to learn the material. Did you rehearse? Did you use spaced rehearsal or massed rehearsal? Tell how well you think you learned the material and what strategy worked best for you. Save this assignment in your portfolio.

Using Your Words

Rehearsing your text or lecture notes by reviewing the information and rephrasing it in your words is another memory enhancement technique that yields good results. To express new information in your words requires that you really know the new information. If you are unable to think of a way to state a new idea, you probably haven't fully learned it. Ask questions and restudy the information you are unsure of. Express the information in your words by speaking aloud or by writing.

GROUP ACTIVITY

Activity J: Putting New Information in Your Words

Apply the oral rehearsing technique to the following paragraph from a psychology textbook. Take several minutes to read and silently rehearse the information. You might want to take notes or underline definitions and main ideas. Then, with a partner from your group, rehearse the paragraph content aloud in your words. You and your partner can collaborate, each rehearsing a part of the paragraph, or you can rehearse the entire paragraph alone while your partner checks what you say against the printed paragraph to make sure you remembered the key points.

The Site of Sound and Balance: The Ear
While many of us think only of the **outer ear** when we consider hearing, this part is little more than a reverse mega-

(From Feldman, R., *Essentials of Understanding Psychology*.
Copyright © 1989 by McGraw-Hill, Inc.
Reprinted by permission of McGraw-Hill, Inc.)

phone, designed to collect and bring sounds into the internal portions of the ear. **Sound** is the movement of air molecules brought about by the vibration of an object. Sounds travel through the air in wave patterns similar to those made by a stone thrown into a still pond.

Once sounds, which arrive in the form of wave vibrations, have been herded into the **auditory canal**, a tubelike passage, they reach the **eardrum**. The eardrum is aptly named because it operates like a miniature drum, vibrating when sound waves hit it. The louder the sound, the more it vibrates. These vibrations are then transmitted into the **middle ear**, a tiny chamber containing just three bones, called, because of their shapes, the **hammer**, the **anvil**, and the **stirrup**. These bones have one function: to transmit vibrations to the **oval window**, a thin membrane leading to the inner ear. Because of their shape, the hammer, anvil, and stirrup do a particularly effective job not only transmitting vibrations but actually increasing their strength, since they act as a set of levers. Moreover, since the opening into the middle ear is considerably larger than the opening out of it, the force of sound waves on the smaller area becomes amplified. The middle ear, then, acts as a tiny mechanical amplifier, making us aware of sounds that would otherwise go unnoticed.

Using Advance Organizers

You've seen previews, or "trailers," of movies that give you glimpses of the coming attractions. An **advance organizer** does the same thing for a textbook chapter. The organizer is a feature that appears ahead of new chapter material to present the concepts included in the chapter. The organizer might be in one of these forms:

- Outline

- List of questions

- Chapter opener, describing the content of the chapter

These items help you anticipate what you will learn before you read the new chapter. An advance organizer in the form of a chapter opener from a biology textbook is shown on pages 434-435.

23
Plants: The Great Producers

The migration of plants from the seas to the dry land surfaces of the earth more than 400 million years ago ranks among the most important events in the history of the biological world.

Sara A. Fultz, in *Botany* (1983)

The majority of the earth's landscapes—whether alpine meadow, tropical rain forest, rolling farmland, tall stand of timber, scorched desert, urban park, or ocean surface—have a common denominator: Their primary biological component is plants. These photosynthetic organisms can be microscopic and single-celled, like many species of green algae. They can be stately giants like redwood and sequoia trees. Or they can bear flowers and fruit, in an endless variety of colors, fragrances, and forms.

Regardless of individual locale and appearance, plants are collectively the great producers: autotrophs that convert solar

(From *Essentials of Biology* by Janet L. Hopson and Norman K. Wessells. Copyright © 1990 by McGraw-Hill, Inc. Reprinted by permission of McGraw-Hill.)

If a textbook does not have advance organizers, preview the chapter or read the chapter summary if there is one. To preview the chapter, look through the chapter pages, noting the chapter title, headings, and illustrations. Read the first and last paragraphs of the chapter and the first sentence of each paragraph in the chapter.

When a chapter has a summary but no advance organizer, read the summary first before reading the chapter. The summary will identify the important information from the chapter. As a result, when you read the chapter, you will remember more of the new information than if you had not previewed the chapter.

energy into fixed carbon that supplies their own energy needs and also supports most other living organisms, directly or indirectly. They also represent an evolutionary spectrum ranging from some of the earliest eukaryotic cells to the first large organisms that survived on dry land to the diverse modern groups that we see so abundantly around us—and that we rely on so completely for our fruits, vegetables, beverages, spices, wood, grains, fibers, and many of our chemicals and drugs.

This chapter surveys that broad spectrum, including:

- The major characteristics of all plants and the main branches of the plant kingdom
- The basic plant life cycle, with its alternating generations
- The algae, diverse aquatic producers
- The challenges of land and its early colonization
- The nonvascular land plants—the mosses, liverworts, and hornworts
- The seedless vascular plants—the whisk ferns, club mosses, horsetails, and ferns
- How seed plants may have evolved
- The gymnosperms—plants with cones and seeds
- The anthophytes—plants with flowers, fruit, seeds, and a close interrelationship with animals

Activity L: Using an Advance Organizer

Examine one of your textbooks to find out if it has advance organizers for the chapters. Describe the form of the organizers you find. Describe what feature of the textbook you can use if there are no advance organizers.

_____

_____

_____

_____

_____

WRAPPING IT UP

SUMMARY

- Three components of information processing theory are:
    1. Encoding
    2. Storage
    3. Retrieval

- To remember something, you must pay attention to it and intend to remember it.

- You forget most of what you will ever forget about a piece of information within twenty-four hours unless you do something to prevent the loss.

- Effective memorization requires organizing and sorting new information.

- Your memory of new information can be enhanced by observing the following:
    1. Involve all your senses.
    2. Use mnemonics (memory aids).
    3. Use associations (links of new information to images of words).
    4. Use loci (associations of new information with specific places).
    5. Rehearse.
    6. Recite or write information in your words.
    7. Use advance organizers.

THINKING IT OVER

- What material from this chapter did you find most useful?

  _____

  _____

  _____

  _____

  _____

  _____

- How will you apply the information and ideas from this chapter to improve your memory?

  _____

  _____

  _____

  _____

  _____

  _____

  _____

IN YOUR
JOURNAL

Review the goal you set for improving your memory. Describe the progress you've made toward that goal. Describe new goals based on what you've learned in this chapter.

20

TAKING TESTS

OBJECTIVES:

- To plan preparation time for tests and examinations.

- To identify strategies for reviewing in preparation for tests.

- To use strategies for taking objective and essay tests.

- To use strategies for reducing test-taking anxiety.

How Can I Do Well on Tests?

The test is about to begin. Based on your experiences in situations like the one shown in the picture, what might be going through the students' minds?

Some students—maybe you are one of them—mistakenly believe the future of their entire lives depends on how well they do on college tests. Tests are indeed important, but by looking at them realistically—as a way to show what you have learned—you should be able to deal with tests and testing situations more easily. This chapter will help you develop strategies to prepare for and take tests.

GETTING STARTED

You've probably taken many tests during your elementary and high school education. You may also have taken a driver's test and an employment test of some kind.

- Are tests helpful? Explain.

  _____

  _____

  _____

  _____

- What is most difficult about taking tests?

  _____

  _____

  _____

  _____

  _____

- How do you prepare for tests? Describe what you usually do.

  _____

  _____

  _____

  _____

  _____

IN YOUR
JOURNAL

Set a goal for improving your ability to take tests. Identify some aspect of test taking that gives you a problem, and explain how you would like to solve that problem. For example, in testing situations, you might have trouble remembering what you know. Your goal might be to reduce your anxiety before a test.

DISCUSSING YOUR TEST EXPERIENCES

GROUP ACTIVITY

For many people the most memorable experiences with tests tend to be negative ones—the time you couldn't remember something you'd studied over and over, for example. You may also have had positive experiences with tests—feeling that your study methods paid off in a good test score, for example. Discuss your experiences. Include items from the Data Bank in your discussion. Describe some of the experiences that group members have had in common, including strategies that were the most helpful. Write your description.

_____

_____

_____

_____

_____

_____

_____

_____

_____

_____

DATA BANK

- Studying in groups.
- Studying alone.
- Finding a quiet place to concentrate.
- Using active methods.
- Recopying notes.
- Rereading chapters.
- Anticipating instructors' questions.
- Talking to instructors about tests.
- Oral testing by friend/family.
- Reciting from notes/text.
- Making study sheets.
- Making maps or visuals.
- Taking frequent breaks when studying.
- Studying at the last moment.
- Staying up all night.
- Asking friends how and what they are studying.
- Moving around while studying.

STUDYING REGULARLY

To become good at something, you need to practice regularly. Regular practice is as important for test taking as it is for becoming a skilled nurse, architect, cook, musician, or athlete.

DISCOVERY ACTIVITY

- Describe something you practice regularly.

  _____

  _____

  _____

  _____

- How often do you practice?

  _____

- What have you gained from regular practice?

  _____

  _____

  _____

  _____

  _____

By following the guidelines for periodic review of your lecture and textbook notes in Chapter 12 and by scheduling regular study time according to the guidelines in Chapter 7, you should already be fairly well prepared for a test. For especially important tests such as midterms and finals, you need to schedule extra time for studying. A good rule of thumb is to allow a week to prepare for a midterm and two weeks to prepare for a final. Schedule time using the forms for your daily planner and for your weekly schedule (Chapter 7). Plan at least an hour of study time each day for each subject in which you will be tested.

WEEKLY SCHEDULE

Week of _____

Time	Sunday	Monday	Tuesday	Wednesday	Thursday	Friday	Saturday
5:30-6:00							
6:00-6:30							
6:30-7:00							
7:00-7:30							
7:30-8:00							

Time	Sunday	Monday	Tuesday	Wednesday	Thursday	Friday	Saturday
7:00-7:30		*TV*		*TV*		*TV*	*TV*
7:30-8:00	*Job*	*Study Psych* ——————————————————→					*TV*
8:00-8:30							*TV*
8:30-9:00		*Study Soc* ——————————————————→					*TV*
9:00-9:30	*Study Soc*	*Study Soc* ——————————————————→					*TV*
9:30-10:00		*Study CT 115* ——————————————————→					*TV*

PLANNING TO STUDY FOR TESTS

As you plan your study time for tests, remember the following:

1. Allow time to gather and organize all your materials: books, notes, writing materials, markers, index cards, and so on. Set up a special area—a designated desk or table—that you will not have to clean off until after the tests.

2. Several short blocks of study time—30 to 60 minutes—are more productive than longer, concentrated blocks. Take a 5- to 10-minute break between each short block of study time.

3. Plan to study your most difficult subjects when you are at your peak of alertness. You may need to plan extra time for these subjects.

4. Allow time for self-testing or being quizzed by other people. If you involve other people in your preparation for tests, make arrangements as early as possible to meet with them.

5. By the night before the test, you should have completed most of your studying. On this night you should do only a light review.

6. Build in rewards at intervals in your schedule. For instance, after completing the first round of heavy study and the first self-test, reward yourself with a movie or some other diversion.

USING A STUDY CHECKLIST

When your instructor announces a test, list the material the instructor says the test will cover. Your list for a test in a biology course might look like this:

> Hopson and Wessells, Chapters 26 and 27
> handout on pollination
> lectures: sexual reproduction in plants 3—15
>   liquid transport in plants   4—3
> Independent reading: The Sex Life of Plants, pages 1-90
> Important terms—concepts:
>   annual plant
>   biennial plant
>   cotyledon
>   double fertilization
>   mitosis
>   phloem
>   pollination
>   xylem
>   root hair

For other courses, your study checklist might include formulas, problems, theories, and vocabulary. The purpose of a study checklist is to make sure you know what information to study. The checklist, however, is not a substitute for studying. You still need to spend time studying the materials on the list—the chapter pages, your notes, and so on. As you complete your study of each item, check off the item on the checklist.

Activity A: Analyzing Your Study Strategy

In your group, discuss how you prepared for a recent test. Describe the common experiences of the group members. Use the following questions as a guide.

- How much time did you spend studying?

  _____

- Did you study regularly on a daily or weekly basis?

  _____

- How did you know what material to study?

  _____

  _____

- What kinds of material did you study?

  _____

  _____

  _____

  _____

STRATEGIES FOR STUDYING FOR A TEST

The best way to prepare for tests is to do so actively. Three specific strategies for actively preparing for tests can help you improve your ability to take tests—but only if you try them. After trying these strategies, you can decide which ones work best for you and fit most closely with your learning style. The three strategies are:

1. Predicting questions
2. Rehearsing and self-testing
3. Group study

PREDICTING QUESTIONS

By recognizing clues from your instructor and by asking direct questions about an upcoming test, you can often develop a good idea of what the test will cover. If your instructor occasionally praises the textbook, he or she is likely to base test questions on text-book content. On the other hand, if an instructor says something like, "This book is fairly well written but some sections leave a lot to be desired," test questions are likely to be based on lecture material and other assigned readings.

During lectures, notice when the instructor emphasizes certain points by displaying them on the board or chart or by repeating them. Notice word cues the instructor uses such as *most important*, *significant*, *key*, and so on. Information that is emphasized in this way is likely to appear on a test.

If the instructor gives quizzes, add these quizzes to the material you study before a test. Some of the same material is likely to appear on the test. Similarly, questions the instructor asks in class are likely to appear in a slightly different form on a test.

Activity B: Identifying Possible Test Questions

Imagine that you just learned that you will have a test in one of your courses later today. List the kinds of questions a test in that course might ask. Consider clues you've picked up from the instructor and information from both your textbook and lecture notes.

_____

_____

_____

_____

_____

_____

_____

_____

_____

_____

_____

_____

_____

_____

REHEARSING AND SELF-TESTING TECHNIQUES

As you learned in Chapter 19, you rehearse information when you think about it, reread it, talk about it, and recite it aloud. Rehearsing increases your ability to remember information from your notes. The best way to rehearse is actively—by reciting aloud—in segments lasting from 15 to 25 minutes each. Schedule your test preparation so that you have enough time to rehearse orally.

Self-Testing

In Chapters 12 and 17 you learned about self-testing techniques. These techniques help you use your lecture and textbook notes to recall important information. To self-test effectively, create questions based on your lecture or textbook notes—notes that should be in the Cornell split-page style. Folding your notes so that you see only the questions, recall the answers. Then follow these steps:

1. Circle the questions you miss on your first round of self-testing.
2. Restudy the circled items.
3. Retest yourself on the circled items.
4. Retest yourself on *all* the items—both the ones you initially got right and the ones you missed.

Self-Testing With Chapter Outlines

You may need to self-test on textbook material, but you may not have made split-page notes. Instead you may have made a vertical or horizontal outline of chapter material, or you may have made marginal notes in the textbook itself. To self-test using a *vertical outline*, follow these steps:

1. Cover the outline with another sheet of paper.

2. Slide the paper down to reveal a topic or main idea.

3. Try to recall the supporting details for the topic or main idea.

4. Check your recall by sliding the paper down to reveal the details.

To self-test using a *horizontal outline*, follow these steps:

1. Cover the right side of the paper, and recall the supporting details for the topic or main idea.

2. Cover the left side of the paper, and recall the topic or main idea that the details support.

Self-Testing With Marginal Questions

To self-test using marginal questions, follow these steps:

1. Cover the textbook page (except for the margins).

2. Recall the information that answers the questions.

3. Uncover the page and check your answers.

Self-Testing With SQ4R Notes

If you took notes on textbook material using the SQ4R method, use these notes to self-test in the same way you use split-page notes.

Self-Testing With Charts, Maps, or Other Visuals

The study chart on page 449 shows a chart a student developed to help remember African language groups and their characteristics. The same information is also shown as a study map on page 451 and as a study sheet on page 452.

Study Chart

Major Niger-Congo Language Groups

Group	Major Languages	Characteristics
West Atlantic	Wolof Fulani	Word beginnings and endings change according to grammar.
Mande	Bambara Malinke Mende	Distinguishes between free and dependent nouns. Tone inflection of phrases rather than single words.
Kwa	Ga Yoruba Igbo (Ibo) Akan	Short words. Nouns begin with vowels. Long proper names.
Adamawa-Eastern	Sango Baya	Reflects pidgin forms of French and other African languages.
Benue Congo	Swahili Xhosa Kongo Luba Zulu Ganda Rwanda Lingala	Repeated syllables as prefixes of successive words in the same sentence.
Gur (Voltaic)	Mossi	Parallel prefixes and suffixes with suffixes dominant.

By putting information from your notes or from a textbook into a visual format, you'll remember some of the information even if you don't study the visual format afterward. If you do study the visual format, you'll remember even more. The visual image you store in your mind can help you recall important information while you're taking a test.

The study sheet (on page 452) is less graphic than the chart (on page 449) or map (on page 451). If you remember text more easily than graphic images, you may want to use the study sheet. Use larger handwriting than you normally would, and don't crowd the page. If necessary, use more than one sheet of paper to keep the information clear. You can use markers and colors to make the sheet more memorable.

Self-Testing With Concept Cards

Use 3- by 5-inch index cards to write the name of an important concept and several important points about the concept. Two examples of concept cards are shown on page 453. As with other visual study aids, the process of making these cards—aside from whether you study them later—is an effective way to prepare for a test.

Self-Testing With Study Guides and Study Sessions

Some instructors provide study guides that outline the important points to be covered on a test. These study guides are valuable tools for self-testing. The best way to use the guides is to rewrite the topics as questions. If the topics are already written as questions, your job is easier.

Instructors sometimes hold optional study sessions. At these sessions you may receive important information about what will be on a test. Prepare for a test study session by making a list of questions about items from lectures or from your textbook that you are uncertain about. Also ask questions about information that is unclear in your notes. Make sure you find answers to your questions during the session.

Study Map

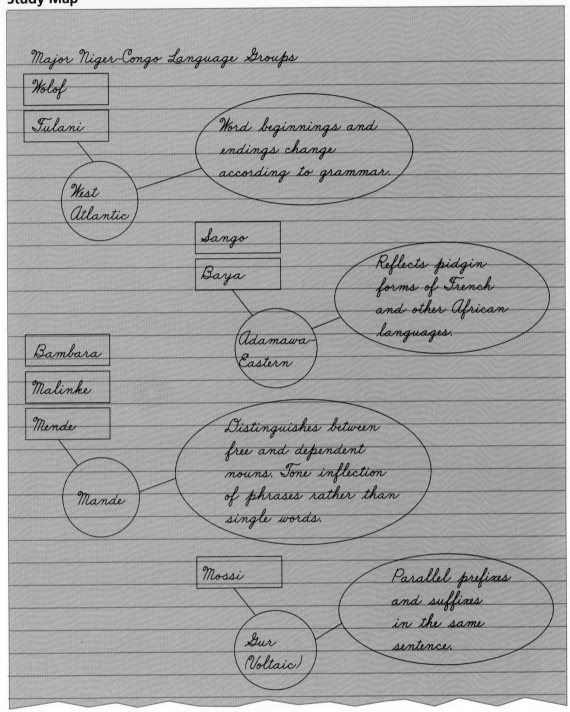

Major Niger-Congo Language Groups

Wolof

Fulani

West Atlantic

Word beginnings and endings change according to grammar.

Sango

Baya

Adamawa-Eastern

Reflects pidgin forms of French and other African languages.

Bambara

Malinke

Mende

Mande

Distinguishes between free and dependent nouns. Tone inflection of phrases rather than single words.

Mossi

Gur (Voltaic)

Parallel prefixes and suffixes in the same sentence.

Study Sheet

Major Niger-Congo Language Groups

West Atlantic   Wolof
                       Fulani

Language Group   Word beginnings and endings
Major Languages   change according to grammar.
Characteristics

Kwa   Ga
                        Yoruba
                        Igbo (Ibo)
                        Akan

                        Short words. Nouns begin with
                        vowels. Long proper nouns.

Mande   Bambara
                        Malinke
                        Mende

                        Distinguishes between free and
                        dependent nouns. Tone inflection of
                        phrases rather than single words.

Study Cards

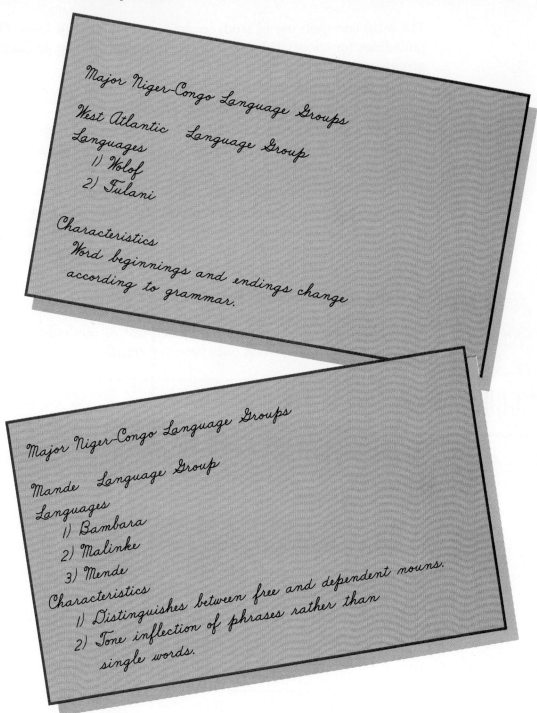

Major Niger-Congo Language Groups

West Atlantic   Language Group
Languages
   1) Wolof
   2) Fulani

Characteristics
Word beginnings and endings change
according to grammar.

Major Niger-Congo Language Groups

Mande   Language Group
Languages
   1) Bambara
   2) Malinke
   3) Mende
Characteristics
   1) Distinguishes between free and dependent nouns.
   2) Tone inflection of phrases rather than
      single words.

Self-Testing With Study Groups

The most common use of study groups is to prepare for tests. These guidelines for successful group interaction apply in test preparation groups:

1. The ideal group size is three. Members should be at approximately the same level of performance in the class.

2. Those who talk and ask questions learn the most. Those who only listen learn less and have the illusion of knowing. (See knowledge illusion on page 456.)

3. If they're available, consult tests from earlier in the term.

4. Keep study sessions short and productive. Take breaks, but specify time limits and keep to them. The greatest complaint that study group users have is that too much time is spent socializing.

GROUP ACTIVITY

Activity C: Discussing Self-Testing Options

• In your group, discuss the different self-testing methods described on pages 446–454. Which ones have you tried?

_____

_____

• How did the methods you tried work for you?

_____

_____

_____

_____

_____

_____

_____

_____

_____

_____

_____

- Which of the methods would work best for you? Why?

_____

_____

_____

_____

_____

_____

_____

_____

_____

_____

_____

_____

_____

_____

_____

_____

_____

_____

_____

STUDYING FOR RECALL VS. RECOGNITION

Like many students, you've probably had a frustrating lapse of memory during a test. You had the feeling that you knew something but couldn't recall it under the pressure of a testing situation. Did you really know the information, or did you just think you did? Does this description of a situation sound familiar?

> Rhonda studied for her sociology test until she was sure she understood the material. When she took the test, however, she seemed to panic. "I know I knew that material," she said, "but I couldn't remember it on the test. I guess I must have test anxiety and can't recall what I know in a testing situation."

- Describe a similar experience you've had.

_____

_____

_____

_____

_____

_____

_____

_____

In the mid-1980s, two cognitive psychologists, Glenberg and Epstein, studied what they called "illusions of knowing." In experiments, they asked people to read a piece of writing and rate how well they felt that they understood the material. The material contained many contradictions that made understanding impossible. Yet, most of the people said they understood the material very well. The researchers have repeated the experiment and have found that people tend to believe they understand something when they do not. They suffer from **knowledge illusion**.

Many students experience the same illusion but don't know what is going on. They "know" the material when they are looking directly at it—for instance while looking at their notes and studying them. During this process students confuse _understanding_ the material with actually _knowing_ it—being able to recall it without any visual clues.

If you find that you suffer from knowledge illusion, you can do something about it: self-test. Follow any of the guidelines for self-testing presented in this chapter:

1. Ask yourself questions, such as the questions you write on your Cornell notes.

2. If you're using split-page notes, keep your paper folded.

3. Recite answers aloud, write them on another piece of paper, or write them in the air with your finger.

4. Do not look at the answers as you try your recall. The idea is to use only your memory, not verbal or visual clues.

A NOTE ABOUT CRAMMING

Cramming for a test—"pulling an all-nighter"—is an extreme form of massed rehearsal. Your brain has no time to absorb or consolidate all of the information you force-feed it. You may remember a small percentage of what you need to know to do well on a test. Chances are, however, that you won't test well.

If you must cram, however, use one or more of the self-testing techniques in which you use your lecture and text-book notes. The most important idea is to use questions to recall and recite key information that will be on the test. Circle missed items, retest, and review as often as time permits.

THE NIGHT BEFORE THE TEST

Some people make the last night before a test into a marathon of frenzied study. They think that by studying into the early morning hours, they are guaranteed to succeed on a test. Nothing could be further from the truth. Getting enough sleep is far more important than cramming in bits of information that you will probably not recall anyway.

Go to sleep at your normal time. If you think you will have trouble getting to sleep, avoid caffeine in the afternoon and evening, take a hot bath, or do something else that relaxes you.

THE MORNING OF THE TEST

The period between the time you wake up and the time you begin taking the test can be critical in helping you do well on the test. Here are some useful tips:

1. Allow enough time to go through your normal routine, including shower, breakfast, exercise—whatever you usually do. If you normally skip breakfast, however, eat something on the day of the test. At the least, you can probably tolerate a bagel, granola bar, or a piece of fruit. Having some food in your stomach will help prevent the queasy feeling brought on by nervousness.

2. Wear comfortable clothing. Sweats and other loose garments are favorites. Wear your watch unless it is prohibited from the test site because it has calculator functions.

3. Do not study. Whatever you do, don't join the gaggle of people who cluster outside the classroom making last minute comparisons of what they did and did not study. You don't have time to learn anything new, and participating in these sessions can only raise your anxiety level.

4. Sit in your usual seat in the classroom or as close as possible to your regular seat. Some of your memories are geared to certain vantage points. You may recall a visual memory of the instructor saying something; if you're in a different location, you may not be able to activate this visual cue.

PORTFOLIO

Assignment 1:
Describing Your Test Preparation Strategies

Now that you've studied several test-preparation strategies, choose the ones you think will work best for you. Summarize the strategies you will use in preparing for your next test. Include methods you will use for predicting questions, rehearsing, self-study, and group study. Save this assignment in your portfolio.

GENERAL TIPS

After completing your pretest studying, you are faced with the test itself. The following strategies can help you improve your chances of doing well on a test.

1. *Pay attention to all instructions.* Your instructor may give you directions before you begin the test. You may be told to not open the test until you hear or see a signal from the instructor. You may be told how much time you have to complete the test and whether there is a penalty for guessing. You may be told what to do with the test when you finish. All of this important information can affect how well you do on the test.

2. *Preview the test unless you are instructed not to.* Previewing the test gives you an idea of what to expect. This strategy is especially helpful if the test has several different sections.

- Make sure you have all the test pages.

- Look over the test, noting the sections and the kinds of test items.

- Notice the relative number of items and points in each section. The instructor may tell you in advance how many points each section is worth.

- Read and make sure you understand the printed instructions. Notice whether different sections have different instructions. Pay particular attention to instructions about how to mark your answers. Make sure you know whether to circle, check, underline, fill in the blank, fill in between pairs of vertical dotted lines, write on a separate sheet of paper, and so on.

3. *Budget your time.* After you have previewed the test and know how much time you have, decide how much time to spend on each section. Allocate time according to point values. If there are two essays that together are worth as much as all of the objective questions, allow half your time to complete the essays. Check your watch or a classroom clock from time to time to make sure you are following your time budget.

4. *Check your answers.* After completing the test, take time to review your answers. Spot check to be sure the items on the test match the answer sheet. Be sure that you've answered all the test items, unless there's a penalty for guessing. Be sure your essay responses are written as clearly as possible and that you've checked your grammar and spelling.

5. *Consider whether or not to change answers.* In general, you should not change an answer just because you are nervous about the answer you gave. On the other hand, if you're sure your first answer is wrong, by all means change it.

TWO BASIC TYPES OF TESTS

You may already be familiar with the two basic types of tests: objective and essay. **Objective tests** are usually made up of many individual test items calling for answers that you mark, check, circle, or fill in. The questions are designed to test your knowledge of specific facts and details. **Essay tests** require you to respond to a specific question or direction by writing a brief essay. Your essay may be one paragraph or several, depending on the question and how much information you need to provide.

OBJECTIVE TESTS

Objective tests include multiple-choice, true-false, fill-in, and matching items. In general, when you take an objective test, answer all of the easier questions first. As you answer these questions, you may activate your memory of answers to harder questions. When you answer easier questions before you answer harder questions, check to make sure you have answered all the questions on the test.

Multiple Choice

A **multiple-choice** item often has an incomplete statement followed by several lettered or numbered choices that complete the statement. Only one choice makes the statement true. Sometimes a multiple-choice item has a question followed by a series of choices, one of which is the correct answer.

Use these strategies for multiple-choice items:

1. Read the statement or question, and recall the answer before you look at the choices. Then look at the choices. Choose the one that is closest to the answer you recalled.

2. Reread the statement or question with each answer choice. Cross out incorrect choices.

3. If two answer choices are identical except for one or two words, one of the choices is likely to be the answer.

4. If two answer choices are exactly opposite, one is likely to be the answer.

5. Give careful consideration to answer choices such as "all of the above" and "a and c above." Choices such as these are sometimes correct because each "above" answer is only part of the correct answer, as in the following example from an economics test:

The size of the budget surplus or deficit is affected by
a. government purchases
b. transfer payments
c. tax rates
d. all of the above

6. Answer choices that have absolute qualifiers such as *all*, *never*, *none*, *every*, and *always* are usually incorrect.

7. Answer choices that have relative qualifiers such as *usually*, *often*, *some*, *probably*, and *generally* are often correct.

True-False

True-false test items consist of statements or questions followed by the words *true* and *false* or the letters *T* and *F*. You choose the word or letter that correctly identifies each item.
Use these strategies for true-false items:

1. Statements or questions that include absolute qualifiers such as *all*, *never*, *none*, *every*, and *always* are usually false.

2. Statements or questions that have relative qualifiers such as *usually*, *often*, *some*, *probably*, and *generally* are often true.

3. If any part of a statement or question is incorrect, the whole item is incorrect. Here's an example:

> In 1992 Carol Moseley Braun of Illinois became the first African American woman elected to the U.S. House of Representatives.

   Most of the information in the statement is true, except that Carol Moseley Braun was elected to the U.S. Senate. Therefore, the whole statement is false.

4. If a statement or question contains double negatives, cross them out and read the sentence again. Decide if the item is true or false without the double negatives. Here's an example:

> T   F   The novels of Amy Tan are not unlikely to be listed among best selling contemporary American fiction.

After crossing out the double negatives, you will see that the statement actually says the following:

The novels of Amy Tan are likely to be listed among best selling contemporary American fiction.

This statement is true.

Fill-In

Fill-in test items include statements with blanks, requiring you to supply a missing word or phrase.

Use this strategy for fill-in items:

Make sure the answer fits grammatically into the statement. Use clues in the statement to help you figure out the grammatical form of the answer. Here's an example:

Among clues to the ancient Mayan civilization are _____, indicating that the Maya had a system of writing.

The correct answer is *hieroglyphics*. Notice that a plural form of the word is indicated by the verb *are* before the blank.

When you see the article *an* before a blank, you know that the answer must begin with a vowel sound, spelled *a, e, i, o,* or *u*.

Matching Items

In **matching** test items, two sets of words and phrases appear. One set is usually preceded by numbers; and the other, by letters. Indicate an answer by writing the number and letter of two items that make sense together.

Use these strategies for matching items:

1. Read both columns of items before you begin to indicate your answers. Notice if one column has more items in it than the other. If one column has more items than the other, you will not have a one-for-one match of all items; some will be left over.

2. Match the easier pairs first, then return to the harder ones.

ESSAY TESTS

Essay tests test your knowledge of large issues and concepts. They require you to **synthesize**—compress and combine—information that you've learned. Here's an example of an essay question:

> Compare the concept of the citizen soldier during the American Revolution with that of the foot soldier of World War II.

A comparison of the citizen soldier during the American Revolution and the foot soldier of World War II reveals very striking similarities and differences. During the American Revolution...

To answer the question, you need to understand thoroughly both concepts—that of the citizen soldier and that of the foot soldier. Your instructor may not have made this comparison in class.

Your essay will be evaluated on how completely and accurately you answer the question or follow the direction. For this reason, it is important to understand exactly what you are to do before you begin writing. The directions or questions for essay tests include key words that will help you know what to do. The following chart lists some of those words and their meaning.

Key Direction Words in Essay Tests

Compare: Write about the similarities and differences between two or more people, places, or things.

Contrast: Write about the differences between two people, places, or things.

Criticize or *Critique:* Write an evaluation, expressing your opinion and supporting your opinion with facts, examples, and descriptions.

Define: Write the exact meaning of a term. The meaning you write should be specific to the course you are taking. Include examples to make your definition clear.

Describe: Write in detail, giving information about appearance, behavior, qualities, and purpose.

Discuss: Write in detail, describing the positive and negative aspects or identifying opinions pro and con regarding the subject.

Enumerate: Write a description of parts, key points, causes, effects, or benefits. Begin by identifying how many items there are, then write about each one, beginning with "First . . ." or using numerals.

Evaluate: Write about the advantages and disadvantages, pros and cons of situations, events, or issues. Cite experts and give your opinion, supported by facts, examples, and other details.

Illustrate: Write a detailed description, explaining how a process or system works or how an event happened. Your description should include examples.

Outline: Write a description of the main parts and important details. You may need to ask your instructor whether you should create an outline with roman numerals and letters or whether you should write your description in paragraph form.

Prove: Write the facts that explain why a statement is true. These facts are usually ones that have been presented in class or in your textbook.

State: Write as clearly and precisely as possible.

Summarize: Write a clear, condensed description, including only the most important points.

Trace: Write a description of development over time, from the earliest events to the latest.

Use these strategies for essay tests:

1. After you've read and understood the directions, write all your ideas and organize them in a list, outline, or map. Then use this plan to guide your writing.

2. Budget enough time to write and to edit your work, correcting your grammar and spelling.

3. Begin by writing a statement that says exactly what you will do. Try to use the key word in the test instructions. Notice the examples on page 463 that show a test question and the beginning of an answer to that question. Here's another example:

Question: Enumerate the causes of the Seminole War of 1817.

Beginning of an Answer: *The five main causes of the Seminole War of 1817 are....*

Notice how a specific number—five—replaces the key word *enumerate*. To complete the answer, you would describe each cause of the Seminole War.

4. Support your ideas with facts, examples, and details that you recall from your notes.

5. Write neatly. If you make corrections, make them neatly. A neat appearance can improve your grade.

GROUP
ACTIVITY

Activity D: Creating Test Items

With your group, identify each of your courses and the kinds of test items you are likely to have on a test for each course. Brainstorm to develop specific test items based on recent material from one of your courses. Try to create one question for each kind of test item you studied in this part of the chapter: multiple choice, true-false, fill-in, and so on.

Math and Science Tests

Math tests often include problem-solving questions. Solving a math or science problem successfully requires **cumulative knowledge**—knowledge you have built up over time, step by step. In some math and science tests, the steps you take to figure out the answer are worth as many points as the final answer, if not more.

PREPARING FOR MATH AND SCIENCE TESTS

When asked how a student should prepare for problem-solving questions, one instructor said, "Do problems. Then do more problems. After that, finish up by doing more problems." Instructors of mathematics, science, chemistry, physics, and accounting warn against a kind of preparation called cookbooking. **Cookbooking** involves reading the steps in example problems and working the problems by repeating the steps without understanding them. If you simply follow the example "recipe," you are likely to be confused when a problem is stated even slightly differently from the example problem you've been copying. You're thrown off because you really did not understand the process—a common experience among students who have some degree of math anxiety.

To avoid cookbooking, use the following strategies:

1. Practice going over the steps of a practice problem out loud.

2. Explain the steps to someone to be sure that you really understand the problem and the procedure.

3. If you find yourself stuck, discuss the problem with members of your study group, or ask a tutor or your instructor for help.

For math and science tests in general, use these strategies:

1. Read the problem carefully. Make sure you know what information you have to work with and what you are asked to do.

2. Make an estimate based on the information you have. As you work through the problem, compare your calculations to the estimate. If your calculations seem out of line with your estimate, you may need to take different steps to solve the problem.

3. Make notes or diagrams that help you understand what to do and how to proceed. You may need additional information to solve the problem—information you can obtain only by doing interim calculations or solving interim problems.

4. If you have time, solve the problem using simple numbers—numbers you can rapidly calculate to see if the procedure you've decided to use is the right one for the problem. If the problem works with simpler numbers, your procedure is likely to work for the numbers in the test item.

Example Problem

Finding Displacement When Velocities and Times Are Known

A spaceship far from any star or planet accelerates uniformly from 65.0 m/s to +162.0 m/s in 10.0 s. How far does it move?

Given: $v_i = +65.0$ m/s   **Unknown:** displacement, d
$v_f = +162.0$ m/s   **Basic equation:** $d = \frac{1}{2}(v_f + v_i)t$
$t = 10.0$ s

Solution: $d = \frac{1}{2}(v_f + v_i)t$
$= \frac{1}{2}(+162.0$ m/s $+ 65.0$ m/s$)(10.0$ s$)$
$= +1.14 \times 10^3$ m $= +1.14$ km

(Paul Zitzewitz, et. al., from *Merrill Physics: Principles and Problems*)

5. Check your work. Check both the procedure and the calculations. If you can work the problem another way, do so as another way of checking your work. Alternate methods of solution include working the problem backward from your answer, and using opposite calculations—for example, checking by dividing if you multiplied to achieve the answer. Otherwise, after checking your procedure and calculations, read the question again, and evaluate whether your answer makes sense.

OTHER TESTING SITUATIONS

Other tests you might need to take include:

• Lab examinations

• Demonstration examinations (as in a physical education class)

• Standardized tests that measure specific knowledge and **aptitude**—how likely you are to succeed at higher levels of education

Each of these tests requires a slightly different approach.

Lab Examinations

Laboratory examinations usually involve identifying aspects or structures of a physical body or conducting experimental procedures. Since such a wide variety of options may be used in testing, a useful guideline is to listen to and consult with your instructor or lab assistant to be sure you understand the procedures to use in the testing situation. When you study for such examinations, use methods that are similar to those you'll need on the actual test.

Demonstration Examinations

Courses such as nursing, home economics, and physical education might require you to perform some task that will be graded. To do well on such tests, you need to do plenty of practicing beforehand. If you will be tested before an audience or panel, ask friends to act as your audience when you are practicing.

Standardized Tests

These tests include the Scholastic Aptitude Test (SAT), Pre-Professional Skills Test (PPST), National Teacher Examination (NTE), Core Battery test, Nursing School Entrance Examinations, Graduate Record Examination (GRE), and Law School Admission Test (LSAT). These tests are administered, scored, and evaluated in the same way throughout the country. The standardized test procedure ensures that everyone who takes the test does so under the same conditions. As a result, your score on one of these tests indicates how you compare to a national standard—a large number of students across the country. Standardized tests consist mainly of multiple-choice questions covering skills such as reading comprehension, analytical thinking, logical thinking, vocabulary, and mathematical concepts. To prepare for these tests, use one of the study books available for the specific test you will take. Take the practice tests under the same timed conditions that exist during the actual test.

PORTFOLIO

Assignment 2:
Tests You May Need to Take

Describe your educational and career goals. Ask your instructor or counselor what major tests you will need to take as you pursue your goals. Investigate these tests by talking to people who have taken them and by reading some of the study books designed for the tests. Describe skill areas and study methods you can begin using now to prepare for these tests. Save this assignment in your portfolio.

HANDLING TEST ANXIETY

Just about everyone experiences a feeling of excitement at test time. For some people, that excitement results in a sharpened alertness, an eagerness to meet the challenge of a test. For other people, that excitement results in dread, loss of confidence, inability to concentrate, and a number of other symptoms that can prevent them from doing their best on a test.

DISCOVERY
ACTIVITY

• In which group would you place yourself—those who feel eagerness or those who feel dread?

_____

_____

• Describe what happens when you know you're going to take a test.

_____

_____

_____

_____

_____

_____

_____

_____

_____

The difference between positive and negative attitudes toward tests is simply in the way you look at tests. If you're anxious about tests, fearful and paralyzed, you can work to change your attitude. In turn, you are likely to do better on tests. By using a few simple strategies, you can reduce your anxiety before, during, and after tests.

BEFORE TESTS

The best way to reduce anxiety before taking a test is to prepare well for the test. Follow the guidelines presented in this chapter for anticipating test questions and for studying. Aim to overstudy—to know the material so well that you have no doubt about your ability to do well on a test. If you feel anxiety creeping in, tell yourself to stop using your imagination in a negative way.

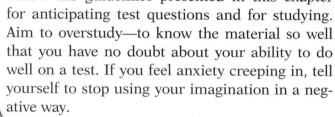

Think of a test as a way of finding out what you know at a particular time. If you assume that a test is a judgment on your life—that if you fail on a test, you're a failure in life—you're giving the test powers that it does not have. Be realistic. A test is just a piece or two of paper; you read the questions or statements and respond to them. You may do well or poorly on a test, but you do not become a different person as a result of taking a test.

Visualize yourself succeeding on the test, and take the steps necessary to achieve that success: study, study, study.

To reduce physical anxiety—shortness of breath, sweaty palms, and insomnia—use these relaxation strategies:

1. **Hand massage.** Use one hand to massage the other, then switch. Use the fingers of one hand to squeeze and release each joint of the fingers of the other hand. Begin at the outermost joint and squeeze-release each joint successively until your hands are relaxed.

2. **Deep breathing.** Sit with your back straight and your feet flat on the floor. Place your hands on your thighs, palms down. Close your eyes. Inhale slowly and very deeply, expanding the diaphragm and abdomen as your lungs fill with air. Exhale

slowly and regularly until your lungs empty. Repeat several times, establishing a regular rhythm. Do not hold your breath or breathe so slowly that you get dizzy. You can combine this deep-breathing exercise with the hand massage.

3. **Progressive relaxation.** Sit comfortably as in the deep-breathing exercise. Squeeze and tense the muscles in your feet. Hold the tension, then release completely. Tense the muscles in your calves. Hold for a moment, then release. Continue by tensing and releasing the muscles in your hips, abdomen, hands, and face. Notice how the muscles feel when you release the tension. After tensing and relaxing your body, from your feet to your head, sit quietly and feel the sensations of total relaxation.

REDUCING ANXIETY DURING TESTS

Keep your attention on the test questions and on the process of answering those questions. Don't allow yourself to be distracted by thoughts of failure or success; just answer the questions. Don't increase your anxiety by saying you must make a certain grade on the test.

If you feel yourself starting to panic, tell yourself to stop. Remind yourself that the test is just a piece or two of paper and that you are answering the questions to the best of your ability. Remind yourself that this is not the end of your life. If necessary, take a moment to do one of the relaxation exercises, then refocus on answering the test questions. Use the strategies you've learned in this chapter for handling different kinds of test questions.

REDUCING ANXIETY AFTER TESTS

The period after you take a test is a critical time. Your reactions following a test affect the way you will take the next test. Maintain a positive attitude. Be realistic. You will probably feel relieved that the test is over. Reward yourself in some way—have a special meal, go to a movie, and avoid worrying about the test results. Keep your mind focused on what you are doing at the moment, not on the possible outcome of the test.

When you receive the test results, remember the purpose of the test—to assess what you know at a given time. Be realistic in your interpretation of the results. If you did well, congratulate yourself on the hard work you did to prepare for the test. If you did not do as well as you expected to, don't let your imagination run away with negative thoughts. Remember that you are the same person you were before you took the test. Your life is not over. Discuss your disappointment with friends or relatives. Then move on.

Use your test results as a learning tool. Study the test items on which you did not do well. Figure out what went wrong, and identify the correct answers. This is an important step toward improving your results on the next test. If you have trouble figuring out what went wrong, confer with a classmate or with your instructor.

Keep copies of your old tests, if possible, and use them as part of your preparation for future tests. Study the items you got right as well as those you got wrong.

GROUP
ACTIVITY

Activity E: Learning From Tests

Analyze a test you've taken recently. In your group identify test items you missed, and discuss what went wrong. Also discuss attitudes and procedures that helped you answer test items correctly.

• What difficulties did some of the members have in common?

_____

_____

_____

_____

_____

_____

_____

_____

_____

_____

_____

_____

_____

_____

- What did you learn from analyzing your test results?

_____

_____

_____

_____

_____

_____

_____

- What strategies helped you answer test items correctly?

_____

_____

_____

_____

_____

_____

_____

WRAPPING IT UP

SUMMARY

- Schedule a week to prepare for a midterm and two weeks to prepare for a final.

- Effective methods of studying for a test are:
    1. Predict questions.
    2. Rehearse.
    3. Self-test.
    4. Study in a group.

- Self-testing is a good strategy for avoiding knowledge illusions—the belief that you know something when you really don't.

- The two basic types of tests are objective tests and essay tests. Using tips for taking different kinds of tests can improve your results. Be sure you understand the directions, budget your time according to the number and point value of test items, answer easier test items first, and check all your answers.

- To handle test anxiety effectively:
    1. Maintain a realistic attitude about the test.
    2. Study for the test.
    3. Use relaxation techniques.
    4. Learn from your test results.

THINKING IT OVER

- What material from this chapter did you find most helpful?

  _____

  _____

  _____

- How will you apply the information and ideas in this chapter to your test-taking situations?

  _____

  _____

  _____

IN YOUR JOURNAL

Describe the progress you've made toward achieving the goal you set in relation to taking tests. Describe new goals you would like to achieve as a result of this chapter.

Appendix

DAILY PLANNING FORM

Date _____

Hour	Item
7:00	
7:30	
8:00	
8:30	
9:00	
9:30	
10:00	
10:30	
11:00	
11:30	
12:00	
12:30	
1:00	
1:30	
2:00	
2:30	

Notes

Date _____

Hour	Item
3:00	
3:30	
4:00	
4:30	
5:00	
5:30	
6:00	
6:30	
7:00	
7:30	
8:00	
8:30	
9:00	
9:30	
10:00	
10:30	

Notes

WEEKLY SCHEDULE

Week of _____

Time	Sunday	Monday	Tuesday	Wednesday	Thursday	Friday	Saturday
5:30- 6:00							
6:00- 6:30							
6:30- 7:00							
7:00- 7:30							
7:30- 8:00							
8:00- 8:30							
8:30- 9:00							
9:00- 9:30							
9:30-10:00							
10:00-10:30							
10:30-11:00							
11:00-11:30							
11:30-12:00							
12:00-12:30							
12:30- 1:00							
1:00- 1:30							
1:30- 2:00							

Notes

Week of _____

Time	Sunday	Monday	Tuesday	Wednesday	Thursday	Friday	Saturday
2:00- 2:30							
2:30- 3:00							
3:00- 3:30							
3:30- 4:00							
4:00- 4:30							
4:30- 5:00							
5:00- 5:30							
5:30- 6:00							
6:00- 6:30							
6:30- 7:00							
7:00- 7:30							
7:30- 8:00							
8:00- 8:30							
8:30- 9:00							
9:00- 9:30							
9:30-10:00							
10:00-10:30							
10:30-11:00							

Notes

Lecture A Excerpt
Instructors' Analysis of Problems With Student Notes

In a recent survey conducted at New Mexico State University (NMSU), instructors from all disciplines across the university were asked to comment on the problems they most often see with student lecture notes. Two comments heard repeatedly were: (1) students do not take enough notes and (2) students do not know how to study notes that they take.

First, instructors commented that students often take scanty notes because they believe that they can remember much of the content of the lecture with just a few words to jog their memory. For instance, students in biology may write down the term "mitochondria" and nothing else. Students believe that they will be able to recall the definition without having written it down. This strategy may carry over from high school when testing occurred more frequently, perhaps once a week. But when many weeks of lectures and notes accumulate, however, relying on memory is a risky business, say NMSU instructors. As a general rule, instructors in the survey said that a student who has fewer than two to three pages of notes per one-hour lecture is probably relying too heavily on memory.

The second point made by the instructors is that students do not know how to study their lecture notes. When students are asked how they prepare for tests, they usually say they just read over their notes before the test. Instructors recommend that students at least review/skim their notes the day they are taken to begin to commit them to memory. Then, when preparing for tests, students must find a way to study other than just reading over their notes. Students need to see if they know the content when they are not looking directly at their notes. Testing each other is one good way for students to get a clear picture of what they know and don't know.

Lecture B Excerpt
Forms of Nonverbal Communication

In their early work in this area, Jurgen Ruesch and Weldon Kees outlined just three categories: sign, action, and object language. Sign language includes gestures used in the place of words, numbers, or punctuation. When an athlete raises his index finger to show his team is "Number One," he is using sign language. Action language includes all those nonverbal movements *not* intended as signs. Your way of walking, sitting, or eating may serve your personal needs, but they also make statements to those who see them. Object language includes both the intentional and unintentional display of material things. Your hairstyle, glasses, and jewelry reveal things about you, as do the books you carry, the car you drive, or the clothes you wear.

(Richard Weaver, from "Forms of Non-verbal Communication," *Understanding Interpersonal Communication*)

Lecture C Excerpt
The Acquisition of Language

Learning a language is tremendously complex. Although you don't realize the difficulty of language acquisition when you learn your first language, you actually complete the majority of the work during the first four or so years of life.

What do we learn when we learn a language? The most obvious thing we learn is the **lexicon** of a language. The lexicon is the store of words, or the vocabulary. Very small children may be seen hard at work building up their store of words (additions to the lexicon), as many as twenty new words per day during the first two years.

The second component of language acquisition is **phonology**, the sounds of a particular language. Researchers think that during the early babbling stages preceding actual speech—say before six months of age—children babble a variety of sounds that prepare them to speak any of the hundreds of human languages. Some of the babbling sounds may not even be part of the language spoken by the community in which the child is born. The community—specifically the child's immediate family—reinforces only certain of the sounds the child babbles, thereby encouraging the child to use the sounds of the family's language. The child eventually forgets the unreinforced sounds and begins imitating more of the sounds of the family's language.

A third component of language is **morphology**, the rules of word construction such as the formation of plurals. It is interesting to note that English-speaking children may correctly learn a plural such as "feet" and then later say "foots." While this may seem like a step backward, it actually reflects increasing linguistic competence.

The child is realizing and generalizing that *s* is added to a noun to form a plural. Therefore "foots" makes more sense than "feet," since "feet" is an exception, an irregular plural. So, such rules as forming plurals and otherwise ordering elements within a word are part of the morphology of a language.

Other elements of language acquisition include *syntax*, *semantics*, and *pragmatics*, which will be discussed in the next lecture.

Lecture D Excerpt
Mood and Memory

In 1968, Sirhan Sirhan assassinated Robert Kennedy in a Los Angeles hotel. Sirhan was in a highly agitated state when he killed Kennedy. When questioned about it immediately afterward, he had no recollection of the event. A hypnotist was called in. The hypnotist re-created the events of the murder. As Sirhan listened, he became agitated and recalled more and more details of the murder. Sometimes while he was in a trance he described events aloud; at other times he recorded his memories by writing them down automatically, without being aware of what he was writing (Bower, 1981). In his non-hypnotized state, Sirhan was never conscious of these memories and even denied that he had committed the murder.

Sirhan Sirhan's case is a dramatic example of *state-dependent memory*. The theory of this type of memory is based on the assumption that events learned in a certain emotional state can be remembered better when one is put back into the same state.

To learn more about the influence of mood on memory, psychologist Gordon Bower conducted a series of laboratory experiments. In one study, he hypnotized a group of subjects and made them feel happy. While they were in that happy state, he gave them a list of words to learn. At another session, he hypnotized them again, but put them in a sad mood and gave them a different list of words to learn. Later, the subjects were hypnotized again and were asked to recall one of the lists they had been given previously. Bower found that the subjects who tried to recall a list in the same mood as that in which they learned could remember more of the words than subjects who tried to recall the list they had learned while in the other mood.

Bower also had subjects keep daily records of the emotional events in their lives. Later, he hypnotized them and asked them to recall the incidents they had recorded. Bower found that subjects who were placed in a sad mood recalled more unpleasant events in their daily lives than subjects who were hypnotized to be in a happy mood. Also, subjects recalled more unpleasant events from their childhood when they were in a sad mood than they recalled happy events when in a happy mood.

One explanation for this mood-dependent recall offered by Bower is that mood serves as a cue for retrieving information. When a memory is stored, it is associated with a specific emotion as well as with specific actions or people. The emotional state later functions as a marker in our memory of the specific event. When we are in the same mood, we are more likely to be able to find the memory thus marked.

There are some practical implications of Bower's research. First, if you want to maximize your recall of material, one way to do so is to recall the material in a circumstance or emotional context similar to the one in which the material was learned. For example, if you match a mood of tension while studying for an exam with a tense mood while taking an exam, you can expect to do better in recalling the studied material. Often, students are relaxed while studying for an exam, but anxious while taking it—a bad match for recall, according to Bower.

(Garrison, from *Introduction to Psychology*)

Answers to Reading Comprehension Questions, Chapter 16

First Selection (pages 335–337)

1. a   4. b
2. c   5. b
3. c

Second Selection (pages 337–339)

1. b   4. c
2. a   5. b
3. d

Third Selection (pages 339–341)

1. c   4. d
2. a   5. c
3. a

CHAPTER 12

Family-Related Problems

Special attention and support should be freely given to troubled families and their members, including single-parent households. Moreover, the bases for violence and abuse within families of all types should be absent.

PREMARITAL BIRTHS AND TEENAGE MOTHERHOOD

MARITAL DISSOLUTION

VIOLENCE IN THE FAMILY
  Spouse Abuse
  Child Abuse
  Child-initiated Violence
  Comment on the Findings

SEXUAL ABUSE OF CHILDREN

RUNAWAYS AND HOMELESS CHILDREN

WHAT IS TO BE DONE?

SUMMARY
Kenneth J. Neubeck, *Social Problems: A Critical Approach*, 3rd edition, McGraw-Hill Publishing Co., 1979. Reprinted by permission of McGraw-Hill Publishing Co.

Sociologists have traditionally viewed the family as a multifunction unit, central to the stability and continuity of human society. Among its functions are economic production, intimacy and nurturance, sexual reproduction, and socialization of the young. Viewed in the abstract, the family may be seen as a social collectivity that protects and aids the individual in confronting the often challenging and sometimes stressful demands of daily life.

In recent decades the nature of the family in the United States has been undergoing change, and a variety of problems related to the family have emerged. There have been significant increases in premarital births and in the numbers of unwed teenage mothers. Rates of marital dissolution also have risen sharply, thus adding to the unprecedented numbers of single-parent households. Researchers have uncovered an unexpectedly high volume of violent behavior within families, most notably in the form of spouse abuse as well as violence and sexual abuse directed at children. One response of children to discord and victimization in the home has been to flee—to become runaways. There are also indications that many children are becoming "pushouts," being made to leave home.

In this chapter we examine these family-related problems. Our attention focuses on the nature of these problems as well as on their extent, causes, and consequences. We begin by looking at premarital births and single teenage mothers.

PREMARITAL BIRTHS AND TEENAGE MOTHERHOOD

The typical image that comes to mind when we hear the term *family* is likely to be mother, father, and children living together in a household. This image belies the reality of what has been taking place in America in recent decades, particularly the surge in the percentage of families living in single-parent households. While much of the change in family composition has occurred as a consequence of increased rates of divorce (a topic addressed later in this chapter), increasing numbers of families *begin* with a single parent.

In 1986 some 3.8 million births were recorded in the United States. As Table 12.1 indicates, 23.4 percent of these births were to unmarried mothers (as compared with 4.0 percent in 1950).[1] While persons under age twenty accounted for only 12.6 percent of all births recorded in 1986, in well over half of these births the under-twenty mother was unmarried. In the under-twenty group the likelihood that the young mother giving birth was unmarried decreased with age: The vast majority of mothers sixteen or under were unmarried, while about half of all eighteen-year-olds were unmarried. In sum, while one in five births in 1986 was to an unwed mother, for teenagers the rate was one in two. Such high rates of premarital births—involving 290,000 births to teenagers in 1986 alone—often have harmful consequences.

Before assessing these consequences we might ask why premarital birth rates are so high, especially among teenagers. A variety of factors seem to be at work.[2] The age of beginning menstruation (and thus susceptibility to becoming pregnant) has been going down over the years, presumably because of overall improvements in the U.S. population's nutrition and health. Thus, the size of the group of young persons at risk for pregnancy has grown.

Perhaps more important is the fact that the percentage of teenagers who are sexually active has been on the upswing in recent years, at least since the mid-1960s. The data available suggest that sixteen is now the average age for a youth's first experience with sexual intercourse. The likelihood of having intercourse has been increasing at all age levels during the teen years, and by age nineteen some four-fifths of all males and two-thirds of all females have had intercourse.[3]

Technology has, of course, provided both males and females with means of pregnancy prevention. One would expect unmarried young people to take advantage of birth control measures, a few of which are highly effective, to reduce the risk of premarital pregnancy; too often, however, they do not do so. Survey data on young unmarried females indicate that a quarter of those who are sexually active *never* use contraceptives, and an additional 45 percent use them only from time to time.[4] Contraceptives frequently are not used by those who are having their first experiences with intercourse, a time when many pregnancies occur.

---

[1] These and more recent data relating to recorded births may be found in *Monthly Vital Statistics,* a federal government publication. See also U. S. Bureau of the Census, *Fertility of American Women: June 1988* (Washington, D.C.: U.S. Government Printing Office, 1989).

---

[2] See *Teenage Pregnancy: The Problem That Hasn't Gone Away* (New York: Alan Guttmacher Institute, 1981).

[3] Ibid.

[4] Ibid. See the data presented in Melvin Zelnick and John F. Kantner, "Sexual and Contraceptive Experience of Young Unmarried Women in the United States, 1976 and 1971," *Family Planning Perspectives,* 9 (March/April 1977): 55–71.

TABLE 12.1 Births to Unmarried Women, by Race of Child and Age of Mother, 1970–86

Race of child and age of mother	1970	1975	1980	1985	1986
Number (in thousands)					
Total live births*	**398.7**	**447.9**	**665.7**	**828.2**	**878.5**
White	175.1	186.4	320.1	433.0	466.8
Black	215.1	249.6	325.7	365.5	380.3
Under 15 years	9.5	11.0	9.0	9.4	9.4
15–19 years	190.4	222.5	262.8	270.9	280.7
20–24 years	126.7	134.0	237.3	300.4	316.2
25–29 years	40.6	50.2	99.6	152.0	165.7
30–34 years	19.1	19.8	41.0	67.3	74.9
35 years and over	12.4	10.4	16.1	28.2	31.6
Percent distribution					
Total*	**100.0**	**100.0**	**100.0**	**100.0**	**100.0**
White	43.9	41.6	48.1	52.3	53.1
Black	54.0	55.7	48.9	44.1	43.3
Under 15 years	2.4	2.5	1.4	1.1	1.1
15–19 years	47.8	49.7	39.5	32.7	32.0
20–24 years	31.8	29.9	35.6	36.3	36.0
25–29 years	10.2	11.2	15.0	18.4	18.9
30–34 years	4.8	4.4	6.2	8.1	8.5
35 years and over	3.1	2.3	2.4	3.4	3.6
Births to unmarried women as percent of all births in racial groups					
Total*	**10.7**	**14.2**	**18.4**	**22.0**	**23.4**
White	5.7	7.3	11.0	14.5	15.7
Black	37.6	48.8	55.2	60.1	61.2
Birth rate†					
Total‡	**26.4**	**24.5**	**29.4**	**32.8**	**34.3**
White	13.8	12.4	17.6	21.8	23.2
Black	95.5	84.2	81.4	78.8	80.9
15–19 years	22.4	23.9	27.6	31.6	32.6
20–24 years	38.4	31.2	40.9	46.8	49.7
25–29 years	37.0	27.5	34.0	39.8	42.0
30–34 years	27.1	17.9	21.1	25.0	26.9

*Includes other races not shown separately.
†Rate per 1,000 unmarried women (never-married, widowed, and divorced) estimated as of July 1.
‡Covers women aged 15–44 years.
Source: U.S. Department of Commerce, U.S. Bureau of the Census, *Statistical Abstract of the United States, 1989* (Washington, D.C.: U.S. Government Printing Office, 1989), p. 66.

Ignorance and misinformation expose millions of sexually active, unmarried teenagers to the risks of pregnancy. In recent years efforts have been under way to provide counseling and effective means of contraception to teenagers, but much more must be done if their startlingly high premarital pregnancy rate is to be reduced. *(Ellis Herwig/The Picture Cube)*

If technology to prevent pregnancy is widely available, why is it so underutilized? The reasons are many.[5] There is still widespread lack of knowledge and misinformation regarding birth control measures and the conditions under which pregnancy may occur. Much of this ignorance stems from the paucity of education on these matters provided to young people, whether by parents, schools, or religious institutions. Sex education (but particularly education in birth control practices) remains a controversial subject in U.S. society. Fears are often expressed that young people will be encouraged into premature sexual activity by such information.

Yet teenagers are already sexually active. Failure to combat lack of knowledge and misinformation thus allows the premarital pregnancy rate to remain high. One study has demonstrated that sex education does not increase the rate of those having intercourse but that it does increase the probability that contraceptives will be used by sexually active teenagers.[6] Yet empirical data along these lines have not begun to be acknowledged by those who see sex education as contributing to teenage sexual activity and the pregnancies that so often follow.

[5] Melvin Zelnick and John F. Kantner, "Reasons for Nonuse of Contraception by Sexually Active Women Aged 15–19," *Family Planning Perspectives,* 11 (September/October 1979): 290–96. Also, in the same issue, see Melvin Zelnick, "Sex Education and Knowledge of Pregnancy Risk Among U.S. Teenage Women."

[6] Melvin Zelnick and J. Kim Young, "Sex Education and Its Association with Teenage Sexual Activity, Pregnancy, and Contraceptive Use," *Family Planning Perspectives,* 14 (May/June 1982): 117–26.

While lack of knowledge and misinformation may contribute to high premarital pregnancy rates, other personal and social factors can get in the way of the utilization of effective birth control measures. Intercourse may occur in an unplanned way, perhaps without original intention. It may also be unplanned in the context of what has been called "date rape," wherein the teenage female is sexually coerced or abused, often while under the influence of alcohol or drugs.

Persons who are struggling over guilt about becoming sexually active may avoid seeking birth control measures, thinking that to do so is to make a concrete commitment to future activity. There may be concern too over comfort or side effects of some contraceptives. There may be a lack of communication between sexual partners over who is responsible for protection. For some teenagers, obtaining and using contraceptives may appear inconvenient, embarrassing, or dangerous (if parents find out). In addition, some simply cannot afford adequate contraceptive measures.

Finally, and often with unhappy results, there are some who *want* to get pregnant—in the hope of coercing the father into marriage or of demonstrating maturity and arrival into "adulthood" or out of a need to have someone to love and who will give love in return.

It is important to note that failure to make effective use of contraceptives has implications for the growing rates of abortion among young females.[7] In 1985 there were 1,588,600 legal abortions reported to government statistical agencies. (The actual rate of abortion may be 10–20 percent higher.) Over a quarter of these abortions occurred in the under-twenty age group. Most persons having abortions are unmarried.[8]

Thus far we have delayed discussion of the consequences of **premarital births and teenage motherhood.**[9] **The evidence shows that to be put into this situation may be self-harmful to the mother and/or harmful to others (in particular to the newborn child). Health implications are the first of many concerns. The younger the age at which pregnancy occurs, the higher the probability that both mother and child will have serious health problems. Young mothers may face complications in giving birth. Newborn children of teenage mothers often have low birth weights and a higher than average incidence of serious birth defects. Infant mortality rates are also high among children born to very young mothers.**

To a large extent these health problems are exacerbated by the fact that a disproportionate percentage of premarital births occur among teenagers from low-income households. Such youths have least ready access to sex education and effective contraceptive measures and are least able to afford abortions or marriage to the male sexual partner. (Low-income teenage couples cannot afford to set up households.) Health services to poor or near-poor young people often preclude proper prenatal care. Economic deprivation frequently has negative effects on dietary and nutritional practices important to the health of the mother and unborn child. Postnatal and "well-baby" care may also not be readily available or affordable.

Aside from health problems, teenage pregnancy commonly restricts the life chances of mother and child in other ways. While public education institutions cannot refuse to serve pregnant unwed girls of eligible school age, many teenagers quit school when they become pregnant. Even more leave upon the births of their children as they face the demands of child care and/or the need for some kind of employment. Once they drop out of school, they are unlikely to return and earn their diplomas, thus

---

[7] See data in *Monthly Vital Statistics.*

[8] Aida Torres and Jacqueline D. Forrest, "Why Do Women Have Abortions?," *Family Planning Perspectives,* 20 (July/August 1988): 169–76.

[9] *Teenage Pregnancy.*

reducing the likelihood of obtaining jobs that provide adequate pay and security. With this process under way, the probability of living in poverty or near-poverty is very high. Consequently, the children of such unions are likely to suffer the often harsh demands of low-income life. Welfare benefits for the children may become a necessary bare means of survival for the most economically desperate. For the fortunate, family and friends (and, less frequently, the biological father) provide a network of support that enables teenage unwed mothers to manage.

All of these demands and responsibilities of teenage parenthood, it should be underscored, are being borne by young persons who have not yet reached physical, emotional, or intellectual maturity. Many are barely out of childhood, even while they struggle to be parents and providers. The result can be serious psychological stress in the face of newfound pressures. The frustrations reveal themselves over time in a number of ways, from ill-conceived attempts at marriage and involvements that may incur additional pregnancies to child abuse and self-harmful behaviors.

At this point it may be obvious that practically nothing has been said about the male partner. This is because in most cases of premarital pregnancy and birth among teenagers the male drops out of sight quickly. The likelihood that marriage will occur in such cases has diminished over the years, as the tradition of forced, or "shotgun," marriages has largely broken down (see Table 12.2). Given the enormous difficulties male teenagers face in supporting a wife and family today and the probability that this means dropping out of school and limiting employment prospects for the foreseeable future, teenage fathers are reluctant to enter into a marital relationship. Moreover, teenage mothers are often unlikely to push them, understanding perhaps that a marriage initiated in such circumstances is unlikely to last.

The public outcry in the last decade or so over teenage pregnancy—termed by some an epidemic—appears to focus on two main concerns. First, such pregnancies objectively announce the fact that teenagers are indeed sexually active. This is a fact that many adults would prefer not to know or would like to see reversed.[10] Second, and perhaps of equal importance, is concern over the costs of teenage pregnancies and their aftermath. This concern is largely voiced in the context of more general antipathy toward persons who must call on public assistance for family support. The increasing proportion over the last twenty years of welfare recipients who are members of female-headed households in which the mother is unmarried seems to be deeply resented. This resentment arises not only out of moral condemnation of unwed motherhood, but also out of concern over the tax burden posed by welfare families.[11]

Yet the public outcry largely neglects the causes of premarital pregnancies as well as the massive problems many teenage mothers face in trying to further the life chances of their children. Moreover, condemnation and resentment of unwed mothers apparently are having little effect on teenage pregnancy rates or decisions by young people to be sexually active.[12]

MARITAL DISSOLUTION

Marital dissolution is a second major contributor to the growing number of families in which only one parent is present. While most persons whose marriages end in divorce do eventually remarry, the problems leading to and flowing from family breakup can be harmful to those involved.

---

[10] "Gallup Poll Shows More Americans Say Premarital Sex Is Wrong," *Family Planning Perspectives*, 20 (July/August 1988): 180–81.

[11] Katherine Bradbury, "Income Maintenance Alternatives and Family Composition," *Journal of Human Resources*, 13 (Summer 1978): 305–31.

[12] See *Teenage Pregnancy in the United States: The Scope of the Problem and State Responses* (New York: Alan Guttmacher Institute, 1989).

TABLE 12.2 Women with a Premaritally Conceived First Child Who Married Before the Birth of the Child, 1970–74 to 1985–88 (Numbers in Thousands)

Race and period of first birth*	Total, 15–24 years		Age at first birth					
			15–17 years†		18 and 19 years		20–24 years	
	Number	Percent	Number	Percent	Number	Percent	Number	Percent
All races								
1985–88	1,359	26.2	214	17.3	422	27.3	723	28.2
1980–84	2,347	36.6	608	27.0	754	35.4	985	43.5
1975–79	2,140	38.6	694	26.7	674	46.6	772	42.4
1970–74	2,132	45.9	732	38.4	766	50.7	634	48.9
White								
1985–88	877	37.5	101	36.6	289	34.6	487	39.4
1980–84	1,647	44.0	417	34.8	521	44.1	709	49.4
1975–79	1,437	52.5	409	42.5	484	60.3	544	52.9
1970–74	1,440	58.1	447	53.7	534	60.5	459	59.7
Black								
1985–88	445	4.7	109	—	124	8.1	212	5.2
1980–84	623	14.8	181	7.7	209	12.4	233	22.3
1975–79	651	8.1	274	2.9	172	9.9	205	13.7
1970–74	636	18.7	268	13.8	208	28.4	160	14.4
Hispanic‡								
1985–88	129	25.6	9	(B)	36	(B)	84	17.9
1980–84	336	27.4	104	26.0	94	4.3	138	44.2
1975–79	262	36.3	76	18.4	74	(B)	112	38.4
1970–74	199	30.7	61	(B)	69	(B)	69	(B)
Not Hispanic								
1985–88	1,230	26.3	204	15.7	387	26.4	639	29.6
1980–84	2,013	38.1	505	27.1	662	39.9	846	43.3
1975–79	1,879	38.9	618	27.7	601	45.9	660	43.0
1970–74	1,934	47.5	672	40.0	697	51.8	565	51.2

Key: B, base too small to show derived statistic.
*Periods are for complete calendar years with the exception of the 1985–88 period, which is for January 1985 to June 1988.
†Excludes births to women who were never married and were 15–17 years old in June 1988.
‡Persons of Hispanic origin may be of any race.
Source: U.S. Department of Commerce, Bureau of the Census, *Fertility of American Women: June 1988* (Washington, D.C.: U.S. Government Printing Office, 1989), p. 9.

America's "divorce rate" can be expressed in different ways.[13] In 1985, some 2,413 million couples were married. In that same year 1,190 million already existing marriages ended in divorce, for a rate of 493 divorces for every 1,000 marriages. This ratio increased from 258 per 1,000 in 1960 and 328 per 1,000 in 1970. In expressing the divorce rate in this way one must remember that the marriages include persons who were formerly divorced.

A second way to approach the divorce rate is in terms of the number of divorces per 1,000 persons in the population. Viewed in these

---

[13] Data are from U.S. Bureau of the Census.

This scene is a familiar one, repeated again and again annually in the United States with varying degrees of ceremony. The probability that such couples will experience divorce seven years on average after marrying is very high. *(Jerry Howard/Stock, Boston)*

terms, the rate was 5.0 divorces per 1,000 persons in 1985. (See Table 12.3.) The rate was up from 2.2 in 1960 and 3.5 in 1970. This approach must be used cautiously because changes in the age composition of the population affect the numerical divorce rate.

The third and most common way of expressing the divorce rate is to look at the number of divorces per 1,000 married women. Table 12.3 indicates that in 1965 there were 10.6 divorces per 1,000 married women. This rate rose to 20.3 in 1975 and has leveled off since 1980. In 1985 the rate was 21.7.

However the divorce rate is expressed, it is clear that marital dissolution has been on a dramatic upswing over the last three decades. Longitudinal statistics show that these recent increases are in reality the extension of a much longer upward trend in divorce rates. Nonetheless, the extent to which this trend has gone of late is having an impact on millions of people.

For example, in the last two decades some 19 million children under age eighteen have seen their parents enter into a divorce.

Before turning to the consequences of marital dissolution, let us consider some of the factors that may help to account for the more recent acceleration of the divorce rate. Social scientists continue to debate these factors and the weight to be attributed to them.[14]

1. Laws pertaining to divorce have changed in recent years. While the upward climb in rates of divorce began well before 1970, prior to that year states would grant a divorce only on such grounds as adultery, cruelty (physical or mental), or desertion. One or the other

---

[14] See Mary Joe Bane, *Here to Stay: American Families in the Twentieth Century* (New York: Basic Books, 1976), and Robert S. Weiss, *Marital Separation* (New York: Basic Books, 1975).

TABLE 12.3 Marriages and Divorces, 1960–85 (Numbers in Thousands)

	Marriages*						Divorces and annulments		
		Rate per 1,000 population						Rate per 1,000 population	
					Unmarried women				Married women 15 years old and over
Year	Number	Total	Men 15 years old and over	Women 15 years old and over	15 years old and over	15–44 years old	Number	Total	
1960	1,523	8.5	25.4	24.0	73.5	148.0	393	2.2	9.2
1965	1,800	9.3	27.9	26.0	75.0	144.3	479	2.5	10.6
1970	2,159	10.6	31.1	28.4	76.5	140.2	708	3.5	14.9
1975	2,153	10.0	27.9	25.6	66.9	118.5	1,036	4.8	20.3
1980	2,390	10.6	28.5	26.1	61.4	102.6	1,189	5.2	22.6
1981	2,422	10.6	28.4	26.1	61.7	103.1	1,213	5.3	22.6
1982	2,456	10.6	28.4	26.1	61.4	101.9	1,170	5.0	21.7
1983	2,446	10.5	28.0	25.7	59.9	99.3	1,158	4.9	21.3
1984	2,477	10.5	28.1	25.8	59.5	99.0	1,169	5.0	21.5
1985	2,413	10.1	26.9	24.8	57.0	94.9	1,190	5.0	21.7

*Beginning 1980, includes nonlicensed marriages registered in California.
Source: U.S. Department of Commerce, Bureau of the Census, *Statistical Abstract of the United States, 1989* (Washington, D.C.: U.S. Government Printing Office, 1989), p. 85.

partner in a marriage had to be found at fault by divorce courts. In 1970 California instituted a no-fault divorce law that allowed married couples to dissolve their marriages in court by mutual agreement. Over half of all states have since adopted a similar law or added no-fault grounds to existing laws. Such legal changes may represent and facilitate more permissive attitudes toward divorce among married persons.

2. The availability of effective means of contraception to married couples is also believed to have had an impact on divorce. Contraception can make extramarital affairs less risky than they otherwise would be—indeed, infidelity is a major source of breakup in first marriages. Moreover, such contraceptive advances as "the pill" have enabled many couples to exert control over the number of children they wish to have. To the degree to which having children mitigates against marital dissolution, not having them may make

divorce a more viable option than it otherwise would be. The average number of children involved in divorce has fallen from 1.33 per divorce in the late 1960s to less than 1.0 at present. (Yet as noted earlier, the number of children affected by divorce over the last twenty years is still substantial. More than half of all divorces involve children even now. See Table 12.4.)

3. Women's participation in the labor force (discussed in Chapter 9) is also a factor to be considered. As women have gained more control over childbearing through contraceptive advances and as they have moved into paid positions outside the home—usually from necessity, but often out of choice—their dependence on the husband-as-supporter has diminished somewhat. As their roles in the family have undergone change, many women locked into unhappy marriages have looked to their work as a way of escape. It is also possible that men, seeing their wives in

TABLE 12.4 Divorces and Annulments—Median Duration of Marriage, Median Age at Divorce, and Children Involved, 1970–85

Duration of marriage, age, and children involved	1970	1975	1977	1978	1979	1980	1981	1982	1983	1984	1985
Median duration of marriage (years)	6.7	6.5	6.6	6.6	6.8	6.8	7.0	7.0	7.0	6.9	6.8
Median age at divorce											
Men (years)	(NA)	32.2	32.4	32.0	32.5	32.7	33.1	33.6	34.0	34.3	34.4
Women (years)	(NA)	29.5	29.9	29.7	30.1	30.3	30.6	31.1	31.5	31.7	31.9
Children involved in divorce (in thousands)	870	1,123	1,095	1,147	1,181	1,174	1,180	1,108	1,091	1,081	1,091
Average number of children per decree	1.22	1.08	1.00	1.01	1.00	0.98	0.97	0.94	0.94	0.92	0.92
Rate per 1,000 children under 18 years of age	12.5	16.7	16.7	17.7	18.4	17.3	18.7	17.6	17.4	17.2	17.3

Key: NA, not available.

Source: U.S. Department of Commerce, Bureau of the Census, *Statistical Abstract of the United States, 1989* (Washington, D.C.: U.S. Government Printing Office, 1989), p. 87.

a position of being able to pursue economic independence, have become less reluctant to dissolve an unhappy marriage.

4. Stresses faced by today's families are likely to exacerbate everyday problems in living and the normal tensions of family life. For example, since the late 1960s U.S. society has experienced economic downturns that have been accompanied by cycles of high inflation; unemployment and a loss in the value of wages have hit moderate- and low-income groups especially hard. Official poverty rates have shown an increase. While economic adversity may bring some families closer, and while others may find divorce a financially unsound option, for still other families economic adversity creates a climate in which divorce takes place. The availability of welfare assistance and other forms of government aid to poverty-stricken female-headed households has probably made divorce more thinkable for some. Divorce rates are highest at lower income levels.

5. Finally, changing attitudes toward marriage may help to account for the upsurge in divorce rates. Investigators such as Robert Weiss suggest that marriage is less likely to be viewed as a sacred, permanent institution

than it was only a few decades ago. Persons entering marriage are more likely to seek self-fulfillment and personal pleasure out of marriage, as opposed to seeing it as an avenue through which to pursue interpersonal commitment and cooperation in meeting social responsibilities. When self-fulfillment and personal pleasure ebb for one or both partners, there may no longer be much reason to stay married. Nor is there likely to be much public pressure on couples to remain together. The subject of divorce remains the focus of much public hand-wringing, but in reality divorce is usually dismissed as reflecting a relationship that just did not "work out."

The consequences of marital dissolution are many. Sharon Price-Bonham and her colleagues have reviewed existing literature on its impact on adults.[15] They point out that divorce involves far-reaching consequences, involving as it does a major life transition. Price-Bonham and col-

---

[15] Sharon Price-Bonham, David W. Wright, and Joe F. Pittman, "Divorce: A Frequent 'Alternative' in the 1970s," in Eleanor D. Macklin and Roger H. Rubin, eds., *Contemporary Families and Alternative Lifestyles* (Beverly Hills, Calif.: Sage Publications, 1983), pp. 125–46.

leagues found that the time of separation prior to formal divorce is often extremely stressful. Depression and psychosomatic symptoms associated with it (e.g., loss of appetite, sleep problems, increased drinking) are quite common. The separation period may be experienced as especially stressful because of such factors as increased parental responsibilities, sudden economic dislocation, change in familiar habits, and grief over the loss of a love object. Compared with married persons, those who are in the process of divorcing and who are newly divorced have been found to have higher rates of mental disturbance, suicide, homicide, accidents, and diseases leading to death.[16]

Adjustment to divorce is a process sometimes described in terms analogous to adjustment to a death. Price-Bonham and colleagues suggest that adjustment requires a variety of conditions, including "breaking away from the former marriage, accepting new roles, building a new lifestyle, and regenerating one's sense of self-concept and trust of others."[17]

The ability to adjust to divorce is influenced by numerous factors. The person who initiated the divorce may experience less stress and readier adjustment, as he or she at least has the advantage of some sense of control over the emerging situation. Economic strain is likely to make adjustment difficult. Having a network of friends and relatives who are supportive in times of need during the pre- and postdivorce period makes adjustment easier. Finally, dating and establishing positive relationships with members of the opposite sex is important to the adjustment process. It should be noted that most persons who divorce also remarry, thereby perhaps signaling an end to the adjustment.

The impact of divorce on children has been much debated. Some social scientists have held that the impact is wholly negative. Others have suggested that children are better off in a single-parent household than in one where the relationship between the parents has obviously fallen apart. Our understanding of the impact on children has been advanced by the research of Judith S. Wallerstein and Joan B. Kelly.[18] These researchers examined a group of 131 children from 60 families who came into contact with a California counseling agency. Meeting with the children at the time of the divorce, eighteen months after, and five years after, Wallerstein and Kelly gained unique data on the impact of divorce on children over time.

At the time of the divorce between their parents, the children were found to be very upset. Younger children expressed fright and confusion over the divorce, often seeing themselves as somehow at fault. Older children were found to be angry and concerned over what this situation might mean for them. Five years later, according to the investigators, the psychological effects of the divorce still lingered for most. While a third of the children were evidently happy and well adjusted, another third showed some signs of unhappiness and the remaining third were seriously dissatisfied.[19]

Andrew J. Cherlin concludes that while all children are likely to be emotionally upset when divorce occurs, most do adjust in a year or two. A minority have long-term psychological problems that can be attributed to the dissolution of their parents' marriage.[20] Yet, considering that 19 million children have seen their parents divorce in the last twenty years, the sheer numbers of those who have been emotionally impaired by this process are substantial.

---

[16] Ibid., pp. 126–27.
[17] Ibid., p. 131.

[18] Judith S. Wallerstein and Joan B. Kelly, *Surviving the Breakup* (New York: Basic Books, 1980).
[19] The researchers were able to interview most of the study's children in a ten-year follow-up. For all too many, the divorce continued to have a troubling impact. See Judith S. Wallerstein and Sandra Blakeslee, *Second Chances* (New York: Ticknor & Fields, 1989).
[20] Andrew J. Cherlin, *Marriage, Divorce, Remarriage* (Cambridge, Mass.: Harvard University Press, 1981), p. 79.

Cherlin does note that the probability of children's successful adjustment to divorce is enhanced by three factors: (1) regular contact with the parent who does not have custody of the children; (2) parental avoidance of involving the children in their differences, so that the latter are not forced to choose sides; and (3) structured, orderly household routine, coupled with an emotionally supportive custodial parent.[21]

Perhaps the most difficult task faced by the parent who is left with the major responsibility for child care is economic. After all the psychological and social adjustments are made and even while they are being attempted, money is frequently a central concern. The fact that the custodial parent is ordinarily the mother adds to the burden, given the subordinate and second-class role women continue to occupy in the labor force (see Chapter 9).

Divorce almost always has a negative economic impact on the single-parent household. The bulk of economic support for the family is typically provided by the husband in intact marriages. When this suddenly disappears or lessens, the standard of living of mothers and children suffers. In most cases of divorce, the father provides little or no child-support money. Even when they are ordered by the courts, child-support payments are received by fewer than half of the women to whom they have been awarded. In 1985, out of the 8.8 million women living with children under twenty-one with no father present, 5.4 million were expecting to receive court-ordered child-support payments. Only 48.2 percent of these women received full payment. In a quarter of the cases the father simply refused to pay. The amount provided to those receiving payments in 1985 averaged $2,220 annually, hardly a boon to most families who have lost a key wage earner.[22]

The economic impact of divorce has been explored in a study by Lenore J. Weitzman.[23] Calculating the incomes of divorced women in relation to their needs in contrast to those of men, Weitzman finds:

> Just one year after legal divorce, men experience a 42 percent improvement in their postdivorce standard of living, while women experience a 73 percent decline.... Divorce is a financial catastrophe for most women.[24]

The women's own words give meaning to Weitzman's statistics.

> We ate macaroni and cheese five nights a week. There was a Safeway special for 39 cents a box. We could eat seven dinners for $3.00 a week.... I think that's all we ate for months.

> I applied for welfare.... It was the worst experience of my life.... I never dreamed that I, a middle class housewife, would ever be put in a position like that. It was humiliating... they make you feel it.... But we were desperate, and I had to feed my kids.

> You name it, I tried it—food stamps, soup kitchens, shelters. It just about killed me to have the kids live like that.... I finally called my parents and said we were coming... we couldn't have survived without them.

> Sometimes when you are so tense about money you go crazy... and you forget what it's like to be twelve years old and to think you can't live without Adidas sneakers... and to feel the whole world has deserted you along with your father.[25]

Many divorced mothers are thus forced into the labor market on a full-time basis and/or

---

[21] Ibid., p. 80
[22] U.S. Bureau of the Census, *Child Support and Alimony: 1985* (Washington, D.C.: U.S. Government Printing Office, 1989), p. 3.

[23] Lenore J. Weitzman, *The Divorce Revolution: The Unexpected Consequences for Women and Children in America* (New York: The Free Press, 1985).
[24] Ibid., p. 339.
[25] Ibid., pp. 339 and 340.
[26] See Terry J. Arendell, "Women and the Economics of Divorce in the United States," *Signs*, 13 (Autumn 1987): 121–

forced to rely on welfare assistance to provide for their families.[26] Divorce and failure to receive adequate child support have contributed to the so-called feminization of poverty (see Chapter 6). Almost 50 percent of the children living in households headed by women are poor. The figure for children in intact husband–wife households is 8 percent.[27] In Andrew Cherlin's words, "the most detrimental aspect of the absence of fathers from one-parent families is not the lack of a male presence but the lack of a male income."[28]

Fortunately, most persons who divorce do remarry—some three-fourths of all divorced women and an even higher percentage of divorced men. Remarriage usually takes place three to four years after divorce. It can ease the economic burden carried by divorced mothers, for many of whom this is the only viable solution. Yet the divorce rate among the remarried is slightly higher than that for those in their first marriage, a fact that should underscore the fragility of marriage as an institution in contemporary times.

VIOLENCE IN THE FAMILY

Ideally, one's family should always exist as an oasis, a place that is safe and satisfying, where one can seek relief from and aid in dealing with the often stressful demands of the outside world. In too many cases today, however, the family setting is just the opposite; it contains levels of tension, conflict, and violence from which flight might be the only rational response. Many persons now admit to being aware of victims of family violence (see Table 12.5.)

Consider this statement by researchers considered experts in their subject matter: "Americans run the greatest risk of assault, physical injury, and even murder in their own homes by members of their own families."[29] Such statements are based not on alarmist rhetoric but on empirical research that has revealed startling rates of husband and wife abuse, parental abuse of their children, and children's abuse of their parents and one another. (By *abuse* we mean acts of physical violence.)[30]

Prior to research by Murray A. Straus and his colleagues, our knowledge of violence in the family was limited. Families in which abuse took place were commonly believed to be abnormal and pathological, their members perhaps victims of mental illness. It was also commonly thought that episodes of violence in the family were almost entirely restricted to the poor. Straus and colleagues have systematically destroyed these views as myths.[31]

The researchers examined 2,143 families who were carefully chosen to be representative of approximately 47 million families in America. The families were not known to have any mentally ill members, and they reflected a broad cross section with regard to age, class, race, and region of the country. An adult from each of the 2,143 families was interviewed and asked a variety of questions bearing on violence in the home. The purpose was to establish, for the first time, the "incidence rate" of family violence. (The incidence rate in this case refers to the frequency with which acts of violence occurred in the year prior to the interviews.) Violence was defined as "an act carried out with the inten-

---

35, and her *Mothers and Divorce* (Berkeley: University of California Press, 1986).

[27] U.S. Bureau of the Census, *Poverty in the United States, 1987* (Washington, D.C.: U.S. Government Printing Office, 1989), p. 11.

[28] Cherlin, *Marriage, Divorce, Remarriage*, p. 81.

[29] Murray A. Straus, Richard J. Gelles, and Suzanne K. Steinmetz, *Behind Closed Doors: Violence in the American Family* (Garden City, N.Y.: Anchor Books, 1980), p. 4.

[30] See Richard Gelles, "Family Violence," *Annual Review of Sociology*, 11 (1985): 347–67.

[31] The data and discussion that follow are drawn from Straus, Gelles, and Steinmetz, *Behind Closed Doors*, and from Murray A. Straus, "A Sociological Perspective on Violence in the Family," in Maurice R. Green, ed., *Violence and the Family* (Boulder, Colo.: Westview Press, 1980), pp. 7–31.

TABLE 12.5 Child Maltreatment Cases Reported, 1976–85

Item	1976	1977	1978	1979	1980	1981	1982	1983	1984	1985
Number of children reported (in thousands)	**669**	**838**	**836**	**988**	**1,154**	**1,225**	**1,262**	**1,477**	**1,727**	**1,928**
Rate per 10,000 children	101	128	129	154	181	194	201	236	273	306
Type of maltreatment										
Deprivation of necessities	70.7	64.0	62.9	63.1	60.7	59.4	62.5	58.4	54.6	55.7
Minor physical injury	18.9	20.8	21.2	15.4	19.8	20.4	16.8	18.5	17.7	15.4
Sexual maltreatment	3.2	6.1	6.6	5.8	6.8	7.5	6.9	8.5	13.3	11.7
Emotional maltreatment	21.6	25.4	23.8	14.9	13.5	11.9	10.0	10.1	11.2	8.9
Unspecified physical injury	0.5	0.4	0.4	2.5	3.1	3.2	4.7	5.2	3.6	4.1
Major physical injury	3.1	3.7	3.5	4.4	3.9	4.1	2.4	3.2	3.3	2.2
Other maltreatment	7.6	7.5	7.4	8.9	7.7	11.7	9.2	8.3	9.6	10.2
Characteristics of child involved										
Age, average (years)	7.7	7.6	7.4	7.5	7.3	7.2	7.1	7.1	7.2	7.1
Sex										
Male	50.0	49.9	49.4	49.5	49.8	49.2	49.5	48.9	48.0	48.1
Female	50.0	50.1	50.6	50.5	50.2	50.5	50.5	51.1	52.0	51.9
Race/ethnicity										
White	61.1	67.7	67.1	65.7	69.4	67.8	64.9	67.5	67.0	(NA)
Black	19.8	19.1	21.1	22.2	18.8	21.7	21.7	19.7	20.8	(NA)
Hispanic	11.1	6.8	8.0	9.2	9.7	8.6	10.9	9.9	9.6	(NA)
Other	8.0	6.3	3.8	2.9	2.0	1.9	2.4	2.9	2.6	(NA)
Characteristics of caretaker										
Age, average (years)	32.6	32.0	32.0	31.9	31.7	31.6	31.4	31.6	31.9	(NA)
Sex										
Male	38.9	39.1	38.0	37.6	37.5	36.8	36.5	36.9	38.5	(NA)
Female	61.1	60.9	62.0	62.4	62.5	63.2	63.5	63.1	61.5	(NA)
Race/ethnicity										
White	65.3	71.5	70.4	72.1	72.7	73.0	70.8	73.1	74.5	(NA)
Black	17.0	15.9	17.2	17.5	16.6	18.6	19.1	17.5	17.5	(NA)
Hispanic	10.0	6.4	9.6	4.9	5.1	4.7	6.1	6.8	5.5	(NA)
Other	7.7	6.2	2.8	5.5	5.6	3.7	4.0	2.6	2.5	(NA)
Family characteristics										
Single-female–headed families	38.5	38.7	40.7	41.8	39.3	43.1	43.4	40.3	37.4	(NA)
Children in household, average (number)	2.3	2.3	2.2	2.2	2.2	2.2	2.2	2.2	2.2	2.3
Families receiving public assistance	45.0	46.5	43.9	48.3	44.2	43.4	43.4	47.4	48.3	(NA)
Characteristics of perpetrator										
Age, average (years)	32.3	31.7	31.7	32.0	31.4	33.8	31.2	31.3	31.5	31.5
Sex										
Male	39.0	39.2	39.0	38.1	41.2	39.3	38.6	40.4	43.0	40.6
Female	61.0	60.8	61.0	61.9	58.8	60.7	61.4	59.6	57.0	59.4
Race/ethnicity										
White	65.1	71.2	71.2	71.2	72.0	71.1	69.0	69.5	69.9	(NA)
Black	17.7	16.5	18.4	19.1	17.6	19.7	19.7	18.7	19.1	(NA)
Hispanic	9.5	6.3	7.4	7.2	8.3	7.5	9.2	9.8	9.3	(NA)
Other	7.7	6.0	3.0	2.5	2.1	1.7	2.1	2.0	1.9	(NA)

[In percent, except as indicated. Total number of children reported is generally a duplicate count in that a child may be reported and therefore enumerated more than once each year. Because of differences in enumeration methods, a relatively small number of states (5 to 10) can provide only unduplicated reports, whereas most states provide only duplicated counts.]

Key: NA, not available.

Source: U.S. Department of Commerce, Bureau of the Census, *Statistical Abstract of the United States, 1989* (Washington, D.C.: U.S. Government Printing Office, 1989), p. 172.

tion of, or perceived as having the intention of, physically hurting another person."[32]

Spouse Abuse

The interviews revealed that incidents of violence between husband and wife had occurred in one in six families in the previous year. While most incidents were relatively minor, involving slapping, shoving, pushing, or throwing things at a person, some were far more serious in terms of real or potential physical harm. In 6 percent of the families, the incidents involved such acts as punching, kicking, biting, hitting with an object, or using a knife or gun. Husbands beat up their wives only slightly more frequently than wives beat their husbands, although it was thought that violence by wives out of self-defense could help to account for this particular finding. What this means is that some 3 million families experience serious acts of spouse abuse each year. Seven and one-half million experience violence of some sort annually.

Child Abuse

The interviews that Straus et al. conducted revealed rates of child abuse that were even higher than rates of spouse abuse. Seven out of ten parents used some form of physical violence on their children in the year prior to the interviews. Again, in most cases this was relatively minor (e.g., spanking). But 14 percent of the children suffered serious attacks. Overall, approximately 6.5 million children in a single year were subject to abuse by being punched, kicked, bitten, hit with an object, beaten up, or attacked with a knife or gun.

Child-initiated Violence

Findings of the research suggest that perhaps one in five children hit a parent the previous

---

[32] Straus, "A Sociological Perspective on Violence in the Family," p. 29.

year, including a parent who was elderly. One in ten used a method in which the risk of physical injury was high. Children also attack one another, at rates higher than their physical attacks on anyone else in the family.

Comment on the Findings

Straus and colleagues readily admit that their findings may underestimate the rate of family violence to an unknown degree. There are several reasons for this. Some of those interviewed may not have recalled or not have chosen to reveal violent incidents. The 2,143 families studied represent only intact families, thus omitting child abuse data for single-parent households. The research also did not examine violence between parents and their children under age three. Finally, the families studied represented 65 percent of those originally selected. It is conceivable that those who chose not to participate in the study may have functioned in families that were more violent than the families willing to be interviewed.

Nonetheless, the data reveal that violence in the family is widespread. Mental illness does not seem to be a major factor among those involved in violent acts; perhaps no more than 10 percent of the family violence that occurs is linked to psychological problems. While rates of violence were found to be highest among low-income families, the researchers' data revealed that violence is common across all income lines.

The next question is "Why?" How does one account for family violence? If mental illness and the ravages of poverty fail to provide more than partial answers, what are the causes of behavior that can leave adults and children injured and even result in loss of life?

According to Straus and colleagues, violence in the family has been around for a long time. Family life may have been even more violent in the past, although this is difficult to ascertain firmly. The reasons underlying family violence cannot be reduced simply to psychological prob-

Studies of family violence have revealed that the rate of child abuse is higher than many people realize. Fortunately public awareness has been on the increase and more cases of abuse are being reported. Still, it is difficult to know of all such cases. This father, shown beating his son with a belt, may never have to answer to authorities for his actions. *(Robert Kalman/The Image Works)*

lems; instead they seem to be rooted largely in the nature of the family itself and influenced by other features of American society as a whole. This is not to say that persons who physically abuse other family members are somehow blameless for their actions. But much family violence is thought to be "situational": There are social and cultural influences that may propel persons toward the use of violence, and in many cases this violence is widely tolerated. What are these social and cultural influences?

First, persons may entertain the use of violence in the family setting as an option partially because they themselves were physically abused or because they observed other family members' violence. Thus, the use of violence to solve interpersonal problems becomes part of the out-

look on life of clinically "normal" people. The use of violence is also constantly reinforced and subtly sanctioned in books, movies, and television shows, as well as through celebration of the activities of society's military forces and police agencies. In this sense the types of data being generated on violence in the family reflect both direct and indirect socialization into the larger culture and the behavior it often tolerates.

A second social and cultural influence pertains to social norms. Norms are rules or standards that define what is socially acceptable behavior. Thus, according to Straus and colleagues, some family violence can be termed *normal violence* in that it is tolerated and accorded legitimacy. As an example of such norms, Straus offers the following: "If someone is doing something wrong and 'won't listen to reason,' it is o.k. to hit."[33]

On the other hand, some violence is seen as socially unacceptable. Termed *abusive violence* by Straus and colleagues, this usually has the potential for inflicting the most serious physical harm. According to Straus, police may define what is considered abusive violence in accordance with the "stitch rule." In many cities police informally observe a norm that holds that unless family disputes result in more than a certain number of stitches, arrests are unlikely to be made. In sum, social norms influence the acceptance or nontolerance of violence within the family.

A third facet of the phenomenon of violence rests with the way in which the family itself is organized. According to Straus and colleagues, family organization can generate conflict between members that may result in incidents of violence. Conflict may be built into the family setting as a consequence of differences in age and sex of family members or differences in roles to be played (e.g., husband vs. wife, parents vs. children). Moreover, when differences do arise they may be felt far more intensely than differences between persons in nonfamily settings, because family members are very involved with one another emotionally.

Family units consider themselves to be collectivities whose business is theirs alone, and others usually share this view. The privacy demanded by and allowed families means that behavior in the home is subject to less public scrutiny and control than is behavior in other institutional settings (e.g., a place of employment, worship, schooling).

Finally, families are subject to a great deal of stress that may help to propel persons into violent behavior. This is particularly the case for low-income families, among whom rates of violence tend to be highest. During their life cycles most families suffer stressful events; at the same time they may be faced with substantial social responsibilities. Husbands and wives, facing stressful life conditions, may include violence in their repertoire of coping mechanisms— hitting out at others who may not even be the cause of the anger they feel. Children, caught up in a situation in which the use of violence may have become a norm, may know of no other way of dealing with their own stressful experiences.

In a study sponsored by the U.S. Department of Justice, researchers found that many of the victims of family violence brought to the attention of the courts continue to be victimized for months or even years after the original case is resolved.[34] The fact that court intervention does not necessarily provide protection for abused family members only serves to underscore the importance of the various social and cultural forces contributing to family violence that social scientists have endeavored to identify.

SEXUAL ABUSE OF CHILDREN

The attention given to violence in the family in recent years, and particularly to child abuse, has inevitably led to concern with what Florence Rush has called "the best kept secret": sexual abuse of children.[35] Long considered not a topic to be discussed in polite company, social scientists have finally begun to explore it in a small-scale way. The little research that has been done indicates that the sexual abuse of children is more widespread than most of us would prefer to believe.[36]

---

[33] Ibid., p. 16.

[34] See "A Study of Patterns in Family Violence," *New York Times* (June 8, 1983): C14.

[35] Florence Rush, *The Best Kept Secret: Sexual Abuse of Children* (New York: McGraw-Hill Book Company, 1980).

[36] Stefanie Doyle Peters, Gail Elizabeth Wyatt, and David Finkelhor, "Prevalence," in David Finkelhor et al., eds., *A*

In one study David Finkelhor surveyed 796 college students. Of 530 female students, 19 percent admitted to having been sexually victimized during childhood. For males, the percentage was lower—8.6 percent.[37] If the victims' experiences were to be projected to the U.S. population as a whole, this would mean that over 30 million persons will have had a sexual encounter with an adult while in childhood. Although our ability to generalize to the population at large from a survey of college students is doubtful, other research is beginning to confirm the widespread incidence of child sexual abuse.

In a more recent study, Finkelhor interviewed parents in 521 Boston families. This carefully selected sample of families had a total of 1,428 children between the ages of six and fourteen. Among the reported findings are these:[38]

1. Nine percent of the parents said one of their own children had been a victim or attempted victim of sexual abuse. (Finkelhor believes the actual rate could be double the 9 percent, given that children frequently do not report it.)
2. Children from every social class and ethnic and racial background were equally vulnerable to sexual abuse.
3. Forty-seven percent of the parents knew of a child who was a victim of sexual abuse; in 37 percent of these cases the victim was six years old or younger.
4. Fifteen percent of the female parents and 6 percent of the male parents had themselves been sexually abused as children. In only a third of the cases were the abusers strangers; 67 percent of the abusers were relatives, acquaintances, or their own parents.

Many of the cases of abuse fail to come to the attention of authorities. In the preceding study, only 56 percent of the parents interviewed reported their children's abuse. What is reported thus is no doubt simply the tip of the iceberg. For example, a quarter of all rapes reported to authorities involve victims who are under twelve. Sexual assault centers and hospitals commonly see children who have been sexually abused, and many children served by youth shelters, runaway services, and juvenile facilities have had such experiences.

Not all cases of child sexual abuse involve such violent acts as rape. Not all come about through the use of force or physical coercion. Nor is sexual intercourse always involved. The bulk of the offenders are thought to be members of the victims' families or family friends. Almost all offenders are male. Faced with demands for sexual activities that many children may not even understand, demands posed by persons who are usually known and trusted, children often simply comply. They may not know they have the right to refuse, or they may be afraid to do so. Abuse may last for long periods of time, even years.

Florence Rush argues that most of the adults who engage in sexual activity with children are not mentally disturbed. They seek out a child for sexual pleasure

> because a child, more than a woman, has less sexual experience, less physical strength, is more trusting of and dependent upon adults and therefore can be more easily coerced, seduced, lured, or forced.[39]

Difficulties arise in dealing with child sexual abuse within the circles of family and friends. Adults to whom complaints are made may not believe the victim, or they may even blame the victim. Children may be reluctant to complain in the first place, feeling confused and power-

Sourcebook on Child Sexual Abuse (Beverly Hills, Calif.: Sage Publications, 1986), pp. 15–59.

[37] David Finkelhor, *Sexually Victimized Children* (New York: The Free Press, 1979).

[38] David Finkelhor, *Child Sexual Abuse* (New York: The Free Press, 1984), Chapter 6.

[39] Rush, *The Best Kept Secret*, pp. 2–3.

PUBLIC PROBLEM, PRIVATE PAIN

The Secret Trauma

We have come to learn that incest is far more common in our society than anyone had realized. Child sexual abuse within families most frequently involves father or stepfather abuse of daughters. This selection illustrates the impacts such abuse may have (impacts that victims can help to heal through counseling, no matter when the abuse took place in their lives).

The most upsetting experience was when I was fourteen. My parents were alcoholics and would stay up till 4 or 5 A.M. drinking and fighting. When my mother would pass out, my father would get my sister and me out of bed for "family discussions." He thought my mother was sexually inhibited and he said he was going to help my sister and me through it so we wouldn't be inhibited too. One night I got up to go to the bathroom and my father was still up. He picked me up bodily, sat me on the table and kissed me. Because he was so drunk and couldn't stop me, I got off the table and after fifteen minutes of argument, I managed to leave and go to bed.

(What about other times?) Right after they were married, when I was about eight and my mother was out, I asked if I could go to bed with him. Being young and without a father, I wanted to be close to him. He said yeah, but when in bed, he asked me if I knew the difference between boys and girls. He said, "Give me your hand." He was going to put it on his penis. I said, "I'd better go to my bed."

(Did you have other sexual experiences with him?) Yes. He'd do little things like say "Give me a kiss," then he'd turn his face so I'd have to kiss him on the mouth. I was careful around him at all times, and tried to avoid physical contact with him. My sister and I never wore just robes or underwear around him.

(What ended it?) I left home at sixteen. (Upset?) Extremely upset. (Effect on your life?) A great effect. It had a much greater effect than being raped by a stranger—someone you'll never see again. I never told my mother. It would have broken her heart and I don't know if she would have believed me. It's so awful on Christmas, birthdays, and es-

pecially Father's Day. I have to send the bastard a card for her sake, and I spend hours in card shops looking for a card that's not mushy—that doesn't say "what a wonderful father you are."

I wanted a father—someone to be close to—not someone I had to be afraid of every moment I was with him. It's very, very sad. My own father left us, so my father image is bad. Because of my father and my stepfather, I felt all men were rotten. It became really hard to relate to men and to trust them. However, I've discovered they have feelings and they're not all bad.

It inhibited me sexually for a long time. There has to be a certain kind of trust for me to have sex with a male. Every time anyone makes a sexual comment or yells at me on the street, I ask myself, "What kind of image am I projecting? Is it the way I walk, or dress, or look? There must be something about me—an aura—that brings that out in people that pass by. Or is it just chance?" The thing that's kept me going is I've been a strong person. I left home early and put myself through school. I'm a fighter. I can't spend the rest of my life brooding about this. I can't jump off bridges, so I just move on.

I've thought of another effect and this is a biggy! My mother is a very sexually inhibited person. She became an alcoholic and thereby avoided it [sex]. After marrying my stepfather, my mother gained an incredible amount of weight and became unattractive to my stepfather. I realize that I did the same thing; I gained about fifty pounds and still can't get rid of the extra weight. I ate constantly also to make myself unattractive to men and to not have to deal with them.

(What did you find most helpful in dealing with the experiences with your stepfather?) Myself. Getting away from the household. And I took psychology courses in college to get more understanding of what had happened.

Source: Diana E. H. Russell, *The Secret Trauma: Incest in the Lives of Girls and Women*, pp. 246–47. Copyright © 1986 by Diana E. H. Russell. Reprinted by permission of Basic Books, Inc., Publishers, N.Y.

less. Concerned adults may interpret the incidents as less than serious, often to avoid rupturing interpersonal relationships with the offenders for personal, social, or even economic reasons.

Father or stepfather and daughter incest, found to be the most common form of child sexual abuse in David Finkelhor's study of college students, is a case in point. In many families in which incest takes place, the mother is helpless. Ashamed to reveal what is happening to others, fearful of involving law enforcement officials, often ignorant of other sources of assistance, and dependent on her husband for economic support for herself and other family members, the mother often withdraws and is frequently depressed. As a consequence, most offenders in cases of incest go undetected by outside authorities and are rarely elevated to the status of criminal.

Perhaps one of the most revealing pieces of research on incest and nonfamilial sexual abuse of children is that conducted by Diana Russell in San Francisco.[40] A carefully selected sample of 930 women residents was interviewed and asked about their experiences as victims of such abuses. The women were first asked if they had ever experienced "incestuous abuse," which

> includes any kind of exploitative sexual contact or attempted sexual contact that occurred between relatives, no matter how distant the relationship, before the victim turned eighteen years old.[41]

Russell found that 16 percent of the women had had at least one experience with incestuous abuse (e.g., sexual propositions, unwanted touching or kissing, forced intercourse) with a relative. In three-fourths of these cases, the incestuous abuse had taken place before the victim was fourteen years of age.

Russell also asked whether the women had been victims of sexual abuse apart from that involving relatives (and also omitting unwanted sexual behavior from a partner in the teenage dating years). If we add these cases to those noted in the preceding paragraph, the experiences of abuse are greatly magnified. Russell found that *38 percent* of the women had had at least one experience with incestuous and/or nonfamilial sexual abuse before reaching age eighteen. And in two-thirds of all the cases, the abuse was experienced before age fourteen.

We do not know if Russell's study has produced results that can be safely generalized to America's female population at large. But it seems safe to say that both incestuous and nonfamilial sexual abuse of children and teens are much more common than many of us would like to believe.

Amazingly, there are a few professionals in the mental health field who argue that adult sexual encounters with children are in many cases harmless and in some cases even positive.[42] That such views are in the minority is largely due to evidence on the often harmful consequences of sexual abuse.[43] These consequences include genital injury, venereal disease, and pregnancy. Moreover, there are emotional effects. These may be expressed in a variety of ways, including loss of appetite, nightmares, bed-wetting, depression and inability to function, and even suicide. Residues of guilt and anger may last long after the occasion of abuse.

While child sexual abuse may be our "best kept secret," in recent years our cultural environment has been one in which children are portrayed in erotic terms. There has been a flowering of attention to child and youth sexuality in films and pornographic materials (so-called kiddie porn).[44] Advertisements for such pop-

---

[40] Diana E. H. Russell, *The Secret Trauma: Incest in the Lives of Girls and Women* (New York: Basic Books, 1986).
[41] Ibid., p. 59.

[42] Ibid., pp. 38–39.
[43] For views of some who have been sexually abused as children, see Ellen Bass and Louise Thornton, eds., *I Never Told Anyone* (New York: Harper & Row Publishers, 1982).
[44] David Finkelhor, "Sexual Abuse: A Sociological Perspective," *Child Abuse and Neglect*, 6 (1982): 99.

ular consumer items as blue jeans have used young girls in adultlike seductive poses to invite attention to the product. Such efforts, motivated by nothing more than a crude quest for profit, may help to legitimate the unspoken and generally unacceptable notion that children can be treated as sex objects. The role of the media in this regard remains speculative, since there is little research on this topic.

RUNAWAYS AND HOMELESS CHILDREN

One response to neglect or abuse within the family is to flee, even if only temporarily. Since the mid-1970s the federal government has provided limited funds to assist runaways through support of youth shelters and telephone hotlines that encourage children to initiate contact with their families. Yet as more has been learned about the runaways, it has become increasingly apparent that many have not simply fled home but have been made to leave. So-called pushouts or "throwaway children," as they have been termed, are effectively homeless. The pushout phenomenon may be viewed as yet another variant of the overall spectrum of child abuse. Runaways ordinarily can go home; they have a home to return to. Pushouts cannot.[45]

At least 1 million children, mostly between the ages of ten and seventeen, leave home each year. As many as half may be pushouts. Some of the pushouts are "economic refugees," evicted by parents facing financial crises who find they cannot support their children. Of the million or more children who leave their homes annually, perhaps half have been victims of some form of parental abuse.[46]

Much of what is known about such children is based on surveys of those served by federally funded youth shelters, of which there are presently 166 around the country. Generalizations about the total runaway–pushout population on the basis of shelter surveys must be made with caution. The shelters serve only about 45,000 children annually, or approximately 5 percent of all who leave home. In any event, it is estimated that the average age of this group is fifteen and that some 60 percent are female. Seventy percent are white. While perhaps 40 percent are school dropouts, most have never been in any kind of trouble that brought them to the attention of juvenile authorities.

What happens to the children who leave home? Runaways are likely to return, usually within twenty-four to forty-eight hours of their disappearance. Of those who do not return in a short period, some will find their way to youth shelters. Others will be picked up by police and placed in jail, either because they must be held for legal disposition as homeless minors or because they have been charged with illegal acts. The latter frequently occur as children away from home struggle to cope with problems of economic survival. Survival may be possible only through such acts as theft and prostitution. Prostitution involves boys as well as girls, and it is estimated that one out of ten homeless children engage in it. Often prostitution results from coercion by adults to whom the children have turned for assistance and protection.[47]

In 1986 police around the nation arrested 138,586 persons under eighteen years of age because they were runaways. The characteristics of those arrested may not reflect the runaway population in general, it should be noted. Of those taken into custody, 55,984 were under age fifteen; 2,210 were under ten. The vast majority (84 percent) were white, and most (58 percent) were female.[48] By 1988, the number of those

---

[45] U.S. Senate, Committee of the Judiciary, *Homeless Youth: The Saga of Pushouts and Throwaways in America* (Washington, D.C.: U.S. Government Printing Office, 1980).

[46] Arlene Rubin Stiffman, "Physical and Sexual Abuse in Runaway Youths," *Child Abuse and Neglect*, 13 (1989): 417–26.

[47] See "A Nation of Runaway Kids," *Newsweek*, 100 (October 18, 1982): 97, and "An Endless Parade of Runaway Kids," *U.S. News & World Report*, 94 (January 17, 1983): 64.

[48] Timothy J. Flanagan and Katherine M. Jamieson, eds., *Sourcebook of Criminal Justice Statistics, 1987* (Washington,

arrested increased 20 percent, to 166,900.[49]

Social science research on children who leave home is limited. However, there is evidence to suggest that, at least for runaways, a variety of factors are influential in determining the decision to flee home. First, children who run away are likely to face a lot of stress within their families.[50] In the words of Tim Brennan and colleagues, families of runaways frustrate "important youth needs and satisfactions, such as the need for security and belonging, the need for autonomy, the need for feelings of competence and self-esteem, the need to be understood."[51] The families of runaways are likely to combine displays of power (e.g., physical punishment, denial of privileges) with apparent withdrawal of love and parental remoteness. Often these processes occur simultaneously with family disruption resulting from death, divorce, or job loss. In all, families of runaways provide little in the way of role models for their children.

Brennan and colleagues have also found that school experiences typically add to the stresses experienced by children who run away. Runaways are more likely than nonrunaways to experience "negative labeling by teachers, blocked access to rewarding roles, low grades, failure tracks, expulsions, suspensions, being beaten by teachers and so on."[52] Thus, bonds to school as well as family are weakened. While there are no doubt some children who leave home simply for adventure and a quest for excitement, these cases are clearly in the minority.

As stated earlier, most runaways return home. The situation of pushouts is much more serious, because they are homeless. A U.S. Senate study, commenting on pushouts and throwaway children, warns of the severity of this family-related problem:

> There is no reason to doubt the numbers of homeless youth will increase. Certainly the wasted lives and talents of these youngsters represent a tremendous loss of human potential to our society. As the size of the homeless population grows, there will be an even larger underclass of bitter, defeated, or angry people in this country.[53]

WHAT IS TO BE DONE?

The picture painted in this chapter is very bleak. One must place these problems in perspective; it is clear that most American families are harmonious and enriching, with children who develop nicely.

With regard to the family-related problem of premarital births and teenage motherhood, some very sensitive issues must be confronted. Youths must be accepted as sexual beings, even if they are only in the process of becoming personally, socially, and intellectually mature. As such, many will make the decision to become sexually active and to engage in intercourse, although the rates will no doubt fluctuate. Knowing this, it seems that the only rational response is to seek to reduce risk of pregnancy. This can be done only by giving teenagers knowledge about contraception and contraceptive devices and seriously promoting birth control as an inviolable prerequisite to premarital sexual behavior. The costs of not doing this—to the unwed mother and child, and to the rest of society—far outweigh the costs of possibly encouraging a small percentage of youths to become sexually active who might not otherwise have done so.

Still, pregnancies will occur. Some teenagers—even when armed with knowledge and

D.C.: U.S. Department of Justice, Bureau of Justice Statistics, 1988), Tables 4.5 and 4.6.

[49] U.S. Department of Justice, *Uniform Crime Reports for the United States, 1988* (Washington, D.C.: U.S. Government Printing Office, 1989), p. 168.

[50] Paul G. Shane, "Changing Patterns Among Homeless and Runaway Youth," *American Journal of Orthopsychiatry*, 59 (April 1989): 208–14.

[51] Tim Brennan, David Huizinga, and Delbert S. Elliott, *The Social Psychology of Runaways* (Lexington, Mass.: Lexington Books, 1978), p. 303.

[52] Ibid.

[53] U.S. Senate, *Homeless Youth*, p. 83.

having ready access to contraceptive resources—will ignore it all. Accidents will occur. Nor is the technology of contraception 100 percent effective. Abortion will no doubt continue to be a highly charged moral and political issue and an avenue rejected by many pregnant teenagers (as well as adults). Some may opt to place their babies for adoption; many will not. If nothing else is done for those who do become mothers, current efforts to provide guidance and support in parenting skills, health assistance, and help in completion of formal education must be greatly expanded. The meager and begrudging help presently offered to young persons who are locked into the responsibility of mothering young babies is a shocking comment on the level of Americans' concern for human life.

Marital dissolution cannot be avoided. In many cases divorce is a solution as well as a problem. The two major areas of deepest concern should be those of (1) adjustment to divorce by adults and children, and (2) economic security for those left most vulnerable by family breakup (commonly the wives and children). The limited steps that are taken to hold fathers to financial responsibility can only be improved. The notion that men who father children have little or no responsibility for the standard of living and life chances of the children after divorce deserves full condemnation.

As for adjustment to divorce, the resources presently available to adults—from professional guidance to self-help groups—should be utilized more fully. The trend toward joint custody, where the divorced parents both play a continual role in parenting, is a positive way of fostering children's emotional adjustment and should be further encouraged. The decline in the number of children on average that are involved in divorce actions is a welcome trend.

Violence in the family seems unstoppable. It is really only in the last few years that family violence has been systematically revealed and widely acknowledged as a problem. The same can be said for the sexual abuse of children. It has been argued that such phenomena have long existed in this society and that the widespread attention they are presently receiving represents shifting attitudes that could well be necessary for behavioral change. Concern with the rights of persons within a family setting is perhaps an extension of concern over the rights of other categories of persons whose treatment is often harmful (e.g., racial minorities, women, the old, the disabled).

The identification of hidden and often tolerated acts in family settings as abuse, outside of the realm of socially acceptable behavior, is at least a start. Such a normative shift is at the very least likely to mean that situations involving violence and other forms of serious abuse are more likely to be brought to the attention of law enforcement and social service agencies. However, the ability of such agencies to respond and successfully alter the behaviors in question will have to be considerably expanded. At present social service agencies are overwhelmed with "business," and they are—far more than law enforcement agencies—understaffed and precariously funded. None of this, unfortunately, addresses the broader social and cultural determinants of family turmoil and abuse. Attitudinal shifts and increased intervention efforts are thus likely to do little more than stem the tide, barring more radical transformations in the self-concept of the American family (and of American society in general).

So long as families are troubled, children will run away. The runaway phenomenon is best understood as an indicator of the existence of child abuse and/or neglect. Thus, our comments regarding the desirability of attitude shifts and increased intervention to aid families are again applicable. But the pushout phenomenon is something else again. Ideally, there would be reason and opportunity for intervention *before* parents deny children their homes. Yet it is likely that many children will have no choice but to try and make a life outside their family setting. For most, youth and economic circumstance virtually dictate that they find their way to families who want them. An expansion of foster family care and small-group homes is required to meet the immediate needs of pushouts.

SUMMARY

Family-related problems have attracted widespread attention in recent years. The rising rates of premarital pregnancy and teenage unwed motherhood have contributed to an increase in single-parent households. Teenage pregnancies reflect the fact that more teenagers are sexually active than in the past, along with their frequent failure to employ effective contraceptive measures. Teenage mothers and their children are at higher than average risk for health-related problems, and their life chances are frequently diminished.

Rates of marital dissolution have also been on the increase and have made a contribution to the number of single-parent households. Divorce rates may have gone up because of more permissive divorce laws; contraceptive advances that permit women more control over childbearing; female participation in the labor force and the possibility of economic independence from a husband; stresses faced by families, particularly economic ones; and changing attitudes toward marriage. Divorce, which involves a major life transition, requires difficult emotional adjustments on the part of adults and children. It almost always has a negative economic impact on the single-parent household. The failure of women to receive adequate child support from their former husbands has contributed to the "feminization of poverty."

Recent research has also revealed high levels of violence within American families, including spouse abuse, child abuse, and violence by children against their parents and against one another. The reasons for such violence cannot be reduced to individual psychological problems in most cases, but lie more with social and cultural factors. Persons learn by observation that violence is often used to solve interpersonal problems and that it is frequently tolerated or accepted as a norm. Conflict that may escalate into violent acts may be built into family life, because of differences that arise between members. Families are permitted a great deal of privacy in handling their own affairs and thus are not subject to much control from without that would impede the expression of violence. Finally, there is the contribution of stress on the family, to which violence may be a response.

As such family-related problems as child abuse have become more widely recognized, the often hidden problem of sexual abuse of children has come to light. Child sexual abuse is more common than we might prefer to believe and commonly involves children and adults (almost always male adults) who are either relatives or family acquaintances. For the most part, offenders are thought to be psychologically undisturbed people who take advantage of the vulnerability and trust of children for their own needs. Most cases of abuse fail to come to the attention of law enforcement and social service agencies. While a few mental health professionals have tried to suggest that children's sexual encounters with adults may in many cases be harmless or even positive, reports of harmful physical health and emotional outcomes suggest otherwise. The treatment of children as possible sex objects by the mass media and in pornography may contribute to child sexual abuse.

One response by children to family turmoil, abuse, or neglect is to run away. Not only are runaways likely to have experienced ill treatment by their families, but they—more than nonrunaways—have negative experiences with teachers and schooling. While runaways usually return to their homes, many other children have no homes to return to. So-called pushouts, or throwaway children, are made to leave by their families. Pushouts and runaways who remain away from home face problems of economic survival that can propel them into such illegal activities as theft and prostitution.

What is to be done? The family-related problem of premarital births and unwed teenage motherhood makes apparent the need for sex education and encouragement of the use of effective contraceptive measures as a norm for sexually active youth. Greater support in such areas as parenting, health, and completion of formal education for pregnant teenagers who decide to be mothers is imperative.

The two areas of major concern with regard to divorce are adjustment to it and the economic stabilization of the custodial parent (commonly the mother) and children. Ways must be found to hold fathers financially responsible for children involved in divorces. The trend toward joint custody—wherein divorced mothers and fathers continue to share in parenting—is a positive step in the adjustment area. The fact that fewer children are involved in divorces (although the number is still substantial) is also a positive trend that may help ease adjustment and economic strains.

As violence in the family and child sexual abuse have become recognized as serious, widespread problems, there has been reduced tolerance of these problems; this may help bring about behavioral change. At the very least it is becoming more likely that family violence and child sexual abuse will be brought to the attention of law enforcement and social service agencies. More resources that would allow such agencies to respond and successfully alter the behaviors in question are needed.

Such intervention may also help to reduce the number of children who flee their homes as runaways; it may also reduce the number of pushouts. The latter, because of their youth and economic circumstances, do need alternative homes where they are wanted. Expanded networks of foster family care and small-group homes are required to meet the immediate needs of such homeless children.

DISCUSSION QUESTIONS

1. Despite lip-service paid to the need for sex education, many parents and religious officials continue to protest and resist its implementation in public schools. Simulate a dialogue between those for and those against school sex education.
2. Alarmed by the increasing rate of divorce, some experts have advocated a mandatory trial marriage period. For those who wished to remain together, a permanent license would then be issued and this marriage would be legally very difficult to dissolve. Discuss the pros and cons of such a policy.
3. Children seem to have fewer rights than adults in general, and this lack extends to their ability to avoid or end abuse. What additional rights do you think should be extended to children under the law? What might be the positive and negative outcomes of doing this?
4. As widespread as child and spouse abuse has become, it is time to raise questions about how to better deter it. What further deterrents are there? What are the obstacles to implementing these deterrents?
5. Running away from home is widely treated as a juvenile "status offense" and is punishable by court action. What arguments could be made for and against eliminating treatment of this behavior as a crime?

SUGGESTED READINGS

Edelman, Marian Wright. *Families in Peril* (Cambridge, Mass.: Harvard University Press, 1989).
Examination of the impact of family instability and poverty on children.
Russell, Diana E. H. *The Secret Trauma: Incest in the Lives of Girls and Women* (New York: Basic Books, 1986).
Incest and its impacts, as told by victims of this sexual abuse.

Teenage Pregnancy in the United States (New York: Alan Guttmacher Institute, 1989).

Overview of the teenage pregnancy problem and state programs designed to intervene.

Wallerstein, Judith S., and Sandra Blakeslee. *Second Chances* (New York: Ticknor & Fields, 1989).

A ten-year follow-up of an original set of interviews of young persons whose parents went through divorce.

Weitzman, Lenore J. *The Divorce Revolution: The Un-* *expected Consequences for Women and Children in America* (New York: The Free Press, 1985).

Legal issues surrounding divorce and child custody, and the economic hardships into which women and children are thrust.

Zinn, Maxine Baca, and D. Stanley Eitzen. *Diversity in American Families* (New York: Harper & Row Publishers, 1987).

The state of the family in America and the changes it has been undergoing.

TEXT CREDITS

Excerpt from the 1993-94 New Mexico State University Undergraduate Catalog; Las Cruces, NM.

Excerpt from the Fall 1993 New Mexico State University Schedule of Classes; Las Cruces, NM.

Blumenthal, et al. *Psychosomatic Medicine*, 49:339-40 (1987). Reprinted by permission of Williams & Wilkins. Material has been adapted for use.

Excerpt from *Reader's Guide to Periodical Literature*, 1992. Copyright © 1992, 1993 by the H. W. Wilson Company. Used by permission.

Excerpt from *The World Book Encyclopedia*, copyright © 1989 by World Book, Inc.

Excerpt from the *Dictionary Catalog of the Research Libraries*, copyright © 1989, courtesy of the New York Public Library, Astor, Lenox and Tilden Foundation.

Excerpt from *Language in Thought and Action*, Fourth Edition by S.I. Hayakawa, copyright © 1978 by Harcourt Brace & Company, reprinted by permission of the publisher.

Listen and Read: MN Lesson Book. Copyright © 1968 Educational Developmental Laboratories, Inc. Used by permission.

Introduction to Psychology, by Garrison, Mark. Copyright © 1992. Used by permission of Glencoe/McGraw-Hill.

Listen and Read: MN Lesson Book. Copyright © 1968 Educational Developmental Laboratories, Inc. Used by permission.

Figure from *An Introduction to Language*, Fourth Edition, by Victoria A. Fromkin and Robert Rodman, Copyright © 1988 by Holt, Rinehart and Winston, Inc., reproduced by permission of the publisher.

By permission. Excerpt from *Merriam-Webster's Collegiate Dictionary*, Tenth Edition. © 1993 by Merriam-Webster Inc., publisher of the Merriam-Webster dictionaries.

Reprinted by permission of Macmillan College Publishing Company from *The Heritage of World Civilizations Volume I: To 1600* by Albert Craig et. al. Copyright © 1994 by Macmillan College Publishing Company, Inc.

Reprinted with the permission of Macmillan College Publishing from *General Geology*, 5th Edition by Robert J. Foster. Copyright © 1988 by Macmillan College Publishing Company, Inc.

Reprinted with the permission of Macmillan College Publishing Company from *The Framing and Ratification of the Constitution* by Leonard W. Levy and Dennis J. Mahoney. Copyright © 1987 by Macmillan College Publishing Company, Inc.

Feldman, R. *Essentials of Understanding Psychology*. Copyright © 1989 by McGraw-Hill, Inc. Reprinted by permission of McGraw-Hill, Inc.

Essentials of Biology by Janet L. Hopson and Norman K. Wessells. Copyright © 1990 by McGraw-Hill, Inc. Reprinted by permission of McGraw-Hill.

Reprinted with the permission of Macmillan College Publishing Company from *The Heritage of World Civilizations Volume I: To 1600* by Albert Craig et. al. Copyright © 1994 by Macmillan College Publishing Company, Inc.

Reprinted from *I Tell You Now: Autobiographical Essays by Native American Writers*, edited by Brian Swann and Arnold Krupat, by permission of the University of Nebraska Press. Copyright © 1987 by the University of Nebraska Press.

"Check Your Coverage," copyright May 24, 1993, *U.S. News and World Report*.

Kottak, C. *Cultural Anthropology*, 6th Edition. Copyright © 1994, 1991, 1987, 1982, 1979, 1978, 1975, 1974 by McGraw-Hill, Inc. Reprinted with permission of McGraw-Hill, Inc.

Franklin, J. and Moss, A. *From Slavery to Freedom: A History of Negro Americans*, 6th Edition. Copyright © 1988, 1980, 1974, 1956, 1947 by McGraw-Hill, Inc. Reprinted with permission of McGraw-Hill, Inc.

Reprinted by permission of Warner Books/New York. From *Taking to the Air: The Rise of Michael Jordan*. Copyright © 1992 by Jim Naughton.

Dornbusch, Rudiger and Fisher, Stanley, *Macroeconomics*, 6th Edition. Copyright © 1994, 1990, 1987, 1984, 1981, 1978, by McGraw-Hill, Inc. Reprinted with permission of McGraw-Hill, Inc.

INDEX

important. *See* Important information; Main ideas, identifying

rephrasing, memory improvement and, 432-433

supporting. *See* Supporting information

Information processing theory, 420-423

encoding and, 420-421

retrieval and, 422-423

storage and, 421-422

Institutional support, 162-192. *See also* Faculty support; Library

activities/fitness centers, 168

career/placement service, 170

counseling services, 167-168

financial aid services, 169

learning assistance/resource center, 170-171

student center/union, 168-169

Instructors. *See also* Faculty support

feelings about, 87

how important information is identified by, 215, 218-222

listening to. *See* Listening

reasoning preference and, 98

responsibilities of, 202

special language used by, 219-222

Internal locus of control, 31

Interpreting, 380

Interpretive meaning, 397-404

Introversion/extroversion preference, 83, 92-94

Jobs. *See* Employment

Journal, personal, 4-5, 15

Judging, in critical thinking, 383, 384

Judgments, relativism preference and, 83, 95-96

Knowledge illusion, 456

Lab examinations, 468

Language. *See also* Special language; Vocabulary

identifying important information by, 215, 218-222

loaded words and phrases and, 407-409

Learning assistance/resource center, 170-171

Learning styles, 78-103

aesthetic preference and, 83

college work and, 81

introversion/extroversion preference and, 83

modality preference and, 83

pacing preference and, 83

reasoning preference and, 83

relativism preference and, 83

tactile preference and, 83

thoughts/feelings preference and, 82

time preference and, 82, 83-85

Library, 171-184

card catalog in, 173-174, 176-178

circulating books in, 182-183

finding books in, 177-178

miscellaneous resources in, 183-184

periodicals in, 179-180

reference books in, 180-182

reference librarian and, 173-175

Library of Congress system, 177

Listening, 111, 214-222

active, 215-217

advantages of, 204-205

developing vocabulary by, 261-262

hearing versus, 215

identifying important information and, 215, 217-222

improving skills for, 198-199

in negotiation, 48

for note taking, 198

Literal meaning, 390-397

Loaded words and phrases, 407-409

Loci, memory improvement and, 430-431

Long-term goals, 9, 13, 14

Long-term tasks, planning, 128-129

Main ideas, identifying, 218, 302-317

activating prior knowledge for, 306-307

assessing your skills for, 304

directly stated ideas and, 309-312

group discussion about, 305

implied ideas and, 312-315

silent dialogue with author for, 307-309

Map(s), self-testing with, 448, 450

Mapping, 366-369

Margin(s), in notes, 224-225, 234, 245

Marginal questions, in textbooks, 361-365

Matching test items, 462-463

Previewing, of textbooks. *See*
Textbook preview
Prioritizing
of goals, 10
of tasks in daily plan, 124-
126
Problems (exercises)
importance of doing
independently, 190
as preparation for math and
science tests, 466-467
Process (how-to) pattern of
organization, 289
Procrastination, 129-132
Progress charts, 16-17
Progressive relaxation, to
reduce test anxiety, 471
Public health services, 154

Questions
marginal, in textbooks, 361-
365
marginal, self-testing with,
448
on tests, predicting, 445-446

*Reader's Guide to Periodical
Literature, The*, 179-180
Reading, 112. *See also* Main
ideas, identifying
critical. *See* Critical reading
developing vocabulary by,
260-270
eye movements during, 332-
333
rate of. *See* Reading rate
of texts, 112
Reading rate, 296-299
adjusting, 299
analyzing, 321-322
comprehension and, 335-
343
familiarity with material
and, 298

phrase reading to improve,
333-335
practice to improve, 342-343
reasons for reading and, 298
scanning to improve, 329-
331
skip reading (skimming) to
improve, 324-329
speed reading and, 323
type of material and, 297
Reading textbooks, 112, 200,
346-377
highlighting/underlining
and, 365-366
mapping and, 366-369
marginal questions and,
361-365
outlining chapters and, 358-
361
SQ4R method for, 369-375
Reasoning preference, 83, 97-
98
Recall, recognition versus,
studying for tests and, 455-
457
Reference books, 180-182
Reference librarian, 173-175
Rehearsing
memory improvement and,
431-432
studying for tests by, 447
Relativism preference, 83, 95-
96
Relaxation techniques, 158-
159, 471
Resource center, 170-171
Resources. *See also* Faculty
support; Institutional
support; Library; Support;
Support systems
goal-related, analyzing and
using, 11-12
motivation as, 24
skills as, 25-26
study groups as, 189-190

Responsibilities, of students
and instructors, 202
Retrieving information, 422-
423
Review(s), weekly, 135
Review of notes
periodic, 247-249
preclass, 201
rapid, 244-245
Root words, 270, 271, 272-273

Scanning, 329-331
Schedules
benefits of, 134
of classes, 63-64
color coding, 135
weekly, 134-138
Scheduling classes, 69, 95
Scheduling tasks
daily planning and, 122-127
long-term tasks and, 128-
129
pacing preference and, 89
Science tests, 465-469
Self-advocacy, 43
Self-esteem (self-concept), 27-
29
Self-testing, 447-455
with chapter outlines, 447-
448
with concept cards, 450
horizontal versus vertical,
361
with marginal questions,
448
with SQ4R notes, 448
with study groups, 454
with study guides and study
sessions, 450
using notes for, 247
with visuals, 448-450
while reading textbooks, 356
Shadowing, 216
Short-term goals, 9, 13, 14
Skills, as resource, 25-26

Thesaurus, 269
Thinking, critical. *See* Critical thinking
Thoughts/feelings preference, 82, 86-87
Time management, 109, 118-145
  daily planning and goals and, 122-129
  guidelines for, 133-141
  procrastination and, 129-132
  study time and, 138-141
Time preference, 82, 83-85
Tone, of writer, 400-403
Tracking, of progress toward goals, 14-17
True-false test items, 461-462

Underlining, in textbooks, 365-366
Unitary pacing style, 89

Venn diagrams, for note taking, 232
Visual(s), self-testing with, 448, 450
Visualization
  goal setting and, 7-8
  relaxation techniques and, 158
Visual learners, 100
Visual organizers, for notes, 231-233
Vocabulary, 110, 256-277
  context cues and, 262-265, 352
  definition pattern of organization and, 290
  dictionaries for building, 265-270
  familiarizing yourself with terms before class and, 201

  handling terms with SQ4R method and, 372-373
  inferring word meanings and, 275
  reading for developing, 260-270
  word analysis for building, 270-275

Weekly reviews, 135
Weekly schedules, 134-138
Work. *See* Employment
Writer
  credentials of, 404-405
  tone of, 400-403
Writing. *See also* Reading
  grammar, mechanics, and spelling and, 110
  of research papers, 175, 182